Maturin M. Ballou

Foot-prints of Travel

Or, Journeyings in many Lands

Maturin M. Ballou

Foot-prints of Travel
Or, Journeyings in many Lands

ISBN/EAN: 9783337091163

Printed in Europe, USA, Canada, Australia, Japan

Cover: Foto ©Andreas Hilbeck / pixelio.de

More available books at **www.hansebooks.com**

Frontispiece. CAPTAIN COOK, THE DISCOVERER.

OR,

JOURNEYINGS IN MANY LANDS.

BY

MATURIN M. BALLOU.

Armado. How hast thou purchased this experience?
Moth. By my journey of observation. — SHAKESPEARE.

BOSTON, U.S.A.:
PUBLISHED BY GINN & COMPANY.
1889.

Entered according to Act of Congress, in the year 1888, by
GINN & COMPANY,
in the Office of the Librarian of Congress at Washington.

TYPOGRAPHY BY J. S. CUSHING & Co., Boston, U.S.A.
PRESSWORK BY GINN & Co., Boston, U.S.A.

PREFACE.

In these notes of foreign travel the object has been to cover a broad field without making a cumbersome volume, to do which, conciseness has necessarily been observed. In previous books the author has described much more in detail some of the countries here briefly spoken of. The volumes referred to are "Due-West; or, Round the World in Ten Months," and "Due-South; or, Cuba Past and Present," which were published by Houghton, Mifflin & Co., of Boston. Two other volumes, namely, "Due-North; or, Glimpses of Scandinavia and Russia," and "Under the Southern Cross; or, Travels in Australia and New Zealand," were issued by Ticknor & Co., of the same city. By the kind permission of both publishers, the author has felt at liberty to use his original notes in the preparation of these pages. It should be understood, however, that about one-half of the countries through which the reader is conducted in the present work are not mentioned in the volumes above referred to. The purpose has been to prepare a series of chapters adapted for youth, which, while affording pleasing entertainment, should also impart valuable information. The free use of good maps while reading these Foot-prints of Travel, will be of great advantage, increasing the student's interest and also impressing upon his mind a degree of geographical knowledge which could not in any other way be so easily or pleasantly acquired.

M. M. B.

CONTENTS.

CHAPTER I.

Crossing the American Continent. — Niagara Falls. — Utah. — Representatives of Native Indian Tribes. — City of San Francisco. — Sea Lions. — The Yosemite Valley. — An Indian Hiding-Place. — The Mariposa Grove of Big Trees. — Chinatown in San Francisco. — Through the Golden Gate. — Navigating the Pacific. — Products of the Ocean. — Sea Gulls. — Harbor and City of Honolulu 1

CHAPTER II.

Discoveries of Captain Cook. — Vegetation. — Hawaiian Women on Horse-back. — The Nuuanu Valley. — The Native Staff of Life. — The Several Islands of the Group. — Resident Chinamen. — Raising Sugar-Cane. — On the Ocean. — Yokohama, Japan. — Habits of the People. — A Remarkable Idol. — Tokio, the Political Capital. — The Famous Inland Sea of Japan. — Nagasaki. — Products and Progress of Japan 16

CHAPTER III.

Through the Yellow and Chinese Seas. — Hong Kong. — Peculiarities of the Chinese at Home. — Native Women. — City of Canton. — Charitable Organizations. — Chinese Culture. — National Characteristics. — Sail for Singapore. — A Water-spout. — A Tropical Island. — Local Pen-Pictures. — The Island of Penang. — An Indolent Native Race. — The Cocoanut Tree. — Palm Wine. — Tropical Fruits 32

CHAPTER IV.

Crossing the Indian Ocean. — The Island of Ceylon. — Harbor of Colombo. — The Equatorial Forest. — Native Costumes. — Vegetation of Ceylon. — Prehistoric Monuments. — Departure for Australia. — The

Stars at Sea. — The Great Island-Continent. — The Gold Product. — Divisions of the Country. — City of Adelaide. — Public Garden. — West Australia. — Melbourne, Capital of Victoria. — Street Scenes. — Chinese Quarter 44

CHAPTER V.

Gold-fields of Australia. — Kangaroos. — Big Gum Trees. — Largest Trees in the World. — Wild Bird Life. — Gold-seeking. — City of Sydney. — Botanical Garden. — Public Institutions. — Sheep-raising. — Brisbane, Capital of Queensland. — The Aboriginal Race. — Native Legends. — The Boomerang. — Island of Tasmania. — How named. — Launceston. — Hobart, the Capital. — Local Scenes. — A Prosperous Country 62

CHAPTER VI.

Embark for New Zealand. — The Albatross. — Experiments with Sea Water. — Oil upon the Waves. — Geography of New Zealand. — Mineral Wealth. — City of Dunedin. — Public Schools. — Native Cannibals. — Christchurch. — A Wonderful Bird. — Wellington, Capital of New Zealand. — Habits of the Natives. — The Race of Maori Indians. — Liability to Earthquakes. — A Submerged Volcano in Cook's Strait 81

CHAPTER VII.

City of Auckland, New Zealand. — A Land of Volcanoes. — Suburbs of the Northern Metropolis. — The Kauri-Tree. — Native Flowers. — The Hot Lake District. — A New Zealand Forest. — A Vegetable Boa-constrictor. — Sulphureous Hot Springs. — Fiery Caldrons. — Indian town of Ohinemutu. — Typical Home of the Natives. — Maori Manners and Customs. — The Favorable Position of New Zealand. — Its Probable Future 93

CHAPTER VIII.

Arrival in India. — Insect and Reptile Life. — Madura. — City of Trichinopoly. — Car of Juggernaut. — Temple of Tanjore. — Travelling in India. — Madras. — Street Dancing Girls. — Arrival at Calcutta. — Cremating the Dead. — A Fashionable Driveway. — The Himalayan

Mountains. — Apex of the Globe. — Tea Gardens of India. — A Wretched Peasantry. — Ancient Ruins. — City of Benares. — Worship of Animals. — Cawnpore. — Delhi. — Agra. — A Splendid Tomb . . 105

CHAPTER IX.

Native City of Jeypore. — Poppy and Opium-raising. — Bombay. — The Parsees. — The Towers of Silence. — Historical View of India. — Voyage to the Red Sea. — Cairo, Capital of Egypt. — Local Scenes. — The Turkish Bazaars. — Pyramids of Gizeh. — The Sphinx. — The Desert. — Egypt, Past and Present. — Voyage to Malta. — City of Valetta. — Church of St. John. — Gibraltar. — View from the Signal Station. — English Outposts 122

CHAPTER X.

Tangier, Capital of Morocco. — An Oriental City. — Slave Market. — Characteristic Street Scenes. — Malaga, Spain. — A Neglected Country. — Grenada. — The Alhambra. — The Banished Moors. — Cordova and its Cathedral-Mosque. — Madrid, Capital of Spain. — Museo Art Gallery. — Sunday in the Metropolis. — Toledo. — The Escurial. — Burgos. — San Sebastian. — Bayonne. — Spain, Past and Present. — Bordeaux. — Rural Scenery in France 141

CHAPTER XI.

City of Paris. — Sunday in the French Capital. — The Flower Market. — Notre Dame. — The Morgue. — Père la Chaise. — The Story of Joan of Arc. — Educational Advantages. — City of Lyons. — Marseilles. — Nice. — Cimies. — Mentone. — The Principality of Monaco. — A Gambling Resort. — Mediterranean Scenes. — Over the Corniche Road. — City of Genoa. — Marble Palaces. — Italian Navigation. — The Campo Santo or Burial Ground 164

CHAPTER XII.

Port of Leghorn. — Ancient City of Pisa. — Remarkable Monuments. — The Bay of Naples. — Neapolitan Beggars. — A Favorite Drive. — Out-of-door Life. — Vesuvius. — Art Treasures of the Museum. — Pompeii. — Environs of Naples. — Rome, the "Eternal City." — Local Scenes. — Artists' Models. — Favorite Promenade. — The Colisseum. — St. Peter's. — Florence and its Environs. — Art Treasures. — Home of Dante and Michael Angelo 181

CHAPTER XIII.

Venice. — The Gondola. — On the Grand Canal. — Venetian History. — Piazza of St. Mark. — Cathedral of San Marco. — The Campanile. — Academy of Fine Arts. — Doge's Palace. — Tombs of Titian and Canova. — Milan. — The Wonderful Cathedral. — Original Picture of the Last Supper. — Olden City of Pavia. — Innspruck, Capital of the Tyrol. — Among the Alps. — Salzburg, Birthplace of Mozart. — Industries of German Women 200

CHAPTER XIV.

Vienna, the Northern Paris. — Art Galleries and Museum. — Prague, Capital of Bohemia. — Ancient Dungeons. — Historic Mention. — Dresden, Capital of Saxony. — The Green Vaults. — Berlin, Capital of Prussia. — Hamburg. — Copenhagen, Capital of Denmark. — The Baltic Sea. — Danish Progress. — Thorwaldsen. — Educational. — Palace of Rosenborg. — The Round Tower. — Elsinore and Shakespeare's Hamlet 215

CHAPTER XV.

Gottenburg, Sweden. — Intelligence of the People. — The Gotha Canal. — Tröllhatta Falls. — Christiania, Capital of Norway. — Legal Code. — Public Buildings. — Ancient Viking Ship. — Brief Summers. — Swedish Women in the Field. — Flowers in Arctic Regions. — Norwegian Lakes. — Animals of the North. — Mountains and Glaciers. — A Land of Fjords, Cascades, and Lakes. — Dwellings situated like Eagles' Nests 233

CHAPTER XVI.

Bergen, Norway. — Local Products and Scenes. — Environs of Bergen. — The Angler's Paradise. — Tröndhjem. — Story of King Olaf. — A Cruel Imprisonment. — Journey Northward. — Night turned into Day. — Coast of Norway. — Education. — The Arctic Circle. —

Bodöe. — The Lofoden Islands. — The Maelström. — Hardy Arctic Fishermen. — The Polar Sea. — Varied Attractions of Norway to Travellers and Artists 247

CHAPTER XVII.

Peculiar Sleeplessness. — Tromsöe. — The Aurora Borealis. — Short-lived Summer. — Flowers. — Trees. — Laplanders and their Possessions. — Reindeers. — Customs of the Lapps. — Search for Whales. — Arctic Birds. — Influence of the Gulf Stream. — Hammerfest. — The Far North Cape and the Polar Ocean. — The Midnight Sun. — Stockholm, Capital of Sweden. — Royal Palace. — Historic Upsala. — Linnæus, the Naturalist. — Crossing the Baltic and Gulf of Finland . 261

CHAPTER XVIII.

Åbo. — Helsingfors, Capital of Finland. — Remarkable Fortress of Sweaborg. — Fortifications of Cronstadt. — Up the Neva to St. Petersburg. — Grandest City of Northern Europe. — Street Scenes in Russia. — Occupations of the Sabbath. — The Drosky. — Royal Palaces of the Tzar. — Noble Art Gallery. — Celebrated Library. — Public Monuments. — Winter Season 275

CHAPTER XIX.

Palace of Petershoff. — Peter the Great. — Religious Denominations. — On the Way to Moscow. — Through the Forests. — City of Tver. — The Volga. — Water-ways of Russia. — Picturesque Moscow. — The Kremlin. — Churches. — Cathedral of St. Basil. — Treasury of the Kremlin. — Royal Robes and Crowns. — A Page from History. — University of Moscow. — Sacred Pigeons. — Prevalence of Beggary in the Oriental Capital 288

CHAPTER XX.

Nijni-Novgorod. — Valley of the Volga. — One of the Great Rivers of the World. — Famous Annual Fair-Ground. — Variety of Merchandise. — A Conglomerate of Races. — A Large Temporary City. — From Moscow to Warsaw. — Wolves. — The Granary of Europe. — Polish Peasants. — City of Warsaw. — Topography of the Capital. — Royal Residences. — Botanical Gardens. — Political Condition of Poland. — Commercial Prosperity. — Shameful Despotism 298

CHAPTER XXI.

Munich, Capital of Bavaria. — Trying Employments of the Women. — A Beer-Drinking Community. — Frankfort-on-the-Main. — Luther's Home. — Goethe's Birthplace. — Cologne on the Rhine. — The Grand Cathedral. — Antwerp, Belgium. — Rubens' Burial Place. — Art Treasures in the Cathedral. — Switzerland. — Bâle. — Lausanne. — Geneva. — Lake Leman. — Vevay. — Berne, Capital of Switzerland. — Lucerne. — Zurich. — Schaffhausen 310

CHAPTER XXII.

London, the Metropolis of the World. — Some of its Institutions. — The Tower of London. — Statistics of the Great City. — Ancient Chester. — Rural England. — Stratford-on-Avon. — Edinburgh, Scotland. — Remarkable Monuments. — Abbotsford. — Rural Scotland. — Glasgow. — Greenock. — Across the Irish Sea to Belfast. — Queen's College. — Dublin, the Capital of Ireland. — Grand Public Buildings . . 321

CHAPTER XXIII.

Nassau, New Providence. — Trees, Flowers, and Fruits. — Curious Sea Gardens. — The Finny Tribes. — Fresh Water Supply. — Tropical Skies. — The Gulf Stream. — Santiago de Cuba. — Cienfuegos. — Sugar Plantations. — Cuban Fruits. — Peculiarities of the Banana. — A Journey across the Island to Matanzas. — Inland Experiences. — Characteristic Scenes. — The Royal Palm 334

CHAPTER XXIV.

Discovery of Cuba by Columbus. — The Native Race. — Historical Matters. — Headquarters of Spanish Military Operations in the West. — Invasion of Mexico by Cortez. — African Slave Trade. — Peculiarities of the Caribbean Sea. — Geography of the Island of Cuba. — City of Matanzas. — Havana, the Capital. — The Alameda. — The Cathedral. — Military Mass. — A Wonderfully Fertile Island. — Reflections. 349

FOOT-PRINTS OF TRAVEL;

OR,

JOURNEYINGS IN MANY LANDS.

CHAPTER I.

THE title of the book in hand is sufficiently expressive of its purpose. We shall follow the course of the sun, but diverge wherever the peculiarities of different countries prove attractive. As the author will conduct his readers only among scenes and over routes which he himself has travelled, it is hoped that he may be able to impart a portion of the enjoyment experienced, and the knowledge gained in many foreign lands and on many distant seas.

Starting from the city of Boston by railway, we pass at express speed through the length of Massachusetts from east to west, until we arrive at Hoosac, where the famous tunnel of that name is situated. This remarkable excavation, five miles in length, was cut through the solid rock of Hoosac Mountain to facilitate transportation between Boston and the West, at a cost of twenty years of labor and sixteen millions of dollars; a sum, which, were it divided, would amount to over five dollars per head for every man, woman, and child in the State.

By a continuous day's journey from Boston, we reach Niagara late at night. The best view of the falls, which form the grandest cataract on the globe, is to be enjoyed from the Canada side of the Niagara River. In the midst of the falls is Goat Island, dividing them into two unequal parts, one of which forms the American, and the other the Horse Shoe Fall, so called from its shape, which is on the Canada side. As we gaze upon this remarkable exhibition of natural force, a column of vapor rises two hundred feet above the avalanche of waters, white as snow where it is absorbed into the skies, the base being wreathed with perpetual rainbows. A canal, starting from a convenient point above the falls and extending to a point below the rapids, utilizes for mill purposes an infinitesimal portion of the enormous power which is running to waste, night and day, just as it has been doing for hundreds of years. It is well known that many centuries ago these falls were six miles nearer to Lake Ontario than they now are, making it evident that a steady wearing away of the rock and soil is all the time progressing. The inference seems to be plain enough. After the lapse of ages these mammoth falls may have receded so far as to open with one terrific plunge the eastern end of Lake Erie. Long before the Falls are reached we hear the mighty roar which made the Indians call the cataract Niagara, or "the thunder of the waters." On leaving here, we cross the river by a suspension bridge, which, from a short distance, looks like a mere spider's web. Over this the cars move slowly, affording a superb view of the Falls and of the awful chasm below.

But let us not dwell too long upon so familiar a theme. After a day and night in the cars, travelling westward, Chicago, the capital of Illinois, is reached. About sixty years ago a scattered tribe of the Pottawatomies inhabited the spot on the shore of Lake Michigan, where is now situated the most important capital of the North Western States. In 1837 the city was formed with less than five thousand inhabitants; at this writing it has nearly a million. Such rapid growth has no parallel in America or elsewhere. This commercial increase is the natural result of its situation at the head of the great chain of lakes. In size it is a little over seven miles in length by five in width, giving it an area of about forty square miles. The city is now the centre of a railroad system embracing fifteen important trunk lines, forming the largest grain, lumber, and live-stock market in the world. One hundred and sixty million bushels of grain have passed through its elevators in a twelvemonth.

On our way westward, we stop for a day at Salt Lake City, the capital of Utah, some sixteen hundred miles from Chicago. The site of the present town was an unbroken wilderness so late as 1838, but it now boasts a population of twenty-six thousand souls. The peculiar people who have established themselves here, have by industry and a complete system of irrigation, brought the entire valley to a degree of fertility unsurpassed by the same number of square miles on this continent. It is not within our province to discuss the domestic life of the Mormons. No portrait of them, however, will prove a likeness which does not clearly depict their twofold features; namely, their thrift and their iniquity. Contact with a truer condition of civilization, and the enforcement of United States laws, are slowly, but it is believed surely, reducing the numbers of the self-entitled "saints." Mormon missionaries, however, still seek to make proselytes in France, Norway, Sweden, and Great Britain, addressing themselves always to the most ignorant classes. These poor half-starved creatures are helped to emigrate, believing that they are coming to a land flowing with milk and honey. In most cases any change with them would be for their advantage; and so the ranks of Mormonism are recruited, not from any truly religious impulse in the new disciples, but through a desire to better their physical condition.

From Utah, two days and a night passed in the cars will take us over the six hundred intervening miles to San Francisco. The route passes through the Sierra Nevada Mountains, presenting scenery which recalls the grand gorges and snow-clad peaks of Switzerland and Norway, characterized by deep canyons, lofty wooded elevations, and precipitous declivities. At the several railway stations specimens of the native Shoshones, Piutes, and other tribes of Indians are seen lazily sunning themselves in picturesque groups. The men are dirty and uncouth examples of humanity, besmeared with yellow ochre and vermilion; their dress consisting of loose flannel blankets and deerskin leggings, their rude hats decked with eagle feathers. The women are wrapped in striped blankets and wear red flannel leggings, both sexes being furnished with buckskin moccasins. The women are fond of cheap ornaments, colored glass beads, and brass ear-rings. About every other one has a baby strapped to her back in a flat basket. Men and squaws wear their coarse jet-black hair in long, untidy locks, hanging over their bronzed necks and faces. War, whiskey, and want of proper food are gradually blotting out the aboriginal tribes of America.

San Francisco, less than forty years of age, is the commercial metropolis of California, which State, if it lay upon the Atlantic coast, would extend from Massachusetts to South Carolina. It covers a territory five times as large as the whole of the New England States combined, possessing, especially in its southern division, a climate presenting most of the advantages of the tropics with but few of the objections which appertain to the low latitudes. The population of San Francisco already reaches an aggregate of nearly four hundred thousand. Owing its first popular attraction to the discovery of gold within its borders, in 1849, California has long since developed an agricultural capacity exceeding the value of its mineral productions. The future promise and possibilities of its trade and commerce defy calculation.

The Cliff House, situated four or five miles from the centre of the city, is a favorite pleasure resort of the population. It stands on a bluff of the Pacific shore, affording an ocean view limited only by the power of the human vision. As we look due west from this spot, no land intervenes between us and the far-away shore of Japan. Opposite the Cliff House, three hundred yards from the shore, there rises abruptly out of the sea, from a depth of many fathoms, a rough, precipitous rock, sixty or seventy feet in height, presenting about an acre of surface. Sea-lions come out of the water in large numbers to sun themselves upon this rock, affording an amusing sight from the shore. These animals are of all sizes, according to age, weighing from fifty to one thousand pounds, and possessing sufficient muscular power to enable them to climb the rock, where a hundred are often seen at a time. The half roar, half bark peculiar to these creatures, sounds harsh upon the ear of the listeners at the Cliff. The law of the State protects them from molestation, but they quarrel furiously among themselves. The sea-lion belongs to the seal family and is the largest of its species.

A week can hardly be more profitably occupied upon our route than by visiting the Yosemite Valley, where the grandeur of the Alpine scenery is unsurpassed, and where there are forests which produce giant trees of over three hundred feet in height and over thirty in diameter. The ascent of the mountain which forms the barrier to the valley, commences at a place called Clark's, the name of the person who keeps the hotel, and which is the only dwelling-house in the neighborhood. The stage is drawn upwards over a precipitous, winding road, by relays of six stout horses, to an elevation of seven thousand feet, leaving behind nearly all signs of human habitation. A mournful air of loneliness surrounds us as we creep slowly towards the summit; but how grand and inspiring are the views which are seen from the various points! One falls to analyzing the natural architecture of these mountain peaks, gulches, and cliffs, fancy making out at times well-defined Roman circuses; again, castellated crags come into view, resembling half-ruined castles on the Rhine; other crags are like Turkish minarets, while some rocky ranges are dome-capped like St. Peter's at Rome. Far below them all we catch glimpses of dark ravines of unknown depths, where lonely mist-wreaths rest like snow-drifts.

Nestling beside the roadway, there are seen here and there pale wild-flowers surrounded by vigorous ferns and creeping vines, showing that even here, in these lofty and deserted regions, Nature has her poetic moods. Birds almost entirely disappear at these altitudes, preferring the more genial atmosphere of the plains, though now and

MIRROR LAKE, YOSEMITE VALLEY.

again an eagle, with broad spread pinions, is seen to swoop gracefully from the top of some lonely pine, and sail with unmoving wings far away across the depth of the valley until hidden by the windings of the gorge. Even the presence of this proud and kingly bird but serves to emphasize the loneliness of these silent heights.

By and by the loftiest portion of the road is reached at what is known as Inspiration Point, whence a comprehensive view is afforded of the far-famed valley. Though we stand here at an elevation of over seven thousand feet above the plains so lately crossed, still the Yosemite Valley, into which we are gazing with awe and admiration, is but about three thousand five hundred feet below us. It runs east and west, appearing quite contracted from this great height, but is eight miles long by over one in width. On either side rise vertical cliffs of granite, varying from three to four thousand feet in height, several of the lofty gorges discharging narrow but strikingly beautiful and transparent water-falls. Upon descending into the valley, we find ourselves surrounded by precipitous mountains, nearly a score in number, the loftiest of which is entitled Starr King, after the late clergyman of that name, and is five thousand six hundred feet in height. But the Three Brothers, with an average height of less than four thousand feet, and Sentinel Dome, measuring four thousand five hundred feet high, seem to the casual observer to be quite as prominent, while El Capitan, which is about three thousand three hundred feet in height, appears from its more favorable position to be the most striking and effective of them all. Eleven water-falls of greater or less magnitude come tumbling into the valley, adding to the picturesqueness of the scene. Of these several falls, that which is known as the Bridal Veil will be sure to strike the stranger as the finest, though not the loftiest. The constant moisture and the vertical rays of the sun carpet the level plain of the valley with a bright and uniform verdure, through the midst of which winds the swift-flowing Merced River, adding completeness to a scene of rare and enchanting beauty.

It was not until so late as the year 1851 that the foot of a white man ever trod the valley, which had for years proven the secure hiding-place of marauding Indians. In their battles with the whites, the latter were often surprised by the sudden disappearance of their foes, who vanished mysteriously, leaving no traces behind them. On these occasions, as was afterwards discovered, they fled to the almost inaccessible Yosemite Valley. Betrayed at last by a treacherous member of their own tribe, the Indians were surprised and nearly all destroyed. There is scarcely a resident in the valley except those connected with the running of the stages during the summer months, and those who are attached to the hotel. It is quite inaccessible in winter. An encampment of native Indians is generally to be seen in the warm months, located on the river's bank, under the shade of a grove of tall trees; the river and the forest afford these aborigines ample food. For winter use they store a crop of acorns, which they dry, and grind into a nourishing flour. They are a dirty, sad-looking race, far more repulsive in appearance than the lowest type of Spanish gypsies one meets in Andalusia.

In returning from the Yosemite to San Francisco, let us do so by the road leading through the Mariposa Grove of Big Trees. These forest monarchs are situated in a thickly wooded glade hundreds of feet up the slope of the Sierra.

We find one of these trees partially decayed towards its base, yet still alive and standing upright with a broad, lofty passage-way through its entire trunk, large enough for our stage, laden with passengers inside and out, to drive through. Though time has made such havoc with this trunk, it still possesses sufficient vitality to bear leaves upon its topmost branches, some three hundred feet above the ground. It is curious that these enormous trees, among the largest upon the globe, have cones only about the size of walnuts, with seeds of hardly a quarter of an inch in length. There are trunks lying upon the ground in this remarkable grove which are believed to be two thousand years of age; and others upright, and in growing condition, which are reckoned by their clearly defined annual rings, to be thirteen hundred years old. The region embraced in what is known as the Yosemite Valley has been ceded by the National Government to the State of California, on the express condition that it shall be kept inviolate in its present wild and natural state for all time.

The streets, alleys, and boulevards of San Francisco present a panorama of human interest rarely excelled in any part of the world. How impressive to watch its cosmopolitan life, to note the exaggerated love of pleasure exhibited on all hands, the devotion of each active member of the community to money-making, the prevailing manners and customs, the iniquitous pursuits of the desperate and dangerous classes, and the readiness of their too willing victims! It is the solitary looker-on who sees more than the actors in the great drama of every-day life. Above all, it is most curious to observe how the lines of barbarism and civilization intersect along these teeming avenues.

There is a district of the city near its very centre, known

as Chinatown, which is at total variance with the general surroundings. It requires but a slight stretch of the imagination after passing its borders to believe one's self in Canton or Hong Kong, except that the thoroughfares in the Asiatic capitals are mere alleys in width, shut in overhead and darkened by straw mats, while here we have broad streets after the American and European fashion, open to the sky. They are, however, lined with Chinese shops, decked in all their national peculiarities, exhibiting the most grotesque signs, while the windows are crowded with outlandish articles, and the whole surrounded by an Oriental atmosphere. This section is almost entirely peopled by Mongolians, and such poor abandoned men and women of other nationalities as seek among these repulsive surroundings to hide themselves from the shame and penalty of their crimes.

It is not proposed in these Foot-Prints of Travel to remain long on this continent. Americans are presumed to be quite familiar with their native land; so we will embark without delay upon a voyage across the Pacific Ocean to Japan, by way of the Sandwich Islands. Once on board ship, we quickly pass through the Golden Gate, as the entrance to the spacious harbor of San Francisco is called, steering south-southwest towards the Hawaiian group, which is situated a little over two thousand miles away. The great seas and oceans of the globe, like the land, have their geographical divisions and local peculiarities, varying essentially in temperature, products, and moods; now marked by certain currents; now noted for typhoons and hurricanes; and now lying in latitudes which are favored with almost constant calms and unvarying sunshine. By a glance at the map we shall see that a vessel taking her course for New Zealand, for instance, by the way of the Sandwich Islands, will pass through a tract of the Pacific Ocean seemingly so full of islands that we are led to wonder how a ship pursuing such a route can avoid running foul of some of the Polynesian groups. But it must be remembered that the distances which are so concisely depicted to our eyes upon the map, are yet vast in reality, while so mathematically exact are the rules of navigation, and so well known are the prevailing currents, that a steamship may make the voyage from Honolulu to Auckland, a distance of four thousand miles, without sighting land. When Magellan, the Portuguese navigator, first discovered this great ocean, after sailing through the straits which bear his name, he called it the Pacific Ocean, and perhaps it seemed "pacific" to him after a stormy voyage in the Caribbean Sea; but portions of its surface are quite as restless and tempest-tossed as are the waters of any part of the globe. The Pacific measures nine thousand miles from north to south, and is ten thousand miles broad between Quito, South America, and the Moluccas or Spice Islands. At the extreme north, where Behring's Strait divides the continents of Asia and America, it is scarcely more than forty miles in width, so that in clear weather one can see the shores of Asia while standing on our own continent.

It is an eight days' voyage by steamship from San Francisco to Honolulu, giving the traveller ample time to familiarize himself with many peculiarities of this waste of waters. Occasionally a whale is sighted, throwing up a small column of water as it rises at intervals to the surface. A whale is not a fish; it differs materially from the finny tribe, and can as surely be drowned as can a man. Whales bring forth living young; they breathe atmospheric air through their lungs in place of water through gills, having also a double heart and warm blood, like land animals. Flying-fish are frequently seen, queer little creatures, resembling the smelts of our northern waters. While exhibiting the nature of a fish, they have also the soaring ambition of a bird. Hideous, man-eating sharks are sure to follow in the ship's wake, watching for some unfortunate victim of a sailor or passenger who may fall overboard, and eagerly devouring any refuse thrown from the cook's galley. At times the many-armed cuttle-fish is seen to leap out of the water, while the star-fish, with its five arms of equal length, abounds. Though it seems so apparently lifeless, the star-fish can be quite aggressive when pressed by hunger, having, as naturalists tell us, a mysterious way of causing the oyster to open its shell, when it proceeds gradually to consume the body of the bivalve. One frail, small rover of the deep is sure to interest the voyager; namely, the tiny nautilus, with its transparent covering, almost as frail as writing-paper. No wonder the ancient Greeks saw in its beautifully corrugated shell the graceful model of a galley, and hence its name, derived from the Greek word which signifies a ship. Sometimes a pale gray, amber-like substance is seen floating upon the surface of the sea, which, upon examination, proves to be ambergris, a substance originally found in the body of the sperm whale, and which is believed to be produced there only. Scientists declare it to be a secretion caused by disease in the animal, probably induced by indigestion, as the pearl is said to be a diseased secretion of the Australian and Penang oysters. Ambergris is not infrequently found floating along the shores of the Coral Sea, and about the west coast of New Zealand, having been ejected by the whales which frequent these waters. When first taken from the animal it is of a soft texture, and is offensive to the smell; but after a brief exposure to the air it rapidly hardens, and then emits a sweet, earthy odor, and is used in manufacturing choice perfumery.

The harbor of San Francisco abounds in big, white seagulls, which fly fearlessly in and out among the shipping, uttering defiant screams, or floating gracefully like corks upon the water. They are large, handsome, dignified birds, and are never molested, being looked upon as picturesque ornaments to the harbor; and they are also the most active of scavengers, removing all sorts of floating carrion and refuse which is thrown overboard. The gulls one sees off the coast of Norway are numbered by thousands, but they are not nearly so large as these bird monarchs of the Pacific. A score of these are sure to accompany us to sea, closely following the ship day after day, living mostly upon the refuse thrown out from the steward's department. In the month of October, 1884, one of these birds was caught by the passengers upon a steamship just as she was leaving the coast of America for Japan. A piece of red tape was made fast to one of its legs, after which it was restored to liberty. This identical gull followed the ship between four and five thousand miles, into the harbor of Yokohama. Distance seems to be of little account to these buoyant navigators of the air.

On approaching the Hawaiian group from the north, the first land which is sighted is the island of Oahu, and soon after we pass along the windward shores of Maui and Molokai, doubling the lofty promontory of Diamond Head. which rears its precipitous front seven hundred feet above the sea. We arrive at the dawn of day, while the rising sun beautifies the mountain tops, the green slopes, the gulches, and fern-clad hills, which here and there sparkle with silvery streamlets. The gentle morning breeze blowing off the land brings us the dewy fragrance of the flowers, which has been distilled from a wilderness of tropical bloom during the night. The land forms a shelter for our vessel, and we glide noiselessly over a perfectly calm sea. As we draw nearer to the shore, sugar plantations, cocoanut groves, and verdant pastures come clearly into view. Here and there the shore is dotted with the low, primitive dwellings of the natives, and occasionally we see picturesque, vine-clad cottages of American or European residents. Approaching still nearer to the city of Honolulu, it seems to be half-buried in a cloud of luxuriant foliage, while a broad and beautiful valley stretches away from the town far back among the lofty hills.

The steamer glides at half speed through the narrow channel in the coral reef which makes the natural breakwater of the harbor. This channel is carefully buoyed on either side, and at night safety-lamps are placed upon each of these little floating beacons, so that a steamship can find her way in even after nightfall. Though the volcanic origin of the land is plain, it is not the sole cause of these reefs and islands appearing thus in mid-ocean. Upon the flanks of the upheaval the little coral animal, with tireless industry, rears its amazing structure, until it reaches the surface of the waves as a reef, more or less contiguous to the shore, and to which ages finally serve to join it. The tiny creature delegated by Providence to build these reefs dies on exposure to the air, its work being then completed. The far-reaching antiquity of the islands is established by these very coralline formations, which could only have attained their present elevation, just below the surface of the surrounding sea, by the growth of thousands of years. This coral formation on the shores of the Hawaiian group is not peculiar to these islands, but is found to exist in connection with nearly all of those existing in the Pacific Ocean.

The lighthouse, placed on the inner side of the coral reef, is a structure not quite thirty feet in height. After reaching the inside of the harbor of Honolulu, the anchorage is safe and sheltered, with ample room for a hundred large vessels at the same time, the average depth of water being some sixteen fathoms. The wharves are spacious and substantial, built with broad, high coverings to protect laborers from the heat of a tropical sun. Honolulu is the commercial port of the whole group of islands, — the halfway house, as it were, between North America and Asia, — California and the new world of Australasia.

CHAPTER II.

UPON landing at Honolulu we find ourselves in a city of some twenty thousand inhabitants, presenting all the modern belongings of a metropolis of the nineteenth century, such as schools, churches, hospitals, charitable institutions, gas, electric lights, and the telephone. Nearly all of the rising generation can read and write, and the entire population are professed Christians. Great is the contrast in every respect between these islands as discovered by Captain Cook in 1778, and their present condition. Originally they exhibited the same barbarous characteristics which were found to exist in other islands of the Pacific Ocean. They had no sense of domestic virtue, and were victims of the most egregious superstitions. "The requisitions of their idolatry," says the historian Ellis, "were severe, and its rites cruel and bloody." Their idolatry has been abandoned since 1819. In the early days the several islands of the group had each a separate king, and wars were frequent between them, until King Kamehameha finally subjected them all to his sway, and formed the government which has lasted to the present time.

Many of the streets of Honolulu afford a grateful shade, the sidewalks being lined by ornamental trees, of which the cocoanut, palm, bread-fruit, candle-nut, and some others, are indigenous, but many have been introduced from abroad and have become domesticated. The tall mango-tree, with rich, glossy leaves, the branches bending under the weight of its delicious fruit, is seen growing everywhere, though it is not a native of these islands. Among other fruit-trees we observe the feathery tamarind, orange, lime, alligator-pear, citron-fig, date, and rose apple. Of all the flowering trees, the most conspicuous and attractive is one which bears a cloud of brilliant scarlet blossoms, each cluster ball-shaped and as large as a Florida orange. Some of the thoroughfares are lined by pretty, low-built cottages, standing a few rods back from the roadway, with broad, inviting verandas, the whole festooned and nearly hidden by tropical and semi-tropical plants in full bloom. If we drive out to the race-course in the environs, we shall be pretty sure to see King Kalakaua, who is very fond of this sort of sport. He is a man of intelligence and of considerable culture, but whose personal habits are of a low and disgraceful character. He has reached his fifty-second year.

It will be observed that the women ride man-fashion here, — that is, astride of their horses, — and there is a good reason for this. Even European and American ladies who become residents also adopt this mode of riding, because side-saddles are not considered to be safe on the steep mountain roads. If one rides in any direction here, mountains must be crossed. The native women deck themselves in an extraordinary manner with flowers on all gala occasions, while the men wear wreaths of the same about their straw hats, often adding braids of laurel leaves across the shoulders and chest. The white blossoms of the jasmine, fragrant as tuberoses, which they much resemble, are generally employed for this decorative purpose. As a people the Hawaiians are very courteous and respectful, rarely failing to greet all passing strangers with a softly articulated "alo-ha," which signifies "my love to you."

A drive up the Nuuanu valley, which opens with a broad entrance near the city, introduces us to some grand scenery. In ascending this beautiful valley one is constantly charmed by the discovery of new tropical trees, luxurious creepers and lovely wild-flowers. The strangers' burial-ground is passed just after crossing the Nuuanu stream, and close at hand is the Royal Mausoleum,— a stone structure in Gothic style, which contains the remains of the Hawaiian kings, as well as those of many of the high chiefs who have died since the conquest. Some shaded bathing-pools are formed by the mountain streams, lying half hidden in the dense foliage. Here we pass the residence of the late Queen Emma, pleasantly located and flower-embowered. This valley is classic ground in the history of these islands, being the spot where the fierce and conquering invader, King Kamehameha I., fought his last decisive battle, the result of which confirmed him as sole monarch of the Hawaiian group. Here the natives of Oahu made their final stand and fought desperately, resisting with clubs and spears the savage hordes led by Kamehameha. But they were defeated at last, and with their king Kaiana, who led them in person, were all driven over the abrupt and fatal cliff fifteen hundred feet high, situated at the upper end of the valley.

In the environs of the city one passes upon the roadsides large patches measuring an acre or more of submerged land, where is grown the Hawaiian staff of life,— the *taro*, a root which is cultivated in mud and mostly under water, recalling the rice-fields of China and Japan. The vegetable thus produced, when baked and pounded to

HAWAIIANS EATING POI.

a flour, forms a nutritious sort of dough called *poi*, which constitutes the principal article of food for the natives, as potatoes do with the Irish or macaroni with the Italians. This poi is eaten both cooked and in a raw state mixed with water.

Though Oahu is quite mountainous, like the rest of the islands which form the Hawaiian group, still none of these reach the elevation of perpetual snow. The six inhabited islands of the group are Kauai, Oahu, Molokai, Lanai, Maui, and Hawaii, the last containing the largest active volcano of which we have any knowledge; namely, that of Kilauea, to visit which persons cross the Atlantic and Pacific oceans, and also the American continent, between the two. Honolulu was chosen for the capital because it forms the best and almost the only harbor worthy of the name to be found among these islands. In the olden times Lahaina, on the island of Maui, was the city of the king, and the recognized capital in the palmy days of the whale fishery. This settlement is now going to ruin, tumbling to pieces by wear and tear of the elements, forming a rude picture of decay. Should the Panama Canal be completed, it would prove to be of great advantage to these islands, as they lie in the direct course which a great share of navigation must follow. The aggregate population of the group is now about sixty thousand, of whom some thirty-eight thousand are natives. History tells us that Captain Cook estimated these islands to contain over three hundred thousand inhabitants when he discovered them. Perhaps this was an exaggeration, though it is a fact that they are capable of sustaining a population of even much greater density than this estimate would indicate.

The ubiquitous Chinamen are found here as gardeners, laborers, house-servants, fruit-dealers, and poi-makers. What an overflow there has been of these Asiatics from the "Flowery Land!" Each one of the race arriving at the Sandwich Islands is now obliged to pay ten dollars as his landing fee, in default of which the vessel which brings him is compelled to take him away. This singular people, who are wonderfully industrious, notwithstanding their many faults, are equally disliked in these islands by the natives, the Americans, and the Europeans; yet the Chinamen steadily increase in numbers, and it is believed here that they are destined eventually to take the place of the aborigines. The aggregate number now to be found in the group is over twelve thousand. It is evident that many branches of small trade are already monopolized by them, as is the case at Penang, Singapore, and other Pacific islands. On Nuuanu Street every shop is occupied by a Chinaman, dealing in such articles as his own countrymen and the natives are likely to purchase. It does certainly appear as though the aboriginal race would in the near future be obliterated, and their place filled by the Anglo-Saxons and the Chinese, the representative people of the East and the West. The taro-patches of the Hawaiians will doubtless ere long become the rice-fields of the Mongolians.

In the year 1887 there was raised upon these islands a very large amount of sugar, over one hundred thousand tons in all. The entire product, except what was consumed for domestic use, was shipped to this country. Three-quarters of the money invested in sugar-raising here is furnished by American capitalists, and American managers carry on the plantations. A reciprocity treaty between the Sandwich Islands and this country (that is, a national agreement upon matters of mutual interest), and their proximity to the shores of America, have brought this people virtually under the wing of our Government, concentrating their foreign trade almost entirely in the United States, while the youth of the islands, of both sexes, are sent hither for educational purposes. There is no other foreign port in the world where the American flag is so often seen, or more respected than in that of Honolulu.

The Hawaiian Islands are not on the direct route to Japan, and we therefore find it better to return to San Francisco and embark from there, than to await the arrival of a chance steamer bound westward. Our course is not in the track of general commerce, and neither ship nor shore is encountered while crossing this vast expanse of water. Storms and calms alternate; sometimes the ocean is as smooth as an inland lake, and at others in its unrest it tossed our iron hull about as though it were a mere skiff, in place of a ship of three thousand tons' measurement. The roughness of the water is exhibited near the coast and in narrow seas by short, chopping waves; but in the open ocean these are changed to long, heavy swells, covering the expanse of waters with vast parallels separated by deep valleys, the distance from crest to crest being from one hundred and fifty to two hundred feet during a heavy gale. The height of the waves is measured from the trough to the crest, and is of course conjecture only, but in heavy weather it may safely be set down at thirty feet.

Every steamship on the trip westward carries more or less Chinamen, who, having acquired a certain sum of money by industry and self-denial, are glad to return to their native land and live upon its income. Interest is very high in China, and money is scarce. It is curious to watch these second-class passengers. In fine weather they crowd the forward deck, squatting upon their hams in picturesque groups, and playing cards or dominos for small stakes of money. The Chinese are inveterate gamblers, but are satisfied generally to play for very small stakes. When the sea becomes rough and a storm rages, they exhibit great timidity, giving up all attempts at amusement. On such occasions, with sober faces and trembling hands, they prepare pieces of joss-paper (scraps with magic words), bearing Chinese letters, and cast them overboard to propitiate the anger of the special god who controls the sea. The dense, noxious smell which always permeates their quarters, in spite of enforced ventilation and the rules of the ship, is often wafted unpleasantly to our own part of the vessel, telling a significant story of the opium pipe, and a certain uncleanliness of person peculiar to Africans and Mongolians.

After a three weeks' voyage we reach Yokohama, the commercial capital of Japan. When Commodore Perry opened this port in 1854 with a fleet of American men-of-war, it was scarcely more than a fishing village, but it has now a population of a hundred and thirty thousand, with well-built streets of dwelling-houses, the thoroughfares broad and clean, and all macadamized. The town extends along the level shore, but is backed by a half-moon of low, wooded hills, known as the Bluff, among which are the dwellings of the foreign residents, built after the European and American style. A deep, broad canal surrounds the city, passing by the large warehouses, and connected with the bay at each end, being crossed by several handsome bridges. If we ascend the road leading to the Bluff we have a most

MODE OF TRAVELLING IN JAPAN. A JINRIKSHA.

charming and extended view. In the west, seventy miles away, the white, cloud-like cone of Fujiyama, a large volcanic mountain of Japan, can clearly be discerned, while all about us lie the pretty villas of the foreign settlers.

In looking about this commercial capital everything strikes us as curious; every new sight is a revelation, while in all directions tangible representations of the strange pictures we have seen upon fans and lacquered ware are presented to view. One is struck by the partial nudity of men, women, and children, the extremely simple architecture of the dwelling-houses, the peculiar vegetation, the extraordinary salutations between the common people who meet each other upon the streets, the trading bazars, and the queer toy-like articles which fill them; children flying kites in the shape of hideous yellow monsters. Each subject becomes a fresh study. Men drawing vehicles, like horses between the shafts, and trotting off at a six-mile pony-gait while drawing after them one or two persons, is a singular sight to a stranger. So are the naked natives, by fours, bearing heavy loads swung from their shoulders upon stout bamboo poles, while they shout a measured chant by means of which to keep step. No beggars are seen upon the streets; the people without exception are all neat and cleanly. The houses are special examples of neatness, and very small, being seldom more than twenty feet square, and one story in height. All persons, foreigners or natives, take off their shoes before entering upon the polished floors, not only out of respect to the customs of the country, but because one does not feel like treading upon their floors with nailed heels or soiled soles. The conviction forces itself upon us that such universal neatness and cleanliness must extend even to the moral character of the people. A spirit of gentleness, industry, and thrift are observable everywhere, imparting an Arcadian atmosphere to these surroundings. In the houses which we enter there are found neither chairs, tables, nor bedsteads; the people sit, eat, and sleep upon the floors, which are as clean as a newly laid tablecloth.

Here and there upon the roadsides moss-grown shrines bearing sacred emblems are observed, before which women, but rarely men, are seen bending. The principal religions of Japan are Shinto and Buddhism, subdivided into many sects. The Shinto is mainly a form of hero worship, successful warriors being canonized as martyrs are in the Roman Catholic Church. Buddhism is another form of idolatry, borrowed originally from the Chinese. The language of the country is composed of the Chinese and Japanese combined. As we travel inland, places are pointed out to us where populous cities once stood, but where no ruins mark the spot. A dead and buried city in Europe or in Asia leaves rude but almost indestructible remains to mark where great communities once built temples and monuments, and lived and thrived, like those historic examples of mutability, Memphis, Pæstum, Cumæ, or Delhi; but not so in Japan. It seems strange indeed that a locality where half a million of people have made their homes within the period of a century, should now present the aspect only of fertile fields of grain. But when it is remembered of what fragile material the natives build their dwellings, — namely, of light, thin wood and paper, — their utter disappearance ceases to surprise us. It is a curious fact that this people, contemporary with Greece and Rome at their zenith, who have only reared cities of wood and temples of lacquer, have outlived the classic nations whose half-ruined monuments are our choicest models. The Greek and Latin races have passed away, but Japan still remains, without a change of dynasty and with an inviolate country.

In journeying inland we are struck with many peculiarities showing how entirely opposite to our own methods are many of theirs. At the post-stations the horses are placed and tied in their stalls with their heads to the passage-way, and their tails where we place their heads. Instead of iron shoes, the Japanese pony is shod with close-braided rice-straw. Carpenters, in using the fore-plane, draw it towards them instead of pushing it from them. It is the same in using a saw, the teeth being set accordingly. So the tailor sews from him, not towards his body, and holds his thread with his toes. The women ride astride, like the Hawaiians.

A trip of fifteen miles from Yokohama will take us to the town of Kamakura, where we find the remarkable idol of Dai-Butsu. This great Buddha image, composed of gold, silver, and copper, forms a bronze figure of nearly sixty feet in height, within which a hundred persons may stand together, the interior being fitted at the base as a small chapel. A vast number of little scraps of paper bearing Japanese characters, flutter from the interior walls of the big idol, fastened there by pious pilgrims, forming petitions to the presiding deity. As we enter, these scraps, agitated by the winds, rustle like an army of white bats. This sacred figure is as remarkable as the Sphinx, which presides so placidly at the feet of the great Pyramids. As a work of art, its only merits consist in the calm dignity of expression and repose upon its colossal features. It is many centuries old, and how such an enormous amount of bronze metal was ever cast, or how set up in such perfect shape when finished, no one can say. It must have been completed in sections and put together in the place where it stands, the joints being so perfectly welded as not to be obvious. It was formerly covered by a temple which has long since mouldered to dust, but it is certainly none the less effective and impressive, as it now sits surrounded by the natural scenery and the thick woods.

Japanese art, of which we have all seen such laughable specimens, is not without some claims to excellence; otherwise we should not have the myriads of beautifully ornamented articles which are produced by them, exhibiting exquisite finish and perfection of detail. Of perspective they have no idea whatever; the play of light and shade they do not understand; there is no distinction of distances in their pictures. Their figures are good, being also delicately executed, and their choice of colors is admirable. Thus in profile work they get on very well, but in grouping, they pile houses on the sea, and mountains on the houses. In caricature they greatly excel, and, indeed, they scarcely attempt to represent the human face and figure in any other light.

Tokio is the political capital of Japan, and is situated about twenty miles from Yokohama, containing over half a million of people. It has broad streets and good roadways, having adopted many American ideas of city customs and government. The Bridge of Japan is situated in this city, crossing the river which intersects the capital, and is here what the golden milestone was in the Forum at Rome — all distances in the Empire are measured from it. There are many elaborate temples within the city, containing rare bronzes of great value. Priests are constantly seen writing upon slips of paper, inside of the temples, at the request of devotees, which the suppliants pin upon the walls of the temple as a form of prayer. The renowned temple of Shiba is one of the greatest attractions to strangers in Tokio. Here lie buried most of the bygone Tycoons (sovereigns of Japan). The grounds are divided into many departments, tombs, shrines, and small temples. In the main temple there is an amount of gold, silver, and bronze ornaments of fabulous value, leading us to wonder where the raw material could have come from. History knows nothing of the importation of the precious metals, but it is true that they are found in more or less abundance all over the country. Copper of the purest quality is a native product, the exportation of which is prohibited, and mining for the precious metals is carried on to but a very limited extent. The temple of Shiba is situated near the centre of the population, occupying many acres of ground, walled in, and shaded by a thick grove of trees, whose branches are black with thousands of undisturbed rooks and pigeons which are considered sacred. The principal characteristic of the architecture is its boldness of relief, overhanging roofs, heavy brackets, and elaborate carvings. The doors are of solid bronze in bas-relief.

In the suburbs is a hill known as Atago-Yama, from whence there is a grand, comprehensive view of the capital. A couple of miles to the southeast lies the broad, glistening Bay of Tokio, and round the other points of the compass the imperial city itself covers a plain of some eight miles square, divided by water-ways, bridges, and clumps of graceful trees looming conspicuously above the low dwellings. The whole is as level as a checker-board; but yet there is relief to the picture in the fine open gardens, the high-peaked gable roofs of the temples, and the broad white roadways.

A visit to Kioto, which is called the City of Temples, shows us some prominent local peculiarities. The Japanese character presents as much unlikeness to the Oriental as to the European type, and is comparable only to itself. A native believes that the little caricature in ivory or wood which has, perhaps, been manufactured under his own eyes, or even by his own hands, is sacred, and he will address his prayers to it with a solemn conviction of its power to respond favorably. His most revered gods are effigies of renowned warriors and successful generals. African superstition is no blinder than is such adoration, though it be performed by an intelligent people. Some of the native animals, such as foxes, badgers, and snakes, are protected with superstitious reverence. Before one of the temples we see a theatrical performance in progress, which seems rather incongruous, but upon inquiry the object of this is found to be a desire to appease the special gods of this individual temple; in fact, to entertain and amuse them so that they will receive the prayers of the people with favor. The exhibition consists of dancing and posturing by professionals of both sexes, accompanied by the noise of whistles, gongs, bells, and fifes.

At Koby we embark for Nagasaki, sailing the whole length of the famous Inland Sea, a most enchanting three days' voyage among lovely islands, terraced and cultivated here and there like vineyards on the Rhine. The course is characterized by narrow and winding passages, losing themselves in creeks and bays after a most curious fashion, while brown hamlets here and there fringe the coast line.

Nagasaki is in the extreme south of Japan, a city second only to Yokohama in commercial importance. A sad interest attaches to the small but lofty island of Pappenburg, which stands like a sentinel guarding the entrance to the harbor. It is the Tarpeian Rock of the far East. During the persecution of the Christians in the seventeenth century, the steep cliff which forms the seaward side of the island was an execution point, and from here men and women who declined to abjure their faith were cast headlong on the sea-washed rocks five hundred feet below. The harbor is surrounded by lofty elevations. Tall, dark pines and a verdant undergrowth mark the deep ravines and sloping hillsides, upon which European dwellings are seen overlooking the bay. If we climb the path among these hills we occasionally pass a Buddhist temple, and come upon many wild-flowers, shaded by oaks and camphor-trees of great size and beautiful foliage, with occasional specimens of the Japanese wax-tree. Still further up, the hills are covered with dark, moss-grown gravestones, bearing curious characters engraven upon them, and marking the sleeping-places of bygone generations. The unbroken quiet of this city of the dead contrasts vividly with the hum of busy life which comes up to us from the town with its population of a hundred thousand souls. As to the products of this locality, they are mostly figured porcelain, embroidered silks, japanned goods, ebony and tortoise-shell finely carved and manufactured into toy ornaments. Every small, low house has a shop in front quite open to the street; but small as these houses are, room is nearly always found in the rear or at the side for a little flower-garden, fifteen or twenty feet square, where dwarf trees flourish amid hillocks of turf and ferns, with here and there a tub of goldfish. Azaleas, laurels, and tiny clumps of bamboos, are the most common plants to be seen in these charming little spots of greenery.

Botanists declare Japan to be one of the richest of all countries in its vegetation. The cultivation of the soil is thoroughly and skilfully systematized, the greatest possible results being obtained from a given area of land. This is partly due to the careful mode of enrichment applied in liquid form. Its flora is spontaneous and magnificent, repaying the smallest attention by a development which is surprising. Next in importance to the production of rice, which is the staple food of the people, come the mulberry and tea plants, one species of the former not only feeding the silkworm, but it also affords the fibre of which Japanese paper is made, as well as forming the basis of their cordage and some descriptions of dress material. In usefulness the bamboo is most remarkable, growing to a height of sixty feet, and entering into the construction of house-frames, screens, many household articles, mats, pipes, and sails. The camphor-tree, which is seen in such abundance, is a grand ornament in the landscape, lofty and broad-spread. The camphor of commerce is extracted from both the stem and the roots of the tree, which, being cut into small pieces, are subjected to a process of decoction.

No sooner have the Japanese been fairly introduced to American and European civilization, than they have promptly taken a stride of four or five centuries at a single leap, from despotism in its most ultra form to constitutional government. When America opened the port of Yokohama to the commerce of the world, it also opened that hermetically sealed land to the introduction of progressive ideas; and though, unfortunately, the elements of civilization which are most readily assimilated are not always the most beneficial, still the result, taken as a whole, has been worthy of the admiration of the world at large.

The natural intelligence of the Japanese has no superior among any race, however much it may have been perverted, or have lain dormant. There is evidence enough of this in the fact that the young men of that country who are sent here for educational purposes, so frequently win academic prizes and honors over our native scholars, notwithstanding the disadvantages under which a foreigner is inevitably placed.

When we speak of the progress of the Japanese as a nation, we must not forget that the national records of the country date from nearly seven hundred years before the birth of Christ, and that a regular succession of Mikados (supreme rulers), in lineal descent from the founders of their dynasty and race, has since that remote date been carefully preserved.

CHAPTER III.

FROM Nagasaki, in following our proposed course, we sail for Hong Kong, through the Yellow and Chinese seas, a distance of eleven hundred miles. This is very sure to be a rough passage, and the marvel is rather that more vessels are not lost here than that so many are. Seamen call it "the graveyard of commerce." As we enter the magnificent harbor of Hong Kong it is found to be surrounded by a range of lofty hills, which shelter it completely from the sweeping winds that so often prevail in this region. It is the most easterly of the possessions of Great Britain, and is kept in a well-fortified condition, the uniforms of the garrison being a striking feature of the busy streets of the city at all hours of the day. The houses in the European section are large and handsome structures, mostly of stone, rising tier upon tier from the main street to a height of some hundreds of feet on the face of the hill immediately back of the town. On and about the lofty Victoria Peak are many charming bungalows, or cottages, with attractive surroundings, which enjoy a noble prospect of the harbor and country. The streets appropriated to the use of the Europeans are spacious and clean, but the Chinese portion of Hong Kong is quite characteristic of the native race,—very crowded and very dirty, seeming to invite all sorts of epidemic diseases, which in fact nearly always prevail more or less severely among the lower classes.

These streets exhibit strange local pictures. The shoemaker plies his trade in the open thoroughfare; cooking is going on at all hours in the gutters beside the roads; itinerant pedlers dispense food made of mysterious materials; the barber shaves his customer upon the sidewalk; the universal fan is carried by the men, and not by the women. The Chinese mariner's compass does not point to the North Pole, but to the South; that is, the index is placed upon the opposite end of the needle. When Chinamen meet each other upon the streets, instead of shaking each other's hands they shake their own. The men wear skirts, and the women wear pantaloons. The dressmakers are not women, but men. In reading a book a Chinaman begins at the end and reads backwards. We uncover the head as a mark of respect; they take off their shoes for the same purpose, but keep their heads covered. We shave the face; they shave the head and eyebrows. At dinner we begin the meal with soup and fish; they reverse the order and begin with the dessert. The old men fly kites while the boys look on; shuttlecock is their favorite game; it is played, however, not with the hands, but with the feet. White constitutes the mourning color, and black is the wedding hue. The women perform the men's work, and the men wash the clothing. We pay our physicians for attending us in illness; they pay their doctors to keep them well, and stop their remuneration when they are ill. In short, this people seem to be our antipodes in customs as well as being so geographically.

A visit to the water-front of the city affords much amusement, especially at the hour when the market boats with vegetables arrive from the country, and from along shore with fish. Here the people swarm like ants more than like human beings; all eager for business, all crowding and talking at the same time, and creating a confusion that would seem to defeat its own object; namely, to buy and to sell. The vegetables are various and good, the variety of fruit limited and poor in flavor, but the fish are abundant and various in size and color. Nine-tenths of the business on the river-front is done by women, and they are very rarely seen without an infant strapped to their backs, while they are carrying heavy burdens in their hands, or are engaged in rowing or sculling their boats. They trade, make change, and clean the fish quite oblivious of the infant at their backs. A transient visitor to China is not competent to speak of the higher class of women, as no access can be had to domestic life. Only those of the common class appear indiscriminately in public, Oriental exclusiveness wrapping itself about the sex here nearly as rigidly as in Egypt. If ladies go abroad at all, it is in curtained palanquins, borne upon men's shoulders, partially visible through a transparent veil of gauze. Anywhere east of Italy woman is either a toy or a slave.

Hong Kong is an island nearly forty miles in circumference, consisting of a cluster of hills rising almost to the dignity of mountains. The gray granite of which the island is mostly composed, furnishes an excellent material for building purposes, and is largely employed for that object, affording a good opportunity for architectural display. A trip of a hundred miles up the Pearl River takes us to Canton, strangest of strange cities. It has a population of a million and a half, and yet there is not a street of over ten feet in width within the walls, horses and wheeled vehicles being unknown. The city extends a distance of five miles along the river, and a hundred thousand people live in boats. At the corners of the streets, niches in the walls of the houses contain idols, before which incense is constantly burning day and night. The most famous temple in the city is that of the Five Hundred Gods, containing that number of gilded statues of Buddhist sages, apostles, and deified warriors. In some of these sacred structures composed of shrines and miniature temples, among other seeming absurdities we see a number of sacred hogs wallowing in their filth. Disgusting as it appears to an intelligent Christian, it has its palliating features. The Parsee worships fire, the Japanese bows before snakes and foxes, the Hindoo deifies cows and monkeys; why, then, should not the Chinese have their swine as objects of veneration? We may destroy the idols, but let us not be too hard upon the idolaters; they do as well as they know. The idol is the measure of the worshipper. The punishment of crime is swift and sure, the number of persons beheaded annually being almost incredible. Friday is the day for clearing the crowded prison at Canton, and it is not uncommon on that occasion to see a dozen criminals beheaded in the prison yard in eight minutes, one sweeping blow of the executioner's sword decapitating each human body as it stands erect and blindfolded.

One is jostled in the narrow ways by staggering coolies with buckets of the vilest contents, and importuned for money by beggars who thrust their deformed limbs in his face. It is but natural to fear contagion of some sort from contact with such creatures, and yet the crowd is so dense that it is impossible to entirely avoid them. Under foot the streets are wet, muddy, and slippery. Why some deadly disease does not break out and sweep away the people is a mystery.

Philanthropic societies are numerous in the cities of China. Indeed, they are hardly excelled by those of America or Europe. They embrace well-organized orphan asylums, institutions for the relief of indigent widows with families, homes for the aged and infirm, public hospitals, and free schools in every district. As is the case with ourselves, some of these are purely governmental charities, while others are supported by liberal endowments left by deceased citizens. There are depots established to dispense medicines among the poor, and others whence clothing is distributed free of cost. It must be remembered that these societies and organizations are not copied from Western models. They have existed here from time immemorial.

No one has ever been able to trace any affinity between the Chinese language and that of any other people, ancient or modern. It is absolutely unique. No other nation except the Japanese has ever borrowed from it, or mingled any of its elements with its own. It must have originated from the untutored efforts of a primitive people. Like the Egyptian tongue, it was at first probably composed of hieroglyphics, expressing ideas by pictured objects, which in the course of time became systematized into letters or signs expressive of sounds and words.

Though we may dislike the Chinese, it is not wise to shut our eyes to facts which have passed into history. They have long been a reading and a cultured people. Five hundred years before the art of printing was known to Europe, books were multiplied by movable types in China. Every province has its separate history in print,

A CHINESE CART

To face p. 36.

and reliable maps of each section of the country are extant. The civil code of laws is annually corrected and published, a certain degree of education is universal, and eight-tenths of the people can read and write. The estimate in which letters are held is shown by the fact that learning forms the very threshold that leads to fame, honor, and official position. The means of internal communication between one part of China and another are scarcely superior to those of Africa. By and by, however, railways will revolutionize this. Gold and silver are found in nearly every province of the Empire, while the central districts contain the largest coal-fields upon the globe. Nearly one-fourth of the human race is supposed to be comprised within the Chinese Empire. They look to the past, not to the future, and the word "progress" has apparently to them no real significance.

In travelling through portions of the country a depressing sense of monotony is the prevailing feeling one experiences, each section is so precisely like another. There is no local individuality. Their veritable records represent this people as far back as the days of Abraham, and, indeed, they antedate that period. In two important discoveries they long preceded Europe; namely, that of the magnetic compass and the use of gunpowder. The knowledge of these was long in travelling westward through the channels of Oriental commerce, by the way of Asia Minor. There are many antagonistic elements to consider in judging of the Chinese. The common people we meet in the ordinary walks of life are far from prepossessing, and are much the same as those who have emigrated to this country. One looks in vain among the smooth chins, shaved heads, and almond eyes of the crowd for signs of intelligence and manliness. There are no tokens of humor or cheerfulness to be seen, but in their place there is plenty of apparent cunning, slyness, and deceit, if there is any truth in physiognomy. With the Japanese the traveller feels himself constantly sympathizing. He goes among them freely, he enters their houses and drinks tea with them; but not so with the Chinese. In place of affiliation we realize a constant sense of repulsion.

We embark at Hong Kong for Singapore by the way of the China Sea and the Gulf of Siam. The northerly wind favors us, causing the ship to rush through the turbulent waters like a race-horse. The Philippine Islands are passed, and leaving Borneo on our port-bow as we draw near to the Equatorial Line, the ship is steered due west for the mouth of the Malacca Straits. Off the Gulf of Siam we are pretty sure to get a view of a water-spout, and it is to be hoped that it may be a goodly distance from us. Atmospheric and ocean currents meet here, from the China Sea northward, from the Malacca Straits south and west, and from the Pacific Ocean eastward, mingling off the Gulf of Siam, and causing, very naturally, a confusion of the elements, resulting sometimes in producing these wind and water phenomena. A water-spout is a miniature cyclone, an eddy of the wind rotating with such velocity as to suck up a column of water from the sea to the height of one or two hundred feet. This column of water appears to be largest at the top and bottom, and contracted in the middle. If it were to fall foul of a ship and break, it would surely wreck and submerge her. Modern science shows that all storms are cyclonic; that is, they are circular eddies of wind of greater or less diameter. The power of these cyclones is more apparent upon the sea than upon the land, where the obstruction is naturally greater. Yet we know how destructive they sometimes prove in our Western States.

Singapore is the chief port of the Malacca Straits, and is an island lying just off the southern point of Asia, thirty miles long and half as wide, containing a population of about a hundred thousand. Here, upon landing, we are surrounded by tropical luxuriance, the palm and cocoanut trees looming above our heads and shading whole groves of bananas. The most precious spices, the richest fruits, the gaudiest feathered birds are found in their native atmosphere. There are plenty of Chinese at Singapore. They dominate the Strait settlements, monopolizing all branches of small trade, while the natives are lazy and listless, true children of the equatorial regions. Is it because Nature is here so bountiful, so lovely, so prolific, that her children are sluggish, dirty, and heedless? It would seem to require a less propitious climate, a sterile soil, and rude surroundings to awaken human energy and to place man at his best. The common people are seen almost naked, and those who wear clothes at all, affect the brightest colors. The jungle is dense, tigers abound, and men, women, and children are almost daily killed and eaten by them.

It is easy to divine the merchantable products of the island from the nature of the articles which are seen piled up for shipment upon the wharves, consisting of tapioca, cocoanut oil, gambia, tin ore, indigo, tiger-skins, coral, gutta-percha, hides, gums, and camphor.

There is no winter or autumn here, no sere and yellow leaf period, but seemingly a perpetual spring, with a temperature almost unvarying; new leaves always swelling from the bud, flowers always in bloom, the sun rising and setting within five minutes of six o'clock during the entire year. Singapore enjoys a soft breeze most of the day from across the Bay of Bengal, laden with fragrant sweetness from the spice-fields of Ceylon.

Each place we visit has its peculiar local pictures. Here, small hump-backed oxen are seen driven about at a lively trot in place of horses. Pedlers roam the streets selling drinking-water, with soup, fruit, and a jelly made from sugar and sea-weed, called agar-agar. Native houses are built upon stilts to keep out the snakes and tigers. The better class of people wear scarlet turbans and white cotton skirts; others have parti-colored shawls round their heads, while yellow scarfs confine a cotton wrap about the waist. Diminutive horses drag heavy loads, though themselves scarcely bigger than large dogs. Itinerant cooks, wearing a wooden yoke about their necks, with a cooking apparatus on one end, and a little table to balance it on the other, serve meals of fish and rice upon the streets to laborers and boatmen, for a couple of pennies each. Money has here, as in most Eastern countries, a larger purchasing power than it has with us in the West. The variety of fruit is greater than in China or Japan, and there are one or two species, such as the delicious mangosteen, which are found indigenous in no other region.

The stranger, upon landing at Singapore, is hardly prepared to find such excellent modern institutions as exist here. Among them are an attractive museum, a public library, a Protestant cathedral, a hospital, public schools, and a fine botanical garden. The island belongs to the English government, having been purchased by it so long ago as 1819, from the Sultan of Johore, — wise forethought, showing its importance as a port of call between England and India.

A two days' sail through waters which seem at night like a sea of phosphorescence, every ripple producing flashes of light, will take us to the island of Penang, the most northerly port of the Straits. It resembles Singapore in its people, vegetation, and climate, enjoying one long, unvarying summer. While the birds and butterflies are in perfect harmony with the loveliness of nature, while the flowers are glorious in beauty and in fragrance, man alone seems out of place in this region. Indolent, dirty, unclad, he does nothing to improve such wealth of possibilities as nature spreads broadcast only in equatorial islands. He does little for himself, nothing for others, while the sensuous life he leads poisons his nature, so that virtue and vice have no relative meaning for him. We speak now of the masses, the common people. Noble exceptions always exist. In size Penang is a little smaller than Singapore. Its wooded hills of vivid greenness rise above the town and surrounding sea in graceful undulations, growing more and more lofty as they recede inland, until they culminate in three mountain peaks. Penang is separated from the mainland by a narrow belt of sea not more than three miles wide, giving it a position of great commercial importance.

The areca-palm, known as the Penang-tree, is the source of the betel-nut, which is chewed by the natives as a stimulant; and as it abounds on the island, it has given it the name it bears. The town covers about a square mile, through which runs one broad, main street, intersected by lesser thoroughfares at right angles. A drive about the place gives us an idea that it is a thrifty town, but not nearly so populous as Singapore. It is also observable that the Chinese element predominates here. The main street is lined by shops kept by them. The front of the dwellings being open, gives the passer-by a full view of all that may be going on inside the household. Shrines are nearly always seen in some nook or corner, before which incense is burning, this shrine-room evidently being also the sleeping, eating, and living room. The islands of Penang and Singapore are free from malarial fevers, and probably no places on earth are better adapted to the wants of primitive man, for they produce spontaneously sufficient nutritious food to support life independent of personal exertion. The home of the Malay is not so clean as that of the ant or the birds; even the burrowing animals are neater. The native women are graceful and almost pretty, slight in figure, and passionately fond of ornaments, covering their arms and ankles with metallic rings, and thrusting silver and brass rings through their ears, noses, and lips.

The cocoanut-tree is always in bearing on the islands of the Straits, and requires no cultivation. Of the many liberal gifts bestowed upon the tropics, this tree is perhaps the most valuable. The Asiatic poet celebrates in verse the hundred uses to which the trunk, the branches, the leaves, the fruit, and the sap are applied. In Penang a certain number of these trees are not permitted to bear fruit. The embryo bud from which the blossoms and nuts would spring is tied up to prevent its expansion; a small incision then being made at the end, there oozes in gentle drops a pleasant liquor called toddy, which is the palm wine of the poet. This, when it is first drawn, is cooling and wholesome, but when it is fermented it produces a strong, intoxicating spirit. The banana is equally prolific and abundant, and forms a very large portion of the food of the common people. In the immediate neighborhood of the town are some plantations conducted by Europeans who live in neat cottages, with enclosures of cultivated flowers, and orchards of fruit-trees. Still further inland are large gardens of bread-fruit, nutmegs, cinnamon, pepper, and other spices. There are also large fields of sugar-cane, tobacco, and coffee. The delicate little sensitive plant here grows wild, and is equally tremulous and subsiding at the touch of human hands, as it is with us. Lilies are seen in wonderful variety, the stems covered with butterflies nearly as large as humming-birds.

Penang originally belonged to the Malay kingdom, but about the year 1786 it was given to an English sea-captain as a marriage-portion with the King of Keddah's daughter, and by him, in course of time, it was transferred to the East India Company. When Captain Francis Light received it with his dusky bride, it was the wild, uncultivated home of a few hundred fishermen. To-day it has a population of nearly a hundred thousand.

CHAPTER IV.

OUR course now lies across the Indian Ocean, westward. The rains which we encounter are like floods, but the air is soft and balmy, and the deluges are of brief continuance. The nights are serene and bright, so that it is delightful to lie awake upon the deck of the steamer and watch the stars now and then screened by the fleecy clouds. In the daytime it is equally interesting to observe the ocean. Large sea-turtles come to the surface to sun themselves, stretching their awkward necks to get a sight of our hull; dolphins and flying-fish are too abundant to be a curiosity; big water-snakes raise their slimy heads a couple of feet above the sea; the tiny nautilus floats in myriads upon the undulating waves, and at times the ship is surrounded by a shoal of the indolent jelly-fish. Mirage plays us strange tricks in the way of optical delusion in these regions. We seem to be approaching land which we never reach, but which at the moment when we should fairly make it, fades into thin air.

Though the ocean covers more than three-quarters of the globe, but few of us realize that it represents more of life than does the land. We are indebted to it for every drop of water distributed over our hills, plains, and valleys; for from the ocean it has arisen by evaporation to return again through myriads of channels. It is really a misnomer to speak of the sea as a desert waste; it is teeming with inexhaustible animal and vegetable life. A German scientist has with unwearied industry secured and classified over nine hundred species of fishes from this division of the Indian Ocean over which our course takes us. Many of these are characterized by colors as dazzling and various as those of gaudy-plumed tropical birds and flowers.

Our next objective point is Colombo, the capital of Ceylon, situated about thirteen hundred miles from the mouth of the Malacca Straits. Here we find several large steamships in the harbor, stopping briefly on their way to or from China, India, or Australia; and no sooner do we come to anchor than we are surrounded by the canoes of the natives. They are of very peculiar construction, being designed to enable the occupants to venture out, however rough the water may chance to be, and the surf is always raging in these open roadsteads. The canoes consist of the trunk of a tree hollowed out, some twenty feet in length, having long planks fastened lengthwise so as to form the sides or gunwales of the boat, which is a couple of feet deep and about as wide. An outrigger, consisting of a log of wood about one-third as long as the canoe, is fastened alongside at a distance of six or eight feet, by means of two arched poles of well-seasoned bamboo. This outrigger prevents any possibility of upsetting the boat, but without it so narrow a craft could not remain upright, even in a calm sea. The natives face any weather in these little vessels.

It will be remembered that to this island England banished Arabi Pacha after the sanguinary battlefield of Tel-el-Keber. It is one of the most interesting spots in the East, having been in its prime centuries before the birth of Christ. It was perhaps the Ophir of the Hebrews, and it still abounds in precious stones and mineral wealth. Here we observe the native women strangely decked with cheap jewelry thrust through the tops and lobes of their ears, in their lips and nostrils, while about their necks hang ornaments consisting of bright sea-shells, mingled with sharks' teeth. If we go into the jungle, we find plenty of ebony, satin-wood, bamboo, fragrant balsam, and india-rubber trees; we see the shady pools covered with the lotus of fable and poetry, resembling huge pond-lilies; we behold brilliant flowers growing in tall trees, and others, very sweet and lowly, blooming beneath our feet. Vivid colors flash before our eyes, caused by the blue, yellow, and scarlet plumage of the feathered tribe. Parrots and paroquets are seen in hundreds. Storks, ibises, and herons fly lazily over the lagoons, and the gorgeous peacock is seen in his wild condition. The elephant is also a native here, and occasionally hunts are organized upon a grand scale and at great expense by English sportsmen who come here for the purpose, and who pay a heavy fee for a license.

Ceylon lies just off the southern point of India; and though it is a British colony, its government is quite distinct from that of the mainland. It forms a station for a large number of troops, and is about three times the size of Massachusetts.

Many of the native women are employed by the large number of English families resident here, especially by officers' wives, as nurses. These last seem to form a class by themselves, and they dress in the most peculiar manner, as we see the children's nurses dressed in Rome, Paris, and Madrid. The Singhalese nurses wear a single white linen garment covering the body to the knees, very low in

A SINGHALESE DANCER.

the neck, with a blue cut-away velvet jacket covered with silver braid and buttons and open in front, a scarlet silk sash gathering the under-garment at the waist. The legs and feet are bare, the ankles covered with bangles, or ornamental rings, and the ears heavily weighed down and deformed with rings of silver and gold.

The vegetation of Ceylon is what might be expected of an island within so few miles of the equator; that is, beautiful and prolific in the extreme. The cinnamon fields are so thrifty as to form a wilderness of green, though the bushes grow but four or five feet in height. The cinnamon bush, which is a native here, is a species of laurel, and bears a white, scentless flower, scarcely as large as a pea. The spice of commerce is produced from the inner bark of the shrub, the branches of which are cut and peeled twice annually. The plantations resemble a thick, tangled undergrowth of wood, without any regularity, and are not cultivated after being properly started. Ceylon was at one time a great producer of coffee, and still exports the berry, but a disease which attacked the leaves of the shrub has nearly discouraged the planters. Among the wild animals are elephants, deer, monkeys, bears, and panthers — fine specimens of which are preserved in the excellent museum at Colombo. Pearl oysters are found on the coast, and some magnificent pearls are sent to Paris and London.

The bread-fruit tree is especially interesting, with its feathery leaves, and its melon-shaped fruit, weighing from three to four pounds. This, the natives prepare in many ways for eating, and as the tree bears fruit continually for nine months of the year, it forms a most important food-supply. Two or three trees will afford nourishment for a hearty man, and half a dozen well cared for will sustain a small family, a portion of the fruit being dried and kept for the non-producing months. Banana groves, and orchards bending under the weight of the rich, nutritious fruit, tall cocoanut-trees with half a ton of ripening nuts in each tufted top, ant-hills nearly as high as native houses, rippling cascades, small rivers winding through the green valleys, and flowers of every hue and shape, together with birds such as one sees preserved in northern museums, — all these crowd upon our vision as we wander about inland.

Ceylon is rich in prehistoric monuments, showing that there once existed here a great and powerful empire, and leading us to wonder what could have swept a population of millions from the face of the globe and have left no clearer record of their past. The carved pillars, skilfully wrought, now scattered through the forest, and often overgrown by mammoth trees, attest both material greatness and far-reaching antiquity. It would seem as though nature had tried to cover up the wrinkles of age with blooming and thrifty vegetation.

We embark at Colombo for Adelaide, the capital of South Australia, steering a course south by east through the Indian Ocean for a distance of about thirty-five hundred miles. On this voyage we find the nights so bright and charming that hours together are passed upon the open deck studying the stars. Less than two thousand can be counted from a ship's deck by the naked eye, but with an opera-glass or telescope the number can be greatly increased. Among the most interesting constellations of the region through which we are now passing, is the Southern Cross. For those not familiar with its location, a good way to find the Cross is to remember that there are two prominent stars in the group known as Centaurus that point directly towards it. That farthest from the Cross is regarded as one of the fixed stars nearest to the earth, but its distance from us is twenty thousand times that of the sun. Stellar distances can be realized only by familiar comparison. For instance: were it possible for a person to journey to the sun in a single day, basing the calculation upon a corresponding degree of speed, it would require fifty-five years to reach this fixed star! Probably not one-half of those who have sailed beneath its tranquil beauty are aware that near the upper middle of the cross there is a brilliant cluster of stars which, though not visible to the naked eye, are brought into view with the telescope. In these far southern waters we also see what are called the Magellanic Clouds, which lie between Canopus and the South Pole. These light clouds, or what seem to be such, seen in a clear sky, are, like the "Milky Way," visible nebulæ, or star-clusters, at such vast distance from the earth as to have by combination this effect upon our vision.

At sea the stars assume perhaps a greater importance than on land, because from them, together with the sun, is obtained latitude and longitude, and thus by their aid the mariner determines his bearings upon the ocean. Forty or fifty centuries ago the Chaldean shepherds were accustomed to gaze upon these shining orbs in worshipful admiration, but with no idea of their vast system. They were to them "the words of God, the scriptures of the skies." It has been left to our period to formulate the methods of their constant and endless procession. All of the principal stars are now well known, and their limits clearly defined upon charts, so that we can easily acquire a knowledge of them. The inhabitants of North America have the constellation of Ursa Major, or the Great Bear, and the North Star always with them; they never wholly disappear below the horizon. When the mariner sailing north of the equator has determined the position of the "Great Bear," two of whose stars, known as "the pointers," indicate the North Star, he can designate all points of the compass unerringly. But in the far South Sea they are not visible; other constellations, however, whose relative positions are as fixed in the Southern Hemisphere, become equally sure guides to the watchful navigator.

Having landed in Australia, before proceeding to visit the several cities of this great island-continent which possesses an area of nearly three millions of square miles, let us review some general facts and characteristics of the country. So far as we can learn, it was a land unknown to the ancients, though it is more than probable that the Chinese knew of the existence of Northern Australia at a very early period; but until about a century ago, it presented only a picture of primeval desolation. The hard work of the pioneer has been accomplished, and civilization has rapidly changed the aspect of a large portion of the great south land. To-day this continent is bordered by thrifty seaports connected by railroads, coasting-steamers, turnpikes, and electric telegraphs. It is occupied by an intelligent European population numbering between three and four millions, possessing such elements of political and social prosperity as place them in an honorable position in the line of progressive nations. So favorable is the climate that nearly the whole country might be turned into a botanical garden. Indeed, Australia would seem to be better entitled to the name of Eldorado (a mythical country abounding in gold), so talked of in the sixteenth century, than was the imaginary land of untold wealth so confidently believed by the adventurous Spaniards, to exist somewhere between the Orinoco and the Amazon.

This new home of the British race in the South Pacific, surrounded by accessible seas and inviting harbors, inspires us with vivid interest. We say "new," and yet, geologically speaking, it is one of the oldest portions of the earth's surface. While a great part of Europe has been submerged and elevated, crumpled up as it were into mountain chains, Australia seems to have been undisturbed. It is remarkable that in a division of the globe of such colossal proportions there was found no larger quadruped than the kangaroo, and that man was the only animal that destroyed his kind. He, alas! was more ferocious than the lynx, the leopard, or the hyena; for these animals do not prey upon each other, while the aborigines of Australia devoured one another.

What America was to Spain in the proud days of that nation's glory Australia has been to England, and that too, without the crime of wholesale murder, and the spilling of rivers of blood, as was the case in the days of Cortez and Pizarro. The wealth poured into the lap of England by these far-away colonies belittles all the riches which the Spaniards realized by the conquests of Mexico and Peru. Here is an empire won without war, a new world called into existence, as it were, by moral forces, an Eldorado captured without the sword. Here, Nature has spread her generous favors over a land only one-fifth smaller than the whole continent of Europe, granting every needed resource wherewith to form a great, independent, and prosperous nation; where labor is already more liberally rewarded, and life more easily sustained, than in any other civilized country except America. It is difficult to believe while observing the present population, wealth, power, and prosperity of the country at large, characterized by such grand and conspicuous elements of empire, that it has been settled for so brief a period, and that its pioneers were from English prisons. The authentic record of life in the colonies of Australia and Tasmania during the first few years of their existence, is mainly the account of the control of lawless men by the strong and cruel arm of military despotism.

Up to the present writing Australia has realized from her soil over three hundred and thirty millions of pounds sterling, or $1,650,000,000. Her territory gives grazing at the present time to over seventy-five million sheep, which is probably double the number in the United States. When it is remembered that the population of this country is sixty millions, and that Australia has not quite four millions, the force of this comparison becomes obvious. The aggregate amount of wool exported to the mother country is twenty-eight times as much as England has received in the same period from the continent of Europe. The combined exports and imports of the United Kingdom of Great Britain and Ireland are a little over one hundred dollars per annum for each one of the population. In Australia the aggregate is a trifle over two hundred dollars per head. The four principal capitals of Australia contain over eight hundred thousand inhabitants. The railroads of the country have already cost over two hundred million dollars, and are being extended annually. New South Wales has in proportion to its population a greater length of railways than any other country in the world, while there are some thirty thousand miles of telegraph lines within the length and breadth of the land.

The country is divided into five provincial governments: New South Wales, Victoria, Queensland, South Australia, and West Australia. The island of Tasmania forms another province, and is separated from Victoria by Bass's Strait, the two being within half a day's sail of each other. Sydney is the capital of New South Wales; Melbourne, of Victoria; Adelaide, of South Australia; Brisbane, of Queensland; Perth, of West Australia; and Hobart, of Tasmania. It may be remarked incidentally that South Australia would more properly be designated by some other title, as it is not South Australia at all. Victoria lies south of it, and so does a portion of West Australia. The government of these several divisions is modelled upon that of New South Wales, which is in fact the parent colony of them all.

New South Wales is governed under a constitution, having two houses of Parliament. The first, a legislative council, is composed of a limited number of members nominated by the Crown, and who hold office for life; the second, or legislative assembly, is composed of members elected by the people and chosen by ballot. All acts, before becoming law, must receive the approval of the Queen of England, though this is nothing more than a mere form. There is a resident governor in each colony, also appointed by the Queen.

As compared with our own land, we find this to be one of strange contradictions. Here, the eagles are white and the swans are black; the emu, a bird almost as large as an ostrich, cannot fly, but runs like a horse. The principal quadruped, the kangaroo, is elsewhere unknown; and though he has four legs, he runs upon two. When the days are longest with us in America, they are shortest here. To reach the tropics, Australians go due-north, while we go due-south. With us the seed, or stone, of the cherry forms the centre of the fruit; in Australia, the stone grows on the outside. The foliage of the trees in America spreads out horizontally; in this south-land the leaves hang vertically. When it is day with us it is night with them. There, Christmas comes in mid-summer; with us in mid-winter. Bituminous and anthracite coal are with us only one color, — black; but they have white bituminous coal, — white as chalk. The majority of trees with us shed their leaves in the fall of the year; with them they are evergreen, shedding their bark and not their leaves.

Adelaide is situated about seven miles from the sea, and is surrounded by an amphitheatre of hills rearing their abrupt forms not far away from the town. The capital is so perfectly level that to be seen to advantage it must be looked upon from some favorable elevation. The colony should be known as Central Australia, on account of its geographical position. It is destined in the near future to merit the name of the granary of the country, being already largely and successfully devoted to agriculture. This pursuit is followed in no circumscribed manner, but in a large and liberal style, like that of our best Western farmers in the United States. Immense tracts of land are also devoted to stock-raising for the purpose of furnishing beef for shipment to England in fresh condition. This province contains nearly a million square miles, and is therefore ten times larger than Victoria, and fifteen times larger than England. It extends northward from the temperate zone, so that nearly one-half of its area lies within the tropics, while it has a coast-line of five hundred miles along the great Southern Ocean. A vast portion of its interior is uninhabited, and indeed unexplored. The total population of the whole colony is about four hundred thousand. Wheat, wool, wine, copper, and meat are at present the chief exports. Over four million acres of land are under the plough. Though gold is found here, it is not so abundant as in other sections of the country. Good wages equalling those realized by the average miners are earned by a dozen easier and more legitimate occupations than that of gold-digging. "Let us cherish no delusions," said a San Francisco preacher on a certain occasion; "no society has ever been able to organize itself in a satisfactory manner on gold-bearing soil. Even Nature herself is deceitful; she corrupts, seduces, and betrays man; she laughs at his labor, she turns his toil into gambling, and his word into a lie!" The preacher's deductions have proved true as regards bodies of miners in California, South Africa, New Zealand, and Australia. And yet the finding of gold mines has stimulated labor, immigration, and manly activity in many directions, and has thus been the agent of undoubted good in other fields than its own.

Adelaide, with a population of a hundred and fifty thousand, has a noble university, quite equal in standing to that of any city in the country. When we remember how youthful she is, it becomes a matter of surprise that such a condition has been achieved in all the appointments which go to make up a great city in modern times. The same remark applies to all of the Australian capitals, none of which are deficient in hospitals, libraries, schools, asylums, art galleries, and charitable institutions generally. Few European cities of twice the size of these in Australia can boast a more complete organization in all that goes to promote true civilization.

The city proper is separated from its suburbs by a belt of park-lands, and the approaches are lined with thrifty ornamental trees. Great liberality and good judgment presided over the laying out of Adelaide. All the streets are broad and regular, running north and south, east and west. There are no mysterious labyrinths, dark lanes, or blind alleys in the city; the avenues are all uniform in width. It is believed that the interior of the continent, which is largely embraced within this province, was at a comparatively recent period covered by a great inland sea. Here are still found mammoth bones of animals, now extinct, which have become an object of careful study to scientists. Africa's interior is scarcely less explored than is Central Australia. There are thousands of square miles upon which the foot of a white man has never trod. Tartary has its steppes, America its prairies, Egypt its deserts, and Australia its "scrub." The plains, so called, are covered by a low-growing bush, compact and almost impenetrable in places, composed of a dwarf eucalyptus. The appearance of a large reach of this "scrub" is desolate indeed, the underlying soil being a sort of yellow sand which one would surely think could produce nothing else; yet, wherever this land has been cleared and properly irrigated it has proved to be remarkably fertile.

All of these colonial cities have botanical gardens, in the cultivation and arrangement of which much skill and scientific knowledge is displayed. In that of Adelaide we see the Australian bottle-tree, which is a native of this country only. It receives its name from its resemblance in shape to a junk-bottle. This tree has the property of storing water in its hollow trunk, — a well-known fact, which has often proved a providential supply for thirsty

BOTANICAL GARDENS AT ADELAIDE, AUSTRALIA.

travellers in a country so liable to severe drought. Here, also, we see the correa, with its stiff stem and prickly leaves, bearing a curious string of delicate, pendulous flowers, red, orange, and white, not unlike the fuchsia in form. The South Sea myrtle is especially attractive, appearing when in flower with round clustering bunches of bloom, spangled with white stars. The styphelia, a heath-like plant, surprises us with its green flowers. We are shown a specimen of the sandrach-tree, brought from Africa, which is almost imperishable, and from which the Mohammedans invariably make the ceilings of their mosques. The Indian cotton-tree looms up beside the South American aloe — this last, with its thick, bayonet-like leaves, is ornamented in wavy lines like the surface of a Toledo blade. The grouping of these exotics, natives of regions so far apart on the earth's surface, yet quite domesticated here, forms an incongruous though pleasing picture.

West Australia, of which Perth is the capital, is eight hundred miles in width and thirteen hundred long from north to south, actually covering about one-third of the continent. It embraces all that portion lying to the westward of the one hundred and twenty-ninth meridian of east longitude, and has an area of about a million square miles. It has few towns and is very sparsely settled, Perth having scarcely eleven thousand inhabitants, and the whole province a population of not over forty-two thousand. Pearl oysters abound upon its coast and form the principal export, being most freely gathered near Torres's Strait, which separates Australia from New Guinea. The latter is the largest island in the world, being three hundred and sixty miles in width by thirteen hundred in length. Its natives are considered the most barbarous of any savages of the nineteenth century.

From Adelaide to Melbourne is about six hundred miles, a distance accomplished by railway. The first sight of Melbourne will surprise the stranger, though he may be fairly well-informed about this capital of Victoria. No one anticipates beholding so grand a capital in this far-away region of the Pacific. Where there was only a swamp and uncleared woods a few years ago, there has risen a city containing to-day a population of four hundred and twenty thousand, embracing the immediate suburbs. This capital is unsurpassed by any of the British colonies in the elegancies and luxuries of modern civilization, such as broad avenues, palatial dwellings, churches, colossal warehouses, banks, theatres, public buildings, and pleasure grounds. It is pleasant to record the fact that one-fifth of the revenue raised by taxation is expended for educational purposes. Of few cities in the new or the old world can this be truthfully said. Universities, libraries, public art-galleries, and museums do not lack for the liberal and fostering care of the government. No city, if we except Chicago and San Francisco, ever attained to such size and importance in so short a period as has Melbourne.

The river Yarra-Yarra runs through the town, and is navigable for large vessels to the main wharves, where it is crossed by a broad and substantial bridge. Above the bridge the river is handsomely ornamented with trees upon its borders; here the great boat-races take place, one of the most popular of all local athletic amusements, and Melbourne is famous for out-door sports of every form, especially ball-playing.

The activity of the streets is remarkable. English

cabs rattle about or stand in long rows awaiting patrons; four-wheeled vehicles of an awkward style, also for hire, abound; messenger-boys with yellow leather pouches strapped over their shoulders hurry hither and thither; high-hung omnibuses with three horses abreast, like those of Paris and Naples, dash rapidly along, well filled with passengers; men gallop through the crowd on horseback, carrying big baskets of provisions on their arms; dog-carts, driven by smart young fellows with a servant behind them in gaudy livery, cut in and out among the vehicles; powerful draught-horses stamp along the way, drawing heavily-laden drays; milk-carts with big letters on their canvas sides make themselves conspicuous, and so do the bakers' carts; while light and neat American wagonettes glide rapidly along among less attractive vehicles. Now and then a Chinaman passes, with his peculiar shambling gait, with a pole across his shoulders balancing his baskets of "truck"; women with oranges and bananas for a penny apiece meet one at every corner, and still the sidewalks are so broad, and the streets so wide, that no one seems to be in the least incommoded. The fruit stores present a remarkable array of tempting fruits, among which are the mandarin and seedless oranges, apricots, green figs, grapes, passion-fruit, pineapples, bananas, and many others, all in fine condition. With the exception of the cities of California, nowhere else can fruit of such choice varieties and so cheap be found as at Melbourne.

Victoria is one of the youngest of the colonies, and was, until the discovery of gold fields within her borders, — that is, in 1851, — a portion of New South Wales; but to-day it is the metropolis of Australia. It has not the many natural beauties of Sydney, but it has numerous compensating advantages, and is the real centre of colonial enterprise upon the continent. The admirable system of street-cars in Melbourne is worthy of all praise, use being made of the underground cable and stationary engine as a motor, a mode which is cheap, cleanly, and popular. Collins Street is the fashionable boulevard of the city, though Burke Street nearly rivals it in gay promenaders and elegant shops. But in broad contrast to these bright and cheerful centres, there are in the northeastern section of the town dirty alleys and by-ways that one would think must prove hot-beds of disease and pestilence, especially as Melbourne suffers from want of a good and thorough system of domestic drainage.

The public library of the city is a large and impressive building, standing by itself, a hundred feet back from the street, on rising ground, and would be creditable to any European or American city. It already contains about a hundred and thirty thousand volumes, and is being constantly added to by public and private bequests. The interior arrangements of the library are excellent, affording ample room for books and all needed accommodation for the public. In these respects it is superior to both the Boston and Astor libraries. Under the same roof is a museum containing an extensive collection, especially of geological specimens, mostly of native product.

Melbourne has its Chinese quarter, like Sydney and San Francisco; it is situated in Little Burke Street, just back of the Theatre Royal, and forms a veritable Chinatown, with its idol temples, opium dens, lottery cellars, cafés, low hovels, and kindred establishments. Here, one requires an experienced guide to enable him to make his way safely and understandingly. The peculiar notices posted upon the buildings in Chinese characters are a puzzle to the uninitiated. The signs over the shops are especially original and peculiar; they do not denote the name of the owner, or particularize the business which is carried on within, but are assumed titles of a flowery character, designed to attract the fancy of the customers. Thus: Kong, Meng & Co. means "Bright Light Firm"; Sun Kum Lee & Co. is in English "New Golden Firm"; Kwong Hop signifies "New Agreement Company"; Hi Cheong, "Peace and Prosperity Firm"; Kwong Tu Tye, "Flourishing and Peaceful Company"; and so on.

It is, as a rule, the worst type of the Chinese who leave their native land to make a new home elsewhere, and it is not to be expected that they will be much improved by intercourse with the Australian "larrikins," who are composed of the lowest and most criminal orders. This refuse of humanity is largely made up of the rabble of London and Liverpool, many of whom have had their passages paid by relatives and interested persons at home solely to get rid of them, while others have worked their passage hither to avoid merited punishment for crimes committed in England.

CHAPTER V.

THE province of Victoria is the special gold-field of Australia, and has produced two-thirds of all the precious metal which statistics credit to the country at large. One of the localities which has proved to be the most prolific in gold is Ballarat, now a charming and populous city, next to Melbourne in importance. It lies nearly a hundred miles north of the capital, at an elevation of fifteen hundred feet above sea-level, and is accessible by railway. This is thought to be the centre of the richest gold-producing district in the world. Beechworth, one hundred and seventy miles northeast of Melbourne, at an elevation higher than that of Ballarat, is nearly as populous, and as prolific in the precious metal. The diggings of Maryborough district, situated a hundred and fifty miles northwest of Melbourne, are famous, and give occupation to some eight thousand miners. Castlemaine, seventy-five miles north of the capital, has proved very profitable in its yield of gold. Nearly forty square miles of gold-bearing lands are being worked by Europeans and Chinese in the district of Ararat, a hundred and fifty miles north of Melbourne. From these several sources of mineral wealth there flows constantly towards the capital a stream of riches, making it probably the greatest gold-producing centre on the globe. There are about fifty thousand people, in all, engaged in gold-mining in the several parts of Victoria, at least ten thousand of whom are Chinese. Still,

A KANGAROO HUNT IN AUSTRALIA.

Page 63.

reliable statistics show that in the aggregate, the corn and wool of this province are alone of more monetary value than is the result from all the gold produced by her mines.

The kangaroos are found in various parts of Victoria, in their wild state. They are usually discovered in the thick woods, sitting upright in circles of a dozen or more, as grave as though engaged in holding a formal council. On such occasions their short forepaws hang limp before them, while their restless heads and delicate ears turn hither and thither in watchful care against surprise. Notwithstanding their huge paunches, big hindquarters, and immense tails, there is something graceful and attractive about these creatures. When they are young they are as playful as kittens. Even when running away from pursuit, — a process performed by enormous leaps, often covering a rod at a flying jump, — there is a certain airy grace and harmony of movement attending their motions. Dogs and horses have more power of endurance than the kangaroo, and are thus enabled to run it down; but neither horse nor dog can achieve the same degree of speed for moderate distances. If the chase occurs in a wood where there are numerous obstacles, like heavy fallen logs, the kangaroo is safe, since he can jump all such impediments without diminishing his speed.

To get a view of the big gum-trees, one visits the Fernshaw Mountain district. We are told of one fallen monarch, which was measured by a government surveyor, having a length upon the ground of four hundred and seventy-four feet. The Pyramid of Cheops is hardly as high as was this tree when it stood erect. The average height of these marvels is from three hundred to four hundred feet. They are situated in a valley protected from winds, and are favorably located to promote their growth, as well as to protect them from sudden gales or tornadoes such as have prostrated large trees in our Yosemite.

The subject of large trees is one of more than ordinary interest; the largest one known in the world is situated in Mascoli, near the base of Mount Etna, on the island of Sicily. It measures one hundred and ninety feet in circumference. It is a chestnut-tree, and still bears fruit in abundance. The oldest tree is believed to be a famous cypress still growing in Oaxaca, Mexico. Humboldt saw it in 1855, when he recorded the measurement as being one hundred and twenty-six feet in circumference and three hundred and eighty-two feet between the out-spread branches. In Nevada, United States, stands what is well known as the "Dead Giant Redwood Tree," which measures one hundred and nineteen feet in circumference, and which is believed to have been growing in the days of Julius Cæsar. Near this mammoth are a dozen other trees, varying in size from seventy-five to one hundred feet in circumference. The "Grizzly Giant," monarch of the Mariposa Grove in California, measures ninety-two feet in circumference. The largest tree in the United States stands near Bear Creek, California, measuring one hundred and forty feet in circumference. It is only by comparison with familiar objects that we can realize these extraordinary dimensions.

We shall be pretty sure to see in the woods of Victoria a most curious example of bird-life and bird-instinct, in the instance of what is known as the bower-bird. This peculiar little creature builds a cunning play-house, a tiny shady bower which it ornaments with vines and highly colored feathers of other birds, besides the yellow blossoms of the

EMU HUNTING IN AUSTRALIA.

wattle-tree and many light-green ferns. In this ingeniously contrived sylvan retreat the feathered architect runs about and holds a sort of carnival, to which others of his tribe gather. Here the little party chirp vigorously, and strut about in a most ludicrous manner.

The glamour of gold-seeking has too much weight in inducing emigration to this region of the South Seas. An industrious and worthy person is sure to make a good living here, and indeed so one might say he would do almost anywhere. He may make a fortune in Australia, but he cannot *pick* it up, — he must *work* it up. The gold nuggets which are occasionally found, never amount to much as regards the benefit of the finder. It is upon the whole a fortunate day for the respectable immigrant who has any degree of ability, when he decides to turn his back upon gold-digging, and adopt some more legitimate business. The great elements of success are the same in Australia as in California, Africa, or Massachusetts; namely, steadiness of purpose, application, and temperance.

Sydney is connected with Melbourne by a railway some six hundred miles in length; but the pleasantest way to reach it, either from the north or the south, is by water. We enter the harbor through an opening which is called Sydney Heads, formed by two frowning cliffs on either side of the entrance. Having left the Heads behind, we pass Botany Bay, seven miles below the city, once a penal colony for English convicts, but now a lovely, rural retreat, which retains nothing of its ill-repute but its name. The aspect of the famous harbor, with its lake-like expanse, its many green islands with handsome residences scattered over them, its graceful promontories, and the abundance of semi-tropical vegetation, all together form the loveliest picture imaginable. It may well be the pride of the citizens of Sydney.

Upon landing, we find great irregularity prevailing in the street architecture. George Street is the main thoroughfare, and is two miles in length, containing many stores furnished as well as the average of those in Vienna or Paris. There are fine business edifices, having massive French plate glass windows which are admirably appointed. The peculiar conformation of the town makes the side streets precipitous, so that a large portion of the city is composed of hilly avenues. Like the old streets of Boston, those of Sydney were the growth of chance, and were not originally laid out, like those of Melbourne and Adelaide. Our Washington Street, Boston, was once a cow-path, while the present site of George Street in Sydney was a meandering bullock-track.

This capital, like the two we have already visited in Australia, has a superb botanical garden covering some forty acres of land. The grounds extend on a gradual incline to the shores of the beautiful bay, forming a semicircle round what is known as Farm Cove, a picturesque indentation of the harbor, close to Government House. One special charm of these delightful grounds is the fact that they are accessible by a walk of about five minutes from the centre of the city. It is not necessary to make an excursion in order to reach them, as is the case with many similar resorts, such as Sydenham in London, Central Park, New York, or the Bois de Boulogne, Paris. Here semi-arctic and semi-tropical plants and trees are found growing together, and all parts of the world seem to be liberally represented. The hardy Scotch fir and delicate palm crowd each other; the india-rubber-tree and the laurel are close friends; the California pine and the Florida orange thrive side by side; so with the silvery fern-tree of New Zealand, and the guava of Cuba. China, Japan, India, Africa, Egypt, and South America have all furnished representative trees and shrubs for the beautifying of these comprehensive gardens.

There is here a fine specimen of the Australian musk-tree, which attains a height of nearly twenty feet, and exhales from leaf and bark a peculiar sweet odor, though not at all like what its name indicates. Here we see also the she-oak-tree, which is said to emit a curious wailing sound during the quietest state of the atmosphere, when there is not a breath of wind to move the branches or the leaves. This tree is found growing near the sea in Australia, and is said to have borrowed the murmur of the conch-shell. It has proved to be the inspiring theme of many a local poet. The flowers in this garden are as attractive as the trees; fuchsias, roses, and camellias are in great perfection and variety, flanked by a species of double pansies and a whole army of brilliant tulips. Flowers bloom in every month of the year in this region, out of doors, and are rarely troubled by the frost.

The excellent university of Sydney is admirably situated, and is the first that was founded in the Southern Hemisphere. The city has also its art-gallery, and free public library, with over a hundred thousand volumes. It has also hospitals, churches, and many charitable institutions, with various schools. Sydney holds high rank as a British colonial city, and deservedly so, having special reason for pride in the complete system of her charitable and educational organizations, her noble public buildings, and the general character of her leading citizens. Land in the city and immediate suburbs is held at prices averaging as high as in Boston and New York, and the wealth of the people is represented to be very great in the aggregate.

Australia in its extreme breadth, between Shark's Bay on the west and Sandy Cape on the eastern shore, measures twenty-four hundred miles; and from north to south, — that is, from Cape York to Cape Atway, — it is probably over seventeen hundred miles in extent. The occupied and improved portions of the country skirt the seacoast on the southern and eastern sides, which are covered with cities, towns, villages, and hamlets. The country occupied for sheep-runs and cattle-ranches is very sparsely inhabited. The reason for this is obvious, since the owner of a hundred thousand sheep requires between two and three hundred thousand acres to feed them properly. The relative proportion as to sheep and land is to allow two and a third acres to each animal.

The great dividing mountain-chain of Australia is near the coast-line in the south and east, averaging perhaps a hundred miles or more from the sea. Nearly all the gold which the land has produced has come from the valleys and hillsides of this range. The gold-diggings of New South Wales have proved to be very rich in some sections; but unlike those of Queensland and Victoria, the precious metal is here found mostly in alluvial deposits.

Many nationalities are represented in Australia and New Zealand, but the majority are English, Scotch, and Irish. The officials of New South Wales especially, look to England for favors which a political separation would cut them off from; among these are honorary titles and crown appointments of a paying nature. The constitution under which the colonies are living is such as to entitle them to be called democracies. In many respects the local government is more liberal and advanced than in England. Church and State, for instance, are here kept quite distinct from each other. As to the legislative power of the colonies, it is seldom interfered with by the home government.

A journey of about five hundred miles northward, either along the coast by steamer, or by railway inland, will take us to Brisbane, the capital of Queensland, which has a population of about fifty thousand. Until 1860 it was an appendage of New South Wales, but was in that year formed into an independent colony. The site of the city is a diversified surface, with the river whose name it bears winding gracefully through it, about twenty-four miles from its mouth; though in a direct line it would be but half that distance to where it empties into Moreton Bay, one of the largest on the coast of Australia. It was discovered by Captain Cook in 1770, and is formed by two long sandy islands running north and south, named respectively Standbroke and Moreton Islands, enclosing between them and the mainland a spacious sheet of water more than thirty miles long and six or eight wide, beautified by fertile islands.

On approaching Brisbane by sea one is puzzled at first to find where the mouth of the river can be, so completely is it hidden by the mangrove swamps which skirt the coast. A pleasant little watering-place is situated close at hand, named Sandgate, which is connected by hourly stages with the city. Several small rivers, all of which, however, are more or less navigable, empty into Moreton Bay, showing that the district inland hereabouts must be well watered. It is less than fifty years since Brisbane was opened to free settlers, having been previously only a penal station for English criminals; but of this taint resting upon the locality, the same may be said as of Sydney, or Hobart, in Tasmania, — scarcely a trace remains.

Queen Street is the principal thoroughfare, and is lined with handsome stores and fine edifices, there being no lack of architectural excellence in either public or private buildings. Like its sister cities, it has a botanical garden, the climate here favoring even a more extensive out-door display of tropical and delicate vegetation than at Melbourne or Sydney. An intelligent spirit of enterprise is evinced by the citizens of Brisbane, and everything goes to show that it is destined to become a populous and prosperous business centre. Its climate, especially, is considered almost perfect. Queensland is very rich in gold-producing mines, but it has also almost endless rolling plains covered with herbage suitable for the support of great herds and flocks, where some fourteen millions of sheep are now yielding meat and wool for export, and where some three millions of cattle are herded. The real greatness of the country is to be found in its agricultural capacity, which is yet to be developed. A very pleasant trip may be enjoyed up the Brisbane River and Bremer Creek, on which latter stream Ipswich is situated. It is twice as far by water as by land, but the sail is delightful, often affording charming views of the city from the river, while at the same time passing suburban residences, flourishing farms, banana-groves, cotton-fields, sugar-plantations, and orange-orchards.

Queensland is more than five times as large as the United Kingdom of Great Britain and Ireland, and it possesses an immense amount of undeveloped resources of the most promising character. The sun shines here with much more tropical ardor than in New South Wales or Victoria. The palm takes the place of the eucalyptus to a certain extent. The tulip-tree, rosewood, sandalwood, and satinwood, which are not observed further south, greet us here. The aborigines are oftener met than elsewhere, as they prefer to live in a more temperate climate than is found southward, and to be where they can have the country more to themselves. They probably do not number over thirty thousand in all, and are slowly but surely decreasing before the advance of the whites. Even when first discovered they were but a handful of people, so to speak, scattered over an immense territory. They have still no distinct notion of the building of houses in which to live, or at least they adopt none, though they have the example of the whites constantly before them. They are very ugly, having black skins, flat noses, wide nostrils, and deep-sunken eyes wide apart. A bark covering, much ruder than anything which would content an American Indian, forms their only shelter, and they often burrow contentedly under the lee of an overhanging rock or hillside.

The Australian blacks have plenty of legends of the most barbaric character, but by no means void of poetical features. They believe that the earth was created by a being of supreme attributes, whom they call Nourelle, and who lives in the sky. They entertain the idea that because the sun gives heat it needs fuel, and that when it descends below the horizon it procures a fresh supply for its fires. The stars are supposed to be the dwellings of departed chiefs. The serpent is believed to contain the spirit of a real devil. To eat the kidney of an enemy, it is thought by them, imparts to the one who swallows it the strength of the dead man. Any number above five, these blacks express by saying, "it is as the leaves," not to be counted. The white man's locomotive is an imprisoned fire-devil, kept under control by water. The lightning is the angry expression of some enraged god.

The most peculiar weapon possessed by these aborigines is one which originated with them, and is known as the boomerang,— of which every one has heard, but which few have seen. It is a weapon whose characteristics have caused its name to pass into a synonym for anything which turns upon the person who uses it. It seems at first sight to be only a flat, crooked, or curved piece of polished wood, about twenty-eight inches long and three-quarters of an inch in thickness. There is nothing remarkable about this weapon until we see a native throw one. In doing this he carefully poises himself, makes a nice calculation as to distance, raises his arm above his head, and brings it down with a sort of swoop, swiftly launching the curved wood from his hand. At first the boomerang skims along near the ground, then rises four or five feet, but only to sink again, and again to rise. As we carefully watch its course, and suppose it just about to stop in its erratic career, and drop, spent, to the ground, it suddenly ceases its forward flight, and rapidly returns to the thrower. It is thought that no white man can exactly learn the trick of throwing this strange weapon, and certainly few ever care to attempt it a second time.

Ethnologists tell us that these blacks belong to the Ethiopian race,— they are the lowest probably of all the human family. The conviction forces itself upon us that they must be the remnant of some ancient people of whom we have no historic record. When Australia was first taken possession of by the whites, it seems to have been, if the term is in any instance admissible, a God-forsaken land; certainly it was the most destitute of natural productions of any portion of the globe. We can well believe that before these blacks came hither, — perhaps a thousand years ago, — this land was untrodden by human beings.

No species of grain was known to these natives; not a single fruit worthy of notice grew wild, and not an edible root of value was produced. The only game of any size was the kangaroo and a few species of birds. Now, the trees, fruits, vegetables, and game of all regions have become domesticated here, proving to be highly productive, whether transplanted from tropical or from semi-tropical regions.

Queensland measures thirteen hundred miles from north to south, and is about eight hundred miles in width, containing a population at the present time of three hundred and forty thousand. The climate may be compared to that of Madeira, and it is entirely free from the hot winds which sometimes render Sydney and Melbourne so uncomfortable. Leaving out West Australia, which is yet so little developed, the country may be divided thus: Queensland is the best and most extensive grazing section; in this respect New South Wales comes next. South Australia is characterized by its prolific grain-fields, and Victoria is richest in auriferous deposits; but there is gold enough in all of these colonies to afford constant stimulus to mining enterprise, fresh discoveries in this line being made every month. It is proposed to separate the north of Queensland from the south, at the twenty-second parallel of latitude, and to form the northern portion into a separate colony. As Queensland is larger than England, France, and Belgium with Holland and Denmark combined, there can be no want of territory for such a political division: population, however, is needed.

We will now turn our steps southward, by the way of Sydney and Melbourne, to Tasmania. At the last-named city we take a coasting steamer passing down the river Yarra-Yarra, the muddiest of water-ways, until Bass's Strait is reached, across which the course is due-south for a hundred and twenty miles. This is a reach of ocean travel which for boisterousness and discomfort can be said to rival the English Channel, between Calais and Dover. As the coast of Tasmania is approached, a tall lighthouse, one hundred and forty feet above sea-level, first attracts the attention, designating the mouth of the Tamar River. While crossing the Strait we are surrounded by a great variety of sea-birds, among which are the cape-pigeon, the stormy petrel, and the gannet, which last is the largest of ocean birds next to the albatross.

On drawing still nearer to the shore, flocks of pelicans are observed upon the rocks, and that most awkward of birds, the penguin, is seen in idle groups. He is a good swimmer, but his apologetic wings are not intended for flying.

We pass up the Tamar River, through a narrow, winding channel for a distance of forty miles before coming to the harbor and town of Launceston. The many tall, smoking chimney-shafts which meet the eye indicate that the town is busy smelting ores, dug from the neighboring mineral hills and valleys. It is a pleasant and thrifty little city, somewhat liable to earthquakes and their attendant inconveniencies. The place has a population of ten or twelve thousand, and is named after a town in Cornwall,

England. We have left Australia proper far behind us, but the Bass Strait which separates that land from Tasmania is evidently of modern formation. The similarity of the vegetation, minerals, animal, and vegetable life of the two countries shows that this island must, at some time in the long-past ages, have been connected with the mainland. And yet the aborigines of Tasmania were a race quite distinct from those of Australia, so different, indeed, as only to resemble them in color. They were a well-formed, athletic people, with brilliant eyes, curly hair, flat noses, and elaborately tattooed bodies. This ingenious and barbaric ornamentation, practised by isolated savage races, seems to have been universal among the inhabitants of the Pacific Islands, though the great distances which separate them, as well as the lack of all ordinary means of intercommunication, would lead to the belief that they could not have borrowed the idea from one another. So late as 1828 there were a few of the Tasmanian aborigines still alive, but to-day there is not a representative of the race in existence.

When the country cast off the disgrace of being a penal colony, the name it bore was very judiciously changed from Van Dieman's Land to that of Tasmania, in honor of its first discoverer, Abel Janssen Tasman, the famous Dutch navigator of the seventeenth century. We should perhaps qualify the words "first discoverer." Tasman was the first accredited discoverer, but he was less entitled to impart his name to this beautiful island than were others. Captain Cook, with characteristic zeal and sagacity, explored, surveyed, and described it, whereas Tasman scarcely more than sighted it. However, any name was preferable to that of Van Dieman's Land, which had become the synonyme for a penal station, and with which is associated the memory of some of the most outrageous and murderous acts of cruelty for which a civilized government was ever responsible.

The whole island has now a population of about one hundred and thirty thousand, and a total area of over twenty-four thousand square miles. It is not quite so large as Ireland. Lying nearer to the Antarctic Circle it is of course cooler than the continent, but the influence of the sea, which completely surrounds it, renders the climate more equable. The general aspect of the country is that of being occupied by thrifty farmers of advanced ideas, such as carry on their calling understandingly, and more like well-populated America than sparsely-inhabited Australia. Our native fruits — apples, peaches, pears, and the like — thrive here in such abundance, as to form a prominent item in the exports, besides promoting a large and profitable industry in the packing of preserved fruits, which are in universal use in Australia and New Zealand. These canned fruits have an excellent and well-deserved reputation. Here, also, we find enormous trees, with a circumference of eighty feet near the ground, and a height of three hundred and fifty feet. Fern-trees, with their graceful palm-like formation, are frequently seen thirty feet in height. The country is well-wooded generally, and traversed by pleasant watercourses; it is singularly fertile, and rich in good harbors, especially upon the east coast. In short, its hills, forests, and plains afford a pleasing variety of scenery, while its rich pastures invite the stockbreeder to reap a goodly harvest in the easiest manner.

Launceston is situated at the head of navigation, on the Tamar, where the town nestles in the lap of a valley surrounded by high elevations. It is regularly laid out in broad streets, lighted by gas, and has a good water-supply brought from St. Patrick's River, fifteen miles east of the city. There are numerous substantial stone buildings, and everything bears a business-like aspect. There is a public library, and several free schools of each grade. The North and South Elk Rivers rise on different sides of Ben Lomond, and after flowing through some romantic plains and gorges, they join each other at Launceston. The sky-reaching mountain just named is worthy of its Scotch counterpart; between it and Launceston is some of the finest river and mountain scenery in all Tasmania. Ben Lomond is the chief object in the landscape, wherever one drives or walks in this part of the island. Tasmania possesses vast mineral wealth. The richest and most profitable tin mine in the world is that of Mount Bischoff, situated about a hundred and fifty miles from Launceston. The Beaconsfield gold mine is only thirty miles from the city, besides several others not much further away, which are rich in their yield of the precious metal.

The journey from here to Hobart, a distance of one hundred and twenty miles, takes us through the length of the island in a southeasterly direction. We pass through lovely glades, over broad plains, across rushing streams, and around the base of abrupt mountains. Hobart was so named in 1804, in honor of Lord Hobart, who was then Secretary of State for the Colonies. It is surrounded by hills and mountains except where the river Derwent opens into lake form, making a deep, well-sheltered harbor, whence it leads the way into the Southern Ocean. Among the lofty hills in this vicinity Mount Wellington towers forty-two hundred feet above the others, so close to the city as to appear to be within rifle range. The shape of the town is square, and it is built upon a succession of hills, very much like Sydney. It has broad streets intersecting each other at right angles, lined with handsome, well-stocked stores and dwelling-houses, serving an active and enterprising population of thirty thousand and more. Of these shops, two or three spacious and elegant bookstores deserve special mention, being such as would be creditable to any American city. It must undoubtedly be a cultured community which affords support to such establishments.

Yet we cannot forget that Hobart has scarcely outlived the curse of the penal association which encompassed its birth. Between thirty and forty years ago, the British government expended here five thousand dollars a day in support of jails and military barracks. The last convict ship from England discharged her cargo at Hobart in 1851, since which year the system has gradually disappeared. The city is supplied with all the necessary charitable and educational institutions, including a public library and art gallery. The street scenes have the usual local color, embracing the typical miner, with his rude kit upon his shoulder, consisting of a huge canvas bag, a shovel, and pick. The professional chimney-sweep, with blackened face and hands begrimed, — he whom we lost sight of in Boston years ago, — is here seen pursuing his antiquated vocation. Market-men have the same peculiar mode of delivering purchases to their customers that we have noticed elsewhere in this country, and are seen galloping about upon wiry little horses, bearing upon their arms large well-filled baskets. Women, with small handcarts full of slaughtered rabbits, cry them for sale at twelve cents a pair, besides which they receive a bounty for killing these pests.

The river Derwent, which rises far inland where the beautiful lakes St. Clair and Sorell are embosomed, broadens into a lake six miles wide where it forms the harbor of Hobart, and is famous for the regattas that are rowed upon its surface. Here, the largest craft that navigates these seas can lie close to the wharf and the warehouses. A visit to the Lake District of Tasmania affords many delightful views, where those inland waters just referred to lie in their lonely beauty, now overhung by towering cliffs, like those bordering a Norwegian arm of the sea, and now edged by pebbly beaches where choice agates and carnelians abound.

The charming cloud-effects which hang over and about the lofty hills which environ the capital of Tasmania, recall vividly those of the Lake of Geneva, near Chillon, while the Derwent itself, reflecting the hills upon its blue and placid surface, forms another pleasing resemblance to Lake Leman. In ascending Mount Wellington, the lion of Tasmanian scenery, when we find ourselves at an elevation of about two thousand feet, it is discovered that we have reached the Old World ocean-floor. Here, there are plenty of remains of the former denizens of the ocean, — fossils, telling the strange and interesting story of terrestrial changes that have taken place in the thousands upon thousands of years that are passed.

About twenty miles from Hobart we find a forest of the remarkable gum-trees of which we have all read, — trees which exceed in height and circumference the mammoth growths of our own Yosemite Valley, and fully equal those of Victoria. The immediate locality which contains them is known as the Huon District. A walk among these forest giants fills one with wonder and delight; their lofty tops seem almost lost in the sky to which they aspire. No church steeple, no cathedral pinnacle reared by the hand of man, but only mountain peaks reach so far skyward.

Tasmania is largely occupied for sheep-runs and wool-raising. The eastern side of the island is studded with lovely homesteads carefully fenced, the grounds about the residences being covered with fruit trees and flower plats. There does not appear to be any waste land, all is carefully improved in the peopled districts. The roads are often lined with thrifty hedges, symmetrically trimmed, frequently consisting of the brilliant, constant flowering, fragrant yellow gorse, and sometimes of the stocky species of scarlet geranium. This sort is not fragrant but becomes very thick by being cut partly down annually, until it makes an almost impenetrable hedge. Prosperity and good taste are everywhere noticeable, amid a succession of landscapes like those of the populous New England States.

SCENE ON THE SOUTH ESK RIVER, TASMANIA.

Page 80.

CHAPTER VI.

WE embark at Hobart by steamship, for Southern New Zealand. After following the course of the river Derwent for a distance of twelve miles, its mouth is reached, where the ship's course is a little south of east, the dull green of the waters on soundings rapidly changing to the navy blue of the ocean. The prevailing winds here are from the west, which with the Australian current and the Antarctic drift, are in our favor, so .the ship speeds cheerily on her way.

The tedium of the voyage is beguiled by watching the graceful movements of the wandering albatross, the fateful bird of nautical romance, which is sure to be seen in considerable numbers below the thirtieth parallel of south latitude. The peculiarities of this sea-bird's flight are a constant marvel, for it scarcely ever plies its wings, but literally sails upon the wind in any desired course. We wonder what secret power can so propel him for hundreds of rods with an upward trend at the close. If for a single moment he lights upon the water to seize some object of food, there is a trifling exertion evinced in rising again, until he is a few feet above the waves, when once more he sails with or against the wind, upon outspread, immovable wings. With no apparent inclination or occasion for pugnacity, the albatross is yet armed with a tremendous beak, certainly the most terrible of its kind possessed by any of the feathered tribe. It is from six to eight inches long, and ends in a sharp-pointed hook extremely strong and hard. It has been humorously said that if he pleased, the albatross might breakfast at the Cape of Good Hope and dine in New York, so wonderfully swift is he in flight and so powerful on the wing.

At night the phosphorescence of these lonely waters lying just north of the Antarctic Circle, between Tasmania and New Zealand, is indeed marvellous. Liquid fire is the only term which will properly express their flame-like appearance. If a bucketful is drawn and deposited upon deck, while it remains still it appears dark and like any other water, but when agitated it emits scintillations of light like the stars. A drop of this water placed under a microscope is found to be teeming with living and active creatures. If we suspend a muslin bag for a few moments over the ship's side, with the mouth open, then draw it up and permit it to drain for a few seconds, placing what remains in a glass tumbler, we shall find the abundance of living forms which it contains quite visible to the naked eye. No two of these minute creatures seem to be of similar form; the variety is infinite, and their activity incessant. Most of these animalcules, however, are so small that if it were not for the microscope we should never know of their existence.

The voyage from Hobart to the Bluff, South New Zealand, usually consumes four days, and it is often a very rough passage. Sailing-vessels making this trip carry a quantity of crude oil, which in extreme cases they employ to still the boisterous sea about them, when "God maketh the deep to boil like a pot." It should be known that our own Benjamin Franklin first suggested, about a century ago, the carrying of oil by vessels for this purpose. This shrewd American philosopher was also the first to suggest, about the same time, that ship-builders should construct the hulls of vessels in water-tight compartments, thus affording sufficient sustaining power to float them when by accident portions of the hull became leaky or broken into. After the lapse of a century both of these precautions have been adopted, and are much used.

As we sight the land, the southwest coast of New Zealand is found to be indented with deep fjords[1] almost precisely like the coast of Norway from Bergen to Hammerfest; and, singular to say, these arms of the sea, like those of the far north, are much deeper than the neighboring ocean. The Bluff, also known as Campbelltown, is situated in the very track of storms, being open to the entire sweep of the Antarctic Ocean. Its shelving side, sloping towards the harbor, forms a sort of lee, or sheltered position, which is occupied by a pretty little fishing-village of some sixty houses, and contains a population of less than a thousand. These people gain their living mostly from the neighboring sea, and from such labor as is consequent upon the occasional arrival of a steamship bound northward. We may here take refreshment at the Golden Age Inn, which is the most southerly house of public entertainment on the globe.

New Zealand did not become a recognized British colony until the year 1840. For three-quarters of a century after Cook's first visit, the native tribes remained in free possession of the country. It is true that England was mistress of these islands by right of discovery, but she made no formal assumption of political domain until the period already named, when it was formed into a colony subordinate to the government of New South Wales. As

[1] Pronounced *feords*.

early as 1815, white men of venturous disposition began to settle in small numbers among the natives; but often their fate was to be roasted and eaten by cannibals. Before 1820, missionaries, no doubt influenced by truly Christian motives, came hither and devoted their lives to this people, — in more senses than one, as it is well known that they not infrequently met with a fate similar to that of other settlers.

New Zealand lies as far south of the equator as Italy does north of it, and is divided into the North and South Islands by Cook's Strait. The South Island is also known as the Middle Island, to distinguish it more fully from Stewart Island, which belongs to the group, and which lies to the south of it. This last-named island is separated from Middle Island by Foveaux Strait some fifteen or twenty miles across the water from the Bluff. It is about fifty miles long by thirty broad, and has a mountain range running through it, the loftiest peak of which is a trifle over three thousand feet high. There are some fishing hamlets here, but there are very few inhabitants. All these islands are popularly believed to have once formed part of a great continent, which is now sunk in the sea.

Unlike Australia, New Zealand is rarely visited by drought. The whole eastern coast abounds in good harbors, while the rivers and streams are ever flowing and innumerable. Though it is a mountainous country, it differs from Switzerland in that it has no lack of extensive plains, which seem to have been left by nature ready to the hand of the farmer, requiring scarcely ordinary cultivation to insure large and profitable crops of grains. This diversity of surface, as well as the fact that these islands extend over thirteen degrees of latitude, give the country a varied climate, but it is a remarkably temperate one, its salubrity far surpassing that of England or any part of the United States. While snow is never seen in the North Island except upon the highest mountains, the plains of the South Island, as far south as Otago, are sometimes sprinkled with it, but only to disappear almost immediately. The rivers are generally destitute of fish, and the forests of game. It is no sportsman's country; but vegetation runs riot, the soil being remarkably fertile, clothing the wild lands with perpetual verdure and vigorous freshness.

The area of the islands known as New Zealand is about one hundred thousand square miles, being a few more than are contained in England, Wales, and Ireland combined. The entire coast line is four thousand miles in length. Out of the seventy million acres of land, forty million are deemed worthy of cultivation. The soil being light and easily worked favors the agriculturist, and New Zealand is free from all noxious animals and venomous reptiles. It is stated that no animal larger than a rat was found here by the discoverers. The remote situation of the country, surrounded by the greatest extent of ocean on the globe, has kept it in a measure unknown to the rest of the world, even in these days of rapid communication with all parts of the earth. Wellington, the capital, is about fifteen thousand miles more or less, from the Colonial Office in London; in other words, New Zealand forms the nearest land to the actual antipodes of England. The precious metals are distributed over the land in gold-bearing quartz reefs, rich alluvial diggings, and in the sands of its many rivers. Mines of tin and iron as well as other minerals are supplemented by an abundant supply of the most important of them all; namely, coal.

There is little of interest to detain us at the Bluff, so we continue on by steamer to Dunedin, the metropolis of Otago district, and indeed, the principal city of New Zealand, if we make the number and wealth of its population the criterion of comparison. The cities of both Australia and New Zealand, but especially those of the latter country, have a habit of locating themselves among and upon a collection of hills, up the sides of which the houses creep in a very picturesque manner. Dunedin is no exception to this rule, rising rather abruptly from the plain, which is the location of the wharves and business houses, to the summit of the surrounding hills. A portion of the plain near the shore, upon which broad streets and substantial blocks of buildings now stand, consists of made land, redeemed at great expense from the shallow water front of the town.

The first settlement here was made so late as 1848, by a colony nearly every member of which came from Scotland, and from this source the city has continued ever since to draw large numbers annually. The Scottish brogue salutes the ear everywhere; the Scottish physiognomy is always prominent to the eye; and indeed, there are several prevailing indications which cause one to half believe himself in Aberdeen, Glasgow, or Edinburgh. This is by no means unpleasant. There is a solid, reliable appearance to everything. People are rosy-cheeked, hearty, and good to look at. The wand of the enchanter, to speak figuratively, touched the place in 1861, from which date it took a fresh start upon the road of prosperity. It was caused by gold being discovered in large quantities near at hand, and from that date the city of Dunedin has grown in population and wealth with marvellous rapidity. Large substantial stone edifices have sprung up on all the main thoroughfares devoted to business purposes, banks, public offices, churches, schools, storehouses, etc., giving an unmistakable aspect of prosperity. The street-cars are mostly operated on the cable principle. Horses could not draw heavily-laden cars up some of the steep streets. The sensation when being conveyed on one of these cars up or down a steep grade of the city, is the same as when ascending or descending some Swiss mountains, by means of the same unseen power. The car is promptly stopped anywhere, to land or to take on a passenger, no matter how steep the grade, by the simple movement of a lever, and is easily started again. The powerful stationary engine situated a mile away, by means of the chain beneath the road-bed quietly winds the car up the declivity however heavily it may be laden, without the least slacking of speed.

The singularly formed hills about Dunedin are not mere barren rocks,— they have their suggestiveness, speaking of volcanic eruptions, of wild upheavals, dating back for thousands of years. Scientists tell us that these islands are of the earliest rock formations. The ground upon which this city stands, like that of Auckland further north, is composed of the fiery outflow of volcanic matter.

Dunedin has all the usual educational and philanthropic institutions which a community of fifty thousand intelligent people demand in our day. It is especially well supplied with primary and other schools. Throughout New Zealand there are over eight hundred registered public schools of the various grades. It is a source of gratification to realize that educational interests are nowhere neglected in these far-away colonies, where the eager pursuit of gold has been so prominent an element in inducing immigration. New

Zealand is nearly as rich in gold deposits as is Australia, and the precious metal is obtained under nearly the same conditions. Much gold has been found here in what are called pockets, under boulders and large stones which lie on the sandy beach of the west coast. This is popularly believed to have been washed up from the sea in heavy weather, but undoubtedly it was first washed down from the mountains and deposited along the shore. Official returns show that New Zealand has produced over two hundred and fifty million dollars in gold since its discovery in these islands.

When Captain Cook first landed here, he fully understood the cannibal habits of the native race, and sought for some practical means of discouraging and abolishing such inhuman practices. Upon his second visit, therefore, he introduced swine and some other domestic animals, such as goats and horned cattle, in the vain hope that they would ultimately supply sufficient animal food for the savages, and divert them from such wholesale roasting and eating of each other. The goats and some other animals were soon slaughtered and consumed, but the swine to a certain extent answered the purpose for which he designed them; that is to say, they ran wild, multiplied remarkably, and were hunted and eaten by the natives; but cannibalism was by no means abolished, or even appreciably checked. Wild hogs, which have sprung from the original animals introduced so many years ago, are still quite abundant in the North Island.

About two hundred miles northward from Dunedin is the city of Christchurch, settled first in 1850, and the chief seat of the Church of England in New Zealand, having a noble cathedral. Littleton is the port of Christchurch, situated eight miles below the city, and connected with it by both river and railway. This metropolis contains about thirty-five thousand people. In its museum there is a most interesting and perfect skeleton of that great bird, the Moa, — indigenous in this country and believed to have been extinct about two thousand years, probably disappearing before any human beings came to these islands. The Maori Indians (pronounced *Mow're*), the native race of New Zealand, can be traced back but six or seven hundred years, and only very imperfectly during that period. They are believed to have come from the islands lying in the North Pacific, presumably from the Sandwich or Hawaiian group. Even the traditions of these natives fail to give us any account of this gigantic bird while it was living, but its bones are found in various sections of the country, principally in caves. What is left of the Moa to-day is quite sufficient to form the greatest ornithological wonder in the world. The head of this reconstructed skeleton in the museum of Christchurch stands sixteen feet from the ground, and its various proportions are all of a character to harmonize with its remarkable height. This skeleton shows the marvellous bird to have been, when standing upright, five feet taller than the average full-grown giraffe. It belonged to the giants who dwelt upon the earth perhaps twenty thousand years ago, in the period of the mammoth and the dodo.

A couple of hundred miles further north will bring us to Wellington, the national capital. After a narrow entrance is passed, the harbor opens into a magnificent sheet of water, in which the largest ships may ride in safety and discharge their cargoes at wharves built close to the busy centre of the town. Here, as in Dunedin, a portion of land has been reclaimed from the sea for business purposes. The city has its asylums, a college, hospital, botanical garden, Roman Catholic cathedral, and a colonial museum, — the latter being of more than ordinary interest in the excellence and completeness of its several departments. A structure which is exhibited here and called the Maori House, built by the natives as a specimen of their domestic architecture, is particularly interesting, being also full of aboriginal curiosities, such as domestic utensils, weapons, and carvings. The house is of ordinary village size, and is ornamented on many of its posts by carved figures, representing native heroes and gods. The province of Wellington stretches northward a hundred and fifty miles and contains seven million acres of land, diversified by two mountain ranges. The population of the capital is a little over twenty thousand. The town impresses one as being a community of shops, and it is a subject of surprise how they can all obtain a living.

A considerable number of natives, mostly in European costume, are seen in the streets of Wellington, loitering about the corners and gazing curiously into shop windows, the girls and women having heavy shocks of unkempt hair shading their great black eyes, high cheek-bones, and disfigured mouths and chins, which last are tattooed in blue dye of some sort. The males tattoo the whole face elaborately, but the women disfigure themselves thus only about the mouth and chin. It is most amusing to see them meet one another and rub noses, which is the Maori mode of salutation. This race has some very peculiar habits: they never eat salt; they have no fixed industry, and no idea of time or its divisions into hours and months; they are, like our North American Indians, constitutionally lazy, are intensely selfish, and seem to care nothing for their dead; they have a quick sense of insult, but cannot as a rule be called pugnacious; they excite themselves to fight by indulging in strange war-dances and by singing songs full of braggadocio; and, after having been thus wrought up to a state of frenzy, they are perfectly reckless as to personal hazard. The Maori is not, however, a treacherous enemy; he gives honorable notice of his hostile intent, warring only in an open manner, thus exhibiting a degree of chivalry unknown to our American Indians. Money with the Maori is considered only as representing so much rum and tobacco. Alcohol is his criterion of value; bread and meat are quite secondary.

The name "Maori" is that which these aborigines gave themselves. If there were any human beings upon these islands when the Maoris first arrived, they doubtless fell a prey to the cannibalistic habits of the newcomers, whose insatiable appetite for human flesh was irrepressible. When discovered by Cook, they were the lowest of savage races; they knew scarcely anything of the mechanic arts, their skill being limited to the scooping out of a boat from the trunk of a tree, and the fabrication of fishing-nets from the coarse fibre of the wild flax. They also made spears, shields, and clubs. They had no beasts of burden, and so their women were made to supply the place. Their agriculture was confined to the raising of sweet potatoes and the taro root, while their more substantial food consisted of fish, rats, wild fowl, and human flesh. Captain Cook estimated, when he first visited them, that the Maoris had passed the period of their best days. He thought that in the century previous to his coming hither they had eaten about one-fourth of their number.

The race is now estimated at only thirty-six or thirty-eight thousand, though it is certain that it embraced a hundred thousand about a century ago. The decrease in ten years is apparent to observant persons, a fact not clearly accounted for by any excess of living on their part, though their daily habits are not very commendable, especially as to drink. They are all most inveterate smokers, — men, women, and children; you can give a Maori maiden nothing more acceptable to her taste and appreciation than a pipe and a plug of smoking-tobacco. As a people, they have manifestly filled the purpose for which Providence placed them upon these islands of the South Sea; and now, like the Moa, they must pass off the scene and give way to another race. So it seems to be with the Red Man of America, and so it was with the now totally extinct natives of Tasmania.

When this capital of Wellington was first settled, the newcomers could build their houses only of wood, the frequency of earthquakes warning them against raising edifices of heavy material or making their dwellings over one or two stories in height. But earthquakes, though now occasionally experienced, are by no means so frequent as formerly. Tremulousness of the earth and rumblings as of distant thunder are heard now and again, in the hills that stretch inland towards the mountains, which is quite sufficient to keep the fact in mind that this is a volcanic region. Earthquake shocks are frequent all over the islands, and it is believed that New Zealand was rent midway, where Cook's Strait divides the North from the South Island, by volcanic explosion. There is known to be an extinct volcano at the bottom of the strait, in front of the entrance to the harbor of Wellington, over which the water is never absolutely calm and where it sometimes boils like a caldron.

CHAPTER VII.

AUCKLAND, the northern metropolis of New Zealand, was formerly the capital of the country until Wellington was selected for the headquarters of the government, as being the more central and accessible from the several islands. So beautiful and picturesque are the bay and harbor that one is not surprised to hear its citizens call it the Naples of New Zealand. Before the European settlers came here this was the locality where the most savage wars were carried on by the natives, and where the most warlike tribes lived in fortified villages. Though the country has virtually no ancient history that is known to us, it has a recognized past extending back for some centuries. When the missionaries first came here about the year 1814, the main subsistence of the natives who lived around what is now Auckland harbor, was human flesh. The first white immigrants, as well as the seamen of chance vessels driven upon the coast, were invariably killed and eaten by the Maoris. Not only did cannibalism prevail here, but it was common in Brazil, in the West Indies, in the other Pacific Islands, along the coast of North America, and among the Indians of Chili, who ate the early navigators who landed upon their shores.

The isthmus upon which the city of Auckland is built is undoubtedly one of the most remarkable volcanic districts in the world, though the agency of subterranean fires is visible enough to the traveller all over the country.

Mount Tongariro, six thousand feet high, is even now in activity, with occasional fiery outbursts. The earthquakes which occur in both the North and the South Islands, cause alternate depressions and elevations. That of 1855 raised the coast line four feet for many miles in length. As in the peninsula of Scandinavia, we here find a grand longitudinal mountain range from the extreme of the South Island through the Auckland district to the far north, forming, as it were, a backbone to the country.

Mount Eden is the nearest elevation to the city, and is seven or eight hundred feet in height. On this hill there are abundant evidences still left of the native fortifications, but of the large Maori population that once covered the peninsula and lived in these *pahs*, or fortified villages, not a soul remains. The harbor is one of the best in Australasia, having ample depth and good wharf facilities, besides being quite sheltered. Its shorter distance from the ports of America gives it an advantage over all others in this region. It is reached from London, across the American continent, in thirty-seven days, while to reach Sydney requires four days more of steam navigation across a boisterous sea.

Auckland occupies a series of hills divided by valleys trending in the direction of the sea or harbor. The slopes and hill-tops are dotted by villas, each of which is surrounded by flowers and ornamental trees. The business part of the town is not particularly attractive, though Queen Street, the principal thoroughfare, contains some fine stores and brick edifices, as well as public buildings of stone. Both the level and the hilly streets are traversed by street railways, upon which horse-power only is used. The population, including the immediate environs, is about sixty-five thousand. The educational interests of the city are well provided for by primary schools, as well as by means for secondary education in a college for boys, and a high school for girls, both taxed to their full capacity.

The Ponsonby suburb and the village of Whou are composed of pleasant residences tastefully ornamented. Parnell forms another suburb, rendered attractive by hedgerows, drooping willows, and prettily arranged gardens. From this point one gets a fine view of the outspread bay lying below, full of various busy maritime craft. Steam ferry-boats are constantly gliding across the harbor, little white-winged cutters bend gracefully to the breeze, the tall masts of sailing-vessels line the piers, and tiny row-boats glance hither and thither. The lofty marine-signal hill looms up across the harbor, in its verdant garb, while volcanic cones, a little way inland on either shore, form an irregular background. Far away and beyond all is seen the swelling bosom of the great Southern Ocean.

This metropolis is situated in the centre of rich timberlands, and also of an abundant coal deposit. Should the Panama Canal be completed, Auckland would be the first port of call and the last of departure between Europe and the colonies of the South Pacific.

The kauri-tree — the pine of this country — is not at all like our North American pine; instead of needles, its foliage consists of leaves of sombre green. It produces a timber which for some purpose is unequalled. It is very slow of growth, is remarkably durable, easily worked, of fine grain, and does not split or warp by atmospheric exposure. It is said that the kauri-tree requires eight hundred years to arrive at maturity. To visit the forest where it is found in the Auckland district, one takes cars from the city to

Helensville, a distance of about forty miles, where the Kaipara River is reached, upon which small steamers ply, taking us directly to the desired spot. Here, the busy saw-mills which are gradually consuming these valuable trees are so situated that vessels of two thousand tons can load at their yards and with their cargo pass directly out to sea. It is singular that while this district is the only place in New Zealand where the kauri-trees are found, nearly every other species of tree native to the country is also found here, among them the rimu, the matai, the white pine, the tooth-leaved beech, and the totara, all in close proximity to the kauri. The commercial prosperity of Auckland is largely due to the harvest reaped from these forests. The kauri-tree grows to an average height of a hundred feet, with a diameter of fifteen feet. It is a clannish tree, so to speak; and when found near to those of other species it groups itself in clumps apart from them. One often sees, however, forests where the kauri reigns supreme, quite unmixed with other trees.

The kauri-gum forms a large figure in the list of exports from Auckland, and the digging and preparing of it for shipment gives employment to many persons. The natives have a theory that the gum descends from the trunks of the growing trees, and through the roots becomes deposited in the ground. But this is unreasonable; the gum is a partially fossilized production, showing that it has gone through a process which only a long period of years could have effected. It is usually found at a depth of five or six feet from the surface. It is undoubtedly a fact that this northerly part of New Zealand was once covered by immense forests of this gum-tree, which have matured and been destroyed by fire and by decay, century after century, and the deposit, which is now so marketable, is from the dead trees, not from the living. Experiments have been tried which have proven that the gum exuded by the growing tree has no commercial value. It is very similar to amber, for which article it is often sold to unskilled purchasers; but its principal use is in the manufacture of varnish.

The immediate neighborhood of Auckland is almost denuded of original trees, but ornamental species are being planted, and flowers are plentiful. The Maoris had distinctive and expressive names for every bird, tree, and flower, before the white man came. There is a lovely little native daisy called tupapa, and a blue lily known as rengarenga, also a green and yellow passion-flower named by the aborigines kowhaia. A glutinous, golden buttercup is known as anata, nearly as abundant as its namesake in America. All these are wild-flowers, cultivated only by Nature's hand. New Zealand seems to be adapted for receiving into its bosom the vegetation of any land, and imparting to it renewed life and added beauty. Its foster-mother capacity has been fully tested, and for years no ship left England for this part of the world, without bringing more or less of a contribution in plants and trees, to be propagated in the new home of the colonists. The consequence is, we find pines and cypresses, oaks and willows, elms and birches, besides fruit-trees of all sorts, which are grown in Europe, thriving here in abundance, in the grounds surrounding the settlers' houses. The range of temperature is here very limited. Summer and winter are only known as the dry and the rainy seasons; flowers, vegetables, grapes, in short, all plants, grow thriftily the whole year round in the open air. Tropical and hardy plants are equally at home; Scottish firs and Indian palms, oranges, lemons, india-rubber trees, and the lime thrive side by side. As in Japan, so it is here. One can gather a pretty bouquet out of doors any day in the year.

At Auckland, we are in the vicinity of the famous Hot Lake District of New Zealand, the veritable wonderland of these regions, to reach which we take the cars for a distance of a hundred and thirty miles, then proceed thirty miles further by stage to the native town of Ohinemutu, on Lake Rotorua. This route carries us in a southeast course and leads into the very heart of the North Island, among the aborigines. The railway passes through a level country or valley, which, however, is bounded on either side, five or six miles away, by lofty hills, presenting a confusion of irregular forms. These hills contain an abundance of mineral wealth in the form of gold, silver, iron, coal, and manganese. Many low-lying marshy fields of native flax are seen, and the Waikato River is three times crossed in its winding course, as we thread our way through the valley. Large plantations, each containing several thousand young pine-trees of the American species, are seen, covering gentle slopes, and many broad acres of level land, where the government is endeavoring to establish artificial forests throughout wide reaches of unwooded country. These trees grow more rapidly here even than in their native soil. Small Maori encampments, composed of a dozen lodges each, are scattered along the way, the lazy tattooed natives — men and women — lingering about the stations, with blackened pipes in their mouths, smoking the rankest sort of tobacco, while they chatter together like Benares monkeys.

The last part of this brief journey, that from Oxford to Ohinemutu, takes us through one of the grandest forests in all New Zealand, extending eighteen or twenty miles, with scarcely a human habitation or sign of life, save the cabin where we change horses, and the occasional flutter of a bird. In this forest, mingled with tall columnar trees of various species, are seen frequent examples of the fern-tree thirty feet in height, and of surpassing beauty, spreading out their plumed summits like Egyptian palms, while the stems have the graceful inclination of the cocoa-nut-tree. The picturesque effect of the birches is remarkable, flanked by the massive outlines and drooping tassels of the rimu. For miles of the way on either side of the narrow road the forest is impenetrable even to the eye, save for the shortest distances, presenting a tangled mass of foliage, vines, and branches such as can be matched only by the virgin forests of Brazil, or the dangerous jungles of India. Ground ferns are observed in infinite variety, sometimes of a silvery texture, sometimes of orange-yellow, but oftenest of the various shades of green. Here, too, we make acquaintance with the sweet-scented manuaka, the fragrant veronica, and the glossy-leaved karaka; this last is the pride of the Maoris.

Specimens of the lofty rimu-tree are seen, about whose tall white stems a parasitic vine (a plant which obtains its nourishment from another plant to which it attaches itself) slowly and treacherously weaves itself, clasping and binding the upright body with such marvellous power of compression as literally to strangle it, until ultimately the vine becomes a stout tree and takes the place of that it has destroyed. The most noted and destructive of these vegetable boa-constrictors is the gigantic rope-like rata, whose Gordian knot nothing can untie. The tree once clasped in its toils is fated, yielding up its sap and life without a struggle to cast off its deadly enemy. Many trees are observed whose stems bear branches only, far above the surrounding woods, laden with bunches of alien foliage, — parasites like the mistletoe. Indeed, this forest seems like vegetation running riot, and with its clumps of dissimilar foliage fixed like storks' nests in the tops of the trees, recalling the same effect which one sees on the St. John's River in Florida.

Once fairly within the area of the Hot Lake District, which is the most active volcanic region of the Antipodes, nothing seems too strange to be true; geysers, vapor-holes, boiling springs, and dry stones burning hot beneath one's feet, surround us, as though the surface of the land covered Nature's chemical laboratory. Sulphur, alkaline, and iron impregnated pools of inviting temperature cause one to indulge in frequent baths, and it seems but natural that the natives in their half-naked condition should pass so much time in the water. Near the shore of Lake Rotorua, where it is shallow, a boiling spring forces its way to the surface of the surrounding cold water, telling of a submerged fiery caldron underlying the lake at that particular point. It is, however, no more significant than the scores of other steam-holes and spouting geysers which force themselves to the surface of the land all about this sulphurous region. In short, the little town of Ohinemutu is built on a thin crust, roofing over as it were a vast fiery furnace, whose remarkable volcanic eccentricities form the marvel of this locality. Here, the traveller eats, drinks, and sleeps above a series of suppressed volcanoes, and is apt to recall the fate of Pompeii. Many of these springs and geysers are so hot that a mere touch of the water will blister the flesh as quickly as contact with red-hot iron. Others are of a temperature suitable for boiling vegetables; and still others by artificial means — that is, the introduction of cold surface water — are rendered of a temperature suitable for bathing purposes. One must walk cautiously among these boiling mud-pits, open springs, and steam-holes, for a misstep might prove fatal. Dangerous caldrons lie on either side of the path, within a few inches of where one may be walking all unsuspiciously.

The natural conclusion as to the cause of these remarkable phenomena would seem to be that the waters of the lakes, rivers, and springs descend by various channels to the fiery regions below, and are returned by the force of the steam thus created, bringing up with them the refuse which is deposited about the surface. Of the hundreds of these boiling springs only a score or so have been analyzed: no two, however, exhibit the same properties. The various chemical combinations seem to be without limit, and bathing in them is considered to be a specific for some skin-diseases, as well as for rheumatic affections. There can be no doubt but that all the medicinal virtues possessed by similar springs in Europe and America are found in these of New Zealand.

Ohinemutu is the most typical home of the natives, and for ages has formed the chief settlement of the Arawa tribe. Nothing could possibly be more grotesque than to see groups of the native women, from the wrinkled old grandams to the girls of a dozen years, bathing at all hours of the day in the warm, steaming pools. It is their daily, almost hourly resort. As a rule, a blanket forms their only covering; and if they are cold, day or night, casting this aside, they at once resort to the hot springs for warmth. Their chief occupations are literally bathing and smoking tobacco, the women using the pipe even more freely than the men. Of regular occupation they have none. A few potatoes are planted and allowed to grow without cultivation, and these with pork form their chief food. The little cooking in which they indulge is usually performed by the boiling springs, in which they hang their potatoes in small wicker baskets; and for baking purposes they use the red-hot stones that are to be found everywhere in this vicinity. These broad, flat stones are the identical ones on which the natives not long ago were accustomed to roast their prisoners of war before eating them.

A certain consistency is discovered in the manners and customs of this people who live so nearly after the style and laws which governed their ancestors, and which have been carefully preserved for hundreds of years. Superstition is born in a Maori. He is a professed Christian in most cases and accepts the Bible, but he is apt to give to it his own interpretation. These children of Nature follow their ancestral traditions modified by Christian influences. The original religion of the natives, if we may call it by that name, consists in a dim belief in a future state, quite undefined even in their own minds. It was largely a sort of ancestor worship, according to the missionaries, with a vague idea of some Being higher than anything human or finite. The sorcery which was universally practised among them filled up a certain measure of religious conviction and observance, nor is this by any means disused among them to-day. Many of the tribes can read and write, and educational facilities are freely offered to the rising generation by the English government.

The Maori differs in many essential particulars from

most savage races with whom we are more familiar. He does not, as has been mentioned, foster a spirit of secret revenge, but when his enmity is aroused, it is openly displayed. This has been a tribal trait with the Maoris for centuries. Before declaring war the Maori always gives his enemy fair notice; still for ages he has been accustomed to go to war upon imaginary grievances, or, to put it more clearly, his great object was to make prisoners of war, and when made to cook and eat them. The early Maoris, and even so late as sixty years ago, looked upon war — what we call civil war — as being the only legitimate object of life.

Though these natives have mostly become Christianized, as we understand the term, still they live more like the lower class of animals than like human beings, seeming to prefer that sort of life even after half a century of intercourse with the whites. They now isolate themselves as a body in what is called the King's Country of the North Island, which embraces the Hot Lake District, where they live under their own laws and customs which are held inviolate by treaty with the English crown. Their decrease in numbers seems to be as rapid in their own district as it is where they are brought into more intimate relations with the whites. The English authorities respect their ownership of lands, and not an acre of it is to be had without just payment for it.

No intelligent person can be blind to the favorable position of New Zealand or to the promise of its future commercial importance. Situated, as it were, in the centre of this Southern Ocean, the future highway of the world, it is accessible from all quarters. On the west, not very far away, lie the busy harbors of Australia, with which her exchanges of merchandise are constant. Within easy reach of India and China on one side, she has California, Mexico, and South America on the other. To the north lie the hundreds of islands which constitute the groups of Polynesia, notable for their voluptuous climate and primitive fertility. With the opening of the Panama Canal or other available means for ships to cross the isthmus of South America, New Zealand will lie directly in the highway between Europe and the gold-fields of the great inland continent, between England and her largest and most promising colony.

The many beautiful islands of the South Sea must sooner or later come under the commercial sway of New Zealand, as they may be explored and civilized. Her admirable harbors, noble estuaries, and navigable rivers are elsewhere unsurpassed. If destined to achieve greatness, these islands, like those of Great Britain, will do so through the development and maintenance of maritime power; and with so many natural advantages as they possess we confidently predict for them this final accomplishment.

CHAPTER VIII.

FROM Auckland we take a steamer for Asia by way of Sydney and other ports of Australia, crossing the Indian Ocean and landing at the extreme southerly point of India, at Tuticorin. It is a quaint old place of little present interest, though it was once famous for its pearl fisheries. We proceed northward by railway to Madura, where, there being no hotel, we take up our quarters in an unoccupied native house, situated in a grove of cocoa-nut-trees. Flies, mosquitoes, and scorpions dispute possession with us, and ugly-looking snakes creep close to the low piazza. Flying-foxes hang motionless from the branches of the trees; clouds of butterflies, many-colored, sunshine-loving creatures, in infinite variety, flit about the bungalow, some with such gaudy spread of wing as to tempt pursuit. Large bronze and yellow beetles walk through the short grass with the coolness and gait of domestic poultry. Occasionally a chameleon turns up its bright eye, as though to take our measure. The redundancy of insect and reptile life is wonderful in Southern India.

The principal attraction to the traveller in Madura, which contains some fifty thousand inhabitants, is a remarkable and very ancient temple supported by two thousand stone columns. It is probably one of the largest and finest monuments of Hindoo art in existence, covering in all its divisions, courts, shrines, colonnades, and tanks, twenty acres of ground. It has nine lofty tower-like gates of entrance and exit, each one of which has the effect of forming an individual pagoda. In the central area of the temple is what is known as the "Tank of the Golden Lily" being a large body of water covering a couple of acres of ground, and leading into which are broad stone steps on all sides. Here individuals of both sexes are seen constantly bathing for religious purification. A grand tank is the adjunct of every Indian temple. This mass of buildings contains many living sacred elephants, deified bulls, enshrined idols, and strange ornamentation, the aggregate cost of which must have been enormous. The elephants rival the beggars in their importunities, being accustomed to receive an unlimited amount of delicacies from visitors, such as fruits, sweetmeats, candies, and the like.

Another hundred miles northward by railway brings us to the city of Trichinopoly, where the famous natural rock five hundred feet in height is crowned by the Temple of Ganesa. The view from this eminence is exceptionally fine. The town far below us looks as though it had been shaken up and dropped there by a convulsion of nature. There is no regularity in the laying out of the place; it is a confused mass of buildings, narrow paths, crooked roads, and low-built mud cabins. In what is called the silversmith's quarter, amid filthy lanes, full of dirty children, mangy dogs, and moping cats, we find hovels containing finely wrought silver ornaments manufactured on the spot by the natives. So original and elegant are these wares that they have a reputation beyond the borders of India. Trichinopoly has over sixty thousand inhabitants. But however much there may be to interest us, we must not tarry long. Two hundred miles still northward bring us to Tanjore, a large fortified city, where we find a mammoth and gorgeously decorated car of Juggernaut, the Indian idol. It makes its annual excursion from the temple through the town, drawn by hundreds of worshippers, who come from great distances to assist at the ceremony. Pilgrims, delirious with fanaticism, used once to throw themselves under the wheels of the huge car and perish. This self-immolation is now almost entirely suppressed by the government, as is the kindred one of the burning of widows upon their husbands' funeral piles. From 1815 to 1826, published statistics show that fifteen thousand widows perished thus in India!

The great temple of Tanjore is fourteen stories in height, and measures two hundred feet from base to top. These temples all resemble each other in general design, and are characterized by grotesqueness, caricature, and vulgar images, as well as by infinite detail in their finish. Though they are gorgeously decked in colors, and gross in ornamentation, still they are so grand in size and on so costly a scale, as to create amazement rather than disgust. It would seem that a people equal to such efforts must have been capable of something better. In all grosser forms of superstition and idolatry, carnal and material elements seem to be essential to bind and attract the ignorant, and this is undoubtedly the governing policy of a religion, embodying emblems so outrageous to Christian sensibility. This grand pagoda at Tanjore, taken as a whole, is the most remarkable religious monument in India. In passing through the southern section of the country, we see many ruined temples in unpopulated districts, which belong to past ages; many mammoth stone elephants and bulls, crumbling by the wear of centuries. Large flocks of goats tended by herdsmen are seen distributed over the plains, and so level is the country, that the eye can make out these groups for miles away on either side of the railroad. Well-cultivated plantations of sugar-cane, plantains, wheat, rice, and orchards of fruit come into view. The old style of irrigation goes on, by means of buckets worked by hand, the same as was practised in the East four thousand years ago, while the very plough, rude and inefficient, which is used upon their plains to-day is after the antique fashion belonging to the same period. Indeed, except that the railroad runs through Southern India, there appears to have been no progress there for thousands of years. A lethargy of the most hopeless character seems to possess the common people. Their mud cabins are not suitable abodes for human beings, and are distanced in neatness by the ant-hills. Such a degraded condition of humanity can hardly be found elsewhere among semi-civilized races. The women are worn by hardships. The men are cadaverous and listless. Clothing among them is the exception; nudity is the rule. It seems strange, but it is true, that one-quarter of the human race goes naked in this nineteenth century.

A day's journey northward by railroad brings us to Madras, situated upon the Bay of Bengal. The city is spread out over a very large territory, with a number of broad, open fields and squares, designed for drilling of troops, some for ball-players, and some for ordinary parks. There is an abundant and handsome growth of trees all about the city, lining the main streets and testifying to the judicious attention given by the authorities to this species of ornamental shade so necessary in a warm climate. The wide streets are admirably kept, and are all macadamized. This applies, however, to the European portion of the town, with its fine, large public buildings, consisting of literary and scientific institutions as well as various educational and charitable ones. The native portion of Madras is contracted and dirty in the extreme, no attention being given to cleanliness or decency. The extensive English fort — Fort George — is one of the best constructed in the East, forming a most prominent feature of the city, and crowning a moderate rise of ground near the shore. Its attractive though warlike surroundings, white walls, flower plats, and green, sloping banks present a charming picture. Fort George was the original name of the city. A noble lighthouse is situated within the fortifications. Near this spot, along the coast to the northward, are the rock-cut temples of Mahabulihuram rendered familiar by Southey's admirable verses.

Dancing-girls are to be seen here, on the streets. They are attached to some native temple, as no religious ceremony or gala day is considered complete without them; and the same may be said of all large private entertainments, no guests ever dancing in the East. They prefer to hire it done for them. These Indian dancing-girls, with a musical accompaniment, tell a story by their performance, expressing grief, joy, jealousy, and other passions so well portrayed, that one easily interprets the pantomime. They preserve strict propriety in their dances, which are curious to witness, their ankles being covered with silver bells, and their wrists and arms similarly decked.

No more unprotected spot could be found on the surf-beaten shore of the Coromandel coast than this where stands Madras. It is so completely exposed to the northeast monsoons as to be inaccessible for sailing-vessels from October to January, and yet it was the first British capital in India. There is usually such a surf on the shore that nothing but the native boats can weather it; and when high winds prevail, it is too much even for them. We embark by steamship from Madras, and after a voyage of nearly a thousand miles up the coast and Hoogly River, land at Calcutta, which is the political capital of India, though since the Suez Canal has been opened, Bombay rivals it commercially.

Calcutta is a very interesting city, very Indian, notwithstanding that so many Europeans live here, and that it has so long been under English rule, but it is by no means entitled to the designation so often given to it, namely, the "City of Palaces." It is quite modern, having no remains of antiquity about it, and in 1686 was but a mud village. As seen from the Hoogly, when one first arrives, it exhibits a strong array of fine public buildings; but a passage of a few rods, diverging from the main thoroughfare, brings the visitor upon the dirty streets, the mean and narrow houses, and general squalor of the native population.

The Burning Ghat, where cremation is going on at all hours of the day, is the first place the stranger visits. The bodies are brought in and placed upon a square pile of wood, raised to a height of four feet, in the open yard. Under the wood there is plenty of combustible material; the torch is applied, and instantly all is hidden by the flames. In three hours nothing but calcined bones and ashes are left. These are carefully gathered and cast into the river. The Ghat is open to the sky, so that the ventilation is perfect, but the atmosphere is nevertheless impregnated with an unpleasant odor. The Hoogly River being one of the outlets of the much-revered Ganges, is considered to be equally sacred. Close by the Burning Ghat, along the river's front, there is a number of sheds, with only partial shelter from the street, where poor dying Hindoos are brought to breathe their last, believing that if they pass away close to the sacred water, their spirits will be instantly wafted to the regions of bliss. Here they are attended by people who make this their business, and it is believed that they often hasten the demise of the sufferers by convenient means. Human life is held of very little account among these people, whose faith bridges the gulf of death, and who were at one time so prone to suicide by drowning in the Ganges, as to render it necessary on the part of the English to establish watchmen every night along the city shore of the sacred river to prevent it.

At the close of each day, about an hour before sunset, all fashionable Calcutta turns out in state for a drive on the Maiden, — the Hindoostanee name for esplanade, — a broad and finely macadamized roadway, extending along the river's bank by the fort and cricket grounds. It is the Indian Hyde Park, or Bengal Champs Elysées (the famous Parisian boulevard). The variety, elegance, and costliness of the equipages in grand livery are surprising. The whole scene is enlivened by the beautiful dresses of the ladies, the dashing costumes and gold lace of the nabobs, the quaint Oriental dress of their barefooted attendants, and the spirited music of the military band. The superb horses in their gold-mounted harnesses dash over the course at a spirited gait; the twilight hour is brief, the shadows lengthen, when a hundred electric lamps flash upon the scene, rivalling the light of day. Then the occupants of the open vehicles, and the equestrians, gather about the Eden Garden, in rows, six or eight deep, and listen to the popular airs, or chat merrily in the intervals. The Cascine at Florence, the Pincio at Rome, the Chiaja at Naples, the Prado at Madrid — none of these famous drives can compare with the Maiden of Calcutta for gayety, variety, and attractiveness.

Calcutta is said to contain a population of a million. It is sometimes visited by cyclones, and the fierceness of these warrings of the elements may be judged by the fact that at the last occurrence of the sort thirty thousand native houses were totally destroyed in half an hour. The Hoogly River often experiences the effect of tidal waves during the monsoons, which dash up from the sea at a speed of twenty miles an hour, causing much destruction. Ships lying off the city on such occasions often part their cables and are driven on shore, while many of the small craft along the eighty miles of river course are entirely destroyed.

A journey of four hundred miles to the northward, the last half of which is performed by narrow-gauge railway, which climbs zigzag fashion over a very hilly country, will enable us to reach Darjeeling, nearly nine thousand feet above the level of the sea. Here we are in proximity to and in full view of the Himalayan range of mountains, the loftiest on the globe. The lowest peak is over twenty thousand feet in height; the highest exceeds twenty-eight thousand. Upon the range rest eleven thousand feet of perpetual snow. There can be no animal life in that Arctic region — only the snow and ice rest there in endless sleep. The Himalayas — meaning the "Halls of Snow" — form the northern boundary of India, and shut out the country from the rest of Asia. Thibet, which lies

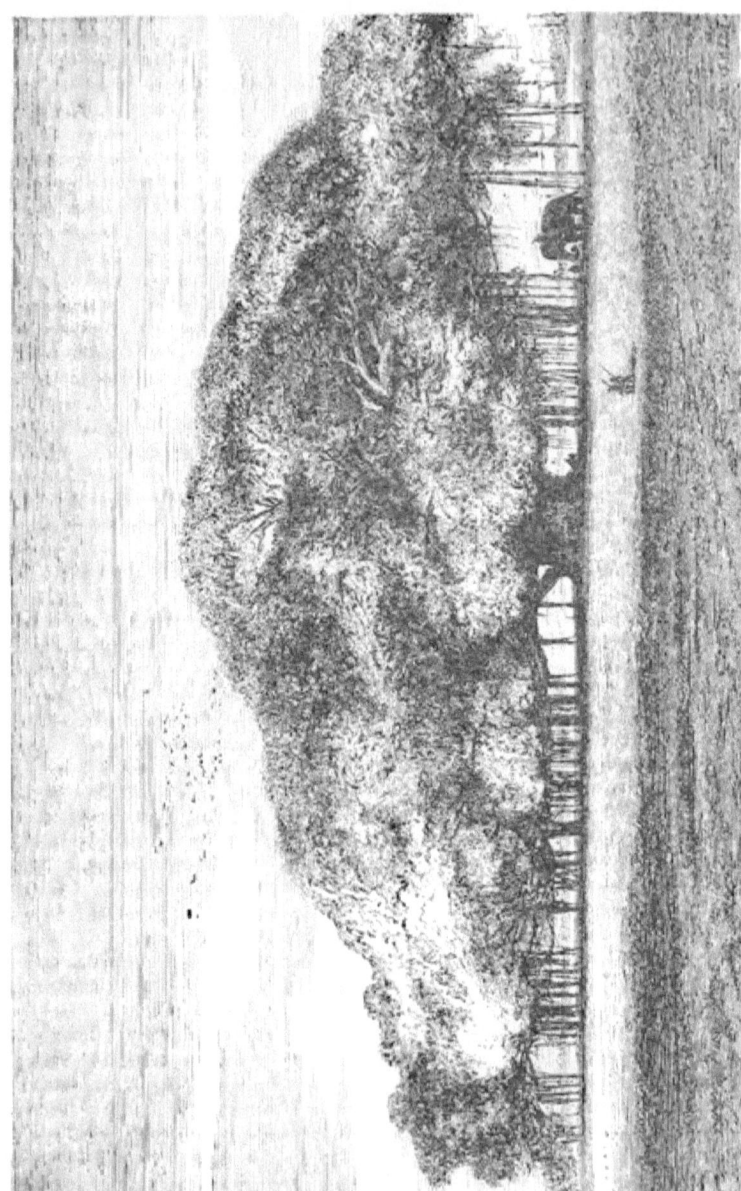

A GREAT BANYAN TREE AT CALCUTTA.

just over the range, whence we view it, is virtually inaccessible by this route, the wild region between being nearly impassable. Bold parties of traders, wrapped in sheepskins, do sometimes force their way over the mountains at an elevation of eighteen thousand feet, but it is a most hazardous thing to do, and the bones of worn-out mules mark the frozen way, telling of suffering and abandonment. The little yak cow, whose bushy tail is manufactured into lace, has been found to be the best and most enduring animal to depend upon when such journeys are performed. She will patiently toil up the steep gorges with a load on her back, and will drop dead in her tracks before she will show any stubbornness or want of courage. The culminating point of the range, and the highest mountain peak in the world, is Mount Everest, which is a little over twenty-nine thousand feet in height above the level of the sea.

Darjeeling is becoming the centre of a great tea-producing district, and thus India bids fair to rival China in a product which has seemed to belong almost exclusively to China from time immemorial. English capitalists are largely embarking in this enterprise, and extensive tea-plantations are already in full process of successful yielding, sending tea annually to the London market. At first it seems strange to see the tea-plant flourishing at such an altitude, covering hundreds of acres of the mountain's sides, on the road descending from Darjeeling, towards the plains of Hindoostan, but it must be remembered that the latitude of this region is just about that of Florida and the West Indies. As to the product of these tea-fields, one realizes no difference in its flavor from that of the Chinese leaf. In England it is known as Assam tea.

As we descend towards the level country, amid many other flowering trees, the magnolia is most prominent. The wild and abundant growth of the rhododendron, which here becomes a forest tree, mingles with a handsome species of cedar, which rises in dark and stately groups and forms a marked feature in the landscape. The general luxuriance of the vegetation is conspicuous, thickly clothing the branches of the trees with mosses, ferns, and creeping vines. Here we observe the cotton-tree, with its red blossoms, which yields a coarse material for native use. Also a species of lotus called "Queen of the Forest," the leaves of which are used by the common people in place of tea. Many bright and exquisitely delicate ferns spring up among the damp undergrowth about the places where we stop to take water for our little, noisy, spluttering engine. Brilliant butterflies float like motes in the sunshine, contrasting with the repulsive whip-snakes seen hanging from the low branches of the trees. Vegetation and animal life seem to be singularly abundant and prolific in these foot-hills of the famous mountain range.

Our course now lies towards Benares, over the plains of Middle India, some five hundred miles from Calcutta. The people on the route seem to be wretchedly poor, living in the most primitive mud cabins thatched with straw. Such squalor and visible poverty can be found nowhere else in any country outside of Ireland, and yet we are passing through a famous agricultural district which ought to support thrifty farmhouses and smiling villages. It abounds in productive rice, wheat, sugar-cane, and vast poppy fields, — these last treacherously beautiful, — and from which the opium of commerce is derived. The presence of such abundance makes the contrast in the condition of the peasantry all the more puzzling. There must be something radically wrong in the modes of the governing power. This part of India is noted for the excellence and prolific yield of its sugar crops. From here, also, indigo and saltpetre are exported in large quantities. Along the route traversed by the railway we see fruit-trees of various sorts native to this section, such as tamarinds, almonds, mangos, oranges, cocoanuts, and other products of the palm family. Temples, centuries in age and quite in ruins, come into view now and again, often adjacent to a cluster of low mud hovels. From the branches of the trees flit birds of such fantastic colors as to cause exclamations of surprise. Occasional specimens of the bird-of-paradise are seen, with its long and graceful tail-feathers glittering in the sunshine and presenting an array of bright colors which are not preserved upon this bird in captivity. Tall flamingoes in snowy plumage, just touched with scarlet on either wing, fly lazily over the ponds, or stand by the banks resting quietly upon one long, slim leg. Parrots abound in carnival hues, and buff-colored doves, with soft white rings of feathers about their necks, coquet lovingly together.

Benares, the first large city on the united Ganges and Jumna, may be called the citadel of Hindooism, containing about a hundred and fifty thousand permanent inhabitants and as many more floating population, composed of pilgrims constantly coming and going. What Jerusalem is to the Jew, Rome to the Roman Catholic, Mecca to the Mohammedan, Benares is to the Hindoo. It is supposed by many to be the oldest known habitation of man. Twenty-five centuries ago, when Rome was unknown and Athens was in its youth, Benares was already famous. It is situated on the left bank of the Ganges, to bathe in which river insures to the devout Hindoo forgiveness of all sins and an easy passport to the regions of the blest. Here, as in Calcutta, cremation is constantly going on beside the river. While we are looking at the scene there comes a family group bearing a body to the funeral pile. It is covered by a linen sheet. In the folded hands are white rosebuds, and orange blossoms encircle the marble brow. There is no apparent lack of heart-felt grief. It is the body of a young maiden decked for her bridal with death. After a few moments the red flames wind themselves ravenously about the youthful body, and quickly all is blackness and ashes.

Benares is mostly supported by the presence of pilgrims, but there is manufactured here a brass ware of such exquisite finish as to defy competition. In her dark alleys and narrow lanes they also produce a fine article of silver embroidery of marvellous delicacy and beauty, greatly prized by travellers as a souvenir. The pilgrims who participate in the river scenes are by no means all of the lower classes; now and then a gorgeously dressed official may be seen, with a long line of attendants, wending his steps towards the river's front. Infirm old men and little children, crazy-looking devotees and comely youths, boys and girls, people of all ages and degrees, are represented in the motley groups who come to these muddy waters for moral purification. There is a singular mingling of races also, for these people do not all speak one tongue. They are from the extreme north and the extreme south of India, while the half-starved vagrants seen among them, and who come from Middle India, could not make themselves understood by people from either extreme. A common purpose moves them, but they cannot express themselves in a common language. Pilgrims are here from Thibet and Cashmere, from the far-off Himalayan country, as well as from Tuticorin, on the Indian Ocean. Numberless idols and symbols of the most vulgar character abound all over the town, in small temples, before which men and women bow down in silent devotion. Idolatry is here seen in its most repulsive form. The delusion, however, is perfect, and these poor creatures are terribly in earnest.

Animals are worshipped, such as bulls, snakes, monkeys, and pigeons. One of the peculiar temples of the city is devoted solely to the worship of monkeys, where hundreds of these mischievous animals find a luxurious home, no one ever interfering with their whims except to pet and to feed them. This temple contains a singular altar, before which devotional rites are performed by believing visitors. On the Ghats, beside the river, these Hindoos pass the happiest hours of their sad lives, coming from the confined, dirty, unwholesome streets and alleys in which they sleep and eat, to pray and to bathe, as well as to breathe the fresh air and to bask in the sun. The hideous fakirs, or begging Oriental monks, make their fixed abode here, living entirely in the open air, most of them diseased, and all misshapen by voluntarily acquired deformity. Their distorted limbs are fixed in attitudes of penance until they become set and immovable. There are pious believers enough to kneel before them and to give them food and money by which means to support their strange and fanatical self-immolation.

We visit at Benares an ancient observatory of more than ordinary interest, erected by a famous Hindoo patron of science, Rajah Manu. Though it is now quite neglected and in partial ruins, a sun-dial, a zodiac, meridian lines, and astronomical appliances are still distinctly traced upon heavy stones arranged for celestial observations. This proves that astronomy was well advanced at Benares hundreds of years before Galileo was born, and it will be remembered that the astronomers of India first settled the fact of the rotation of the earth. The Man-Mundil, as this observatory is called, forms a most important historic link between the days of the Pharaohs and the nineteenth century.

Five hundred miles of travel by way of Cawnpore will bring us to Delhi, where a visit to the crumbling palace of the late king will show us the remains of that famous Peacock Throne, the marvel of the world when the Mogul dynasty was at its zenith — a throne of solid gold, ornamented with rubies, sapphires, and diamonds, the aggregate value of which was thirty million dollars. It was six feet long and four feet broad, surmounted by a gold canopy supported by twelve pillars composed of the same precious metal. The back of the throne was so constructed as to represent a peacock with expanded tail, the natural colors of which were exactly imitated with rubies, sapphires, diamonds, and other precious stones. Delhi was for centuries the proudest metropolis of India; within a circle of twenty miles of the present locality, one city after another has established its capital, ruled in splendor, and passed away. One monument, which we find in the environs, has thus far defied the destructive finger of time, — the Katub-Minar, which stands alone amid hoary ruins, the loftiest single column in the world, but of which there is no satisfactory record. It is not inappropriately considered one of the greatest architectural marvels of India, and whoever erected it achieved a triumph of gracefulness

MOSQUE AT DELHI, INDIA.

and skill. It is built of red stone elaborately ornamented in the form of a minaret, measuring about fifty feet in diameter at the base and ten at the top, with a height from the ground of two hundred and fifty feet, divided into five stories, each fitted with an outer gallery and adorned with colossal inscriptions. The whole exterior is fluted from base to top, narrowing gradually towards the summit.

In the broad main thoroughfare of Delhi — the Chandni Chowk — one constantly meets ponderous elephants, solemn and awkward camels, fine Arabian horses, and the diminutive, toy-like ponies of Cashmere. Daily marriage processions of the most fantastic description crowd the roadway, with the animals just named caparisoned in a gaudy, harlequin style, accompanied by unskilled musicians on foot, whose qualifications evidently consist in being able to make the greatest amount of noise upon a drum, fife, or horn, which are the three instruments employed on these occasions. Some of the white horses in the processions are painted in parts, sky-blue, and some are decked with saffron-yellow. In the ranks are covered bullock-carts with peep-holes, in which ride the women of the harem. Mingled with these are men bearing banners with Hindoo mottoes and ludicrous caricatures, half human and half animal. This is called a marriage procession, but upon careful inquiry it is found to be only a betrothal of children too young to marry. The boy-bridegroom appears upon an elephant, and is dressed like a circus rider; but the future bride, probably a little girl of six or eight years, does not appear: she remains at home to be called upon by this motley crowd, when a brief ceremony takes place, — presents being duly exchanged, — and the farce is then ended.

A journey of nine hundred miles, still over these broad plains of India, will bring us to the city of Agra, which, like Delhi, stands not on the Ganges, but on its great tributary, the Jumna. It is an important city, containing over forty thousand inhabitants. To all who visit this place the first object of interest will be the Taj (pronounced *Tahj*) Mahal, or tomb of the wife of the Emperor Shah-Jehan. It is the most interesting edifice in India and one of the most beautiful in the world. A tomb in this country means a magnificent structure of marble, with domes and minarets, the walls inlaid with precious stones, and the whole surrounded by gardens, fountains, and artificial lakes, covering from ten to twenty acres. Cheap as labor is in India, the Taj must have cost some fifteen millions of dollars, and was seventeen years in building. The Mogul Emperor resolved to erect the most superb monument ever reared to commemorate a woman's name, and he succeeded, for herein Mohammedan architecture reached its height. The mausoleum is situated in a spacious garden, the equal of which can hardly be found elsewhere, beautiful to the eye and delightful to the senses, with fragrant flowers, exotic and indigenous. This grand structure, with the ripeness of centuries upon it, is no ruin; all is fragrant and fresh as at the hour when it was completed. It is of white marble, three hundred feet in height, the principal dome being eighty feet high, and of such exquisite form and harmony is the whole that it seems almost to float in the air.

In the centre of the Taj, beneath the glorious dome, are two raised and ornamented marble frames, covering the resting-place of the emperor and his wife. How appropriate is the inscription at the threshold: "To the memory of an undying love." As we stand beneath the cupola, let us repeat in a low tone of voice a verse from Longfellow's "Psalm of Life"; instantly there will roll through the dimly lighted vault above a soft and solemn repetition, which will sound as though voices were repeating the psalm in the skies. Nothing finer or more lovely in architecture exists than this faultless monument, this ideal of Saracenic art.

By consulting a map of India it will be seen that few regions in the world present such an array of remarkable cities as have sprung up and flourished in the Ganges-Jumna valley. Here we have Agra, Delhi, Cawnpore, Lucknow, Allahabad, Benares, Mirozapur, Patna, Decca, and Murshedabad. What historic associations arise at the bare mention of these Indian cities!

CHAPTER IX.

ON our way southward we pass through the beautiful, though small Indian city of Jeypore, which is under native rule; those we have heretofore visited are subject to Great Britain. It is quite ancient, though there are no ruins here, everything giving evidence of present prosperity, peace, and abundance. The houses are painted in rather gaudy colors, but are neat and pretty. Queer little canvas-covered, two-wheeled carts, their tops shaped like half an egg-shell, are drawn about the town by bullocks at a lively trot. Some are closely curtained, containing women of the harem. Oriental seclusion is the rule with the women. Under the prince who rules here the population exhibits a marked contrast to those of India generally, over which the authority of England extends. There are no mud cabins here, no beggars, no visible want or poverty. The people are decently clothed, and well lodged in neat-looking houses, mostly two stories in height. The streets are broad and well kept, with bright, bubbling fountains here and there. Our excursions in this neighborhood are made upon camels or elephants. Wild animals are abundant, the tiger especially being much dreaded. Here, as at Singapore, men, women and children are daily sacrificed to their rapacious appetites in various parts of the district. It is said to be a fact, that these animals having once tasted human flesh, will be satisfied with none other, but will leave the antelope and smaller game unmolested, though they are known to abound in the vicinity, and lie in wait for days to capture human prey, even invading the villages at night. English hunters visit Jeypore in large numbers annually to capture this dangerous game.

From this native city to Bombay is a distance of seven hundred miles by railway, most of the route being very sparsely inhabited. The larger portion of India is an immense plain, so that the road is generally very monotonous. Nearly seven hundred thousand acres of these plains are cultivated with poppies. A large share of these opium farms, as they may be called, belong to the English government, and are cultivated by their agents. Those which are conducted on private account are very heavily taxed, and are mostly carried on in the interest of the Parsee merchants of Bombay, who have for many years controlled the largest share of the opium trade. We frequently see near these gorgeous poppy-fields ripening acres of grain, which would be stripped of their valuable property by the great flocks of birds, noticed at all times, floating like clouds over our heads, were precautions not taken to drive them away. For this purpose a tall platform is raised upon poles to a height of twenty feet in the centre of each grain-field, with a slight straw shelter over it, upon which a young boy or girl is stationed, and whence they overlook several acres of grain. They have no firearms, but are supplied with a simple sling and a few well-chosen stones: should a bird be seen too near the precious grain, an unerring stone will find him, and his body becomes a warning to the rest of the flock. The precision with which these girls and boys will throw a stone a long distance is marvellous. The monkeys which so abound in Southern India are not to be got rid of in so easy a manner. Birds will not fly after dark, nor much before sunrise, but the monkeys raid the fruit and vegetable fields by night, and are capable of organizing a descent upon some promising point with all the forethought of human thieves.

The opening of communication with England by the Red Sea route has given to Bombay a great business impetus, and it possesses to-day more elements of future greatness than any other city of Asia. The two principal capitals of the country are situated on opposite sides of the great peninsula, Calcutta being on the Bay of Bengal, and Bombay on the Sea of Arabia. We have in the latter a population of a million and over, one hundred thousand of whom are Parsees, a class of merchants originally from Persia, who represent a large share of the wealth of the city. They are by far the most enterprising and intelligent of the natives of India, and are in entire sympathy with the English government. Socially, they keep to themselves, strictly preserving their well-defined individuality. This people settled here more than eight centuries ago, after their expulsion from Persia. Their temples contain no images, nothing but the altars bearing the sacred fire which their fathers brought with them when they landed here so long ago, and which has never been extinguished, according to their traditions. They worship the sun as the representative of God, and fire in all its forms, as well as the ocean, which would seem to be an antagonistic agent; but as their religion recognizes one good and one evil principle ever contending for the mastery of the universe, perhaps these emblems are no contradiction.

One of the first places to which we are attracted in

Bombay is Malabar Hill, a lofty eminence just outside the city. On the top are the five famous "Towers of Silence," which constitute the cemetery of the Parsees. When a death occurs among them, the body is brought here, and after a brief ceremony the corpse is carried into one of the towers, where it is exposed upon a grating. The bearers retire at once, and the door is locked. These towers are open at the top, and on the cornices hundreds of vultures are seen waiting; as soon as the body is left, they swoop down to their awful meal, eagerly tearing and devouring the corpse. The hideous detail is not visible, but the reappearance of those evil birds in a gorged condition is only too significant of what has occurred. The devouring flames which consumed the bodies at Calcutta and at Benares did not shock us like this.

Bombay is made up of fine public buildings, sumptuous dwellings, and low hovels, not mingled indiscriminately, as is often seen in European cities, each class being found clustering in its special locality. In Florence, Rome, or Naples, a half-starved cobbler will be found occupying a stall beneath a palace; but though poverty and riches jostle each other everywhere, the lines of demarcation are more clearly defined in Bombay than elsewhere. A drive along the picturesque shore of the Arabian Sea is an experience never to be forgotten. It will be sure to recall to the traveller the beautiful environs of Genoa, with those winding, rock-cut roads overlooking the Mediterranean Sea. Here the roads are admirably cool and half-embowered in foliage, among which the crimson sagittaria flaunting its fiery leaves and ponderous blossoms, everywhere meets the eye. About the fine villas which are set back a short distance from the roads, delightful gardens of choice flowers are seen, comprising an abundance of tropical plants, tall palms lining the drive-ways up to the houses, where the merchant princes dwell. Most of these are the residences of the Parsees, who in spite of their bigotry and their adherence to ancient superstitions, know how to make their homes beautiful.

In leaving India, a few thoughts naturally suggest themselves. Its history runs back through thousands of years and remotest dynasties, captivating the fancy with numberless ruins, which, while attesting the splendor of their prime, form also the only record of their history. The mosaic character of its population, the peculiarities of its animal kingdom, the luxuriance of its vegetation, the dazzling beauty of its birds and flowers, all crowd upon the memory in charming kaleidoscopic combinations. There can be no doubt of the early grandeur and high civilization of India. To the intellectual eminence of her people we owe the germs of science, philosophy, law, and astronomy. The most perfect of all tongues, the Sanskrit, has been the parent of many others, and now that her lustre has faded, and her children fallen into a condition of sloth and superstition, let us, at least, do her historic justice. Nor should we neglect to heed the lesson she so clearly presents; namely, that nations, like individuals, are subject to the unvarying laws of mutability.

The government of India is a military despotism, England maintaining her rule by force alone over a foreign people numbering four times as many as the whole population of the United States. Order is preserved at a cruel cost of life among an entire race who are totally unrepresented. In travelling from city to city one is not surprised to see many signs of restlessness among the common people, and to hear harsh expressions against British rule. While we recall with a thrill of horror the awful cruelties and the slaughter of human beings during the rebellion of the native race against the English authority in 1857, we do not wonder that a people, so goaded by oppression, should have made a vigorous and bloody struggle to obtain their independence.

We embark at Bombay on a voyage of three thousand miles across the Sea of Arabia and the Indian Ocean, through the Straits of Babelmandeb and the entire length of the Red Sea. The most southerly point of the voyage, taking us within fourteen degrees of the equator, carries us into an extremely warm temperature. The ship holds on her southwest course day after day, lightly fanned by the northeast monsoon, towards the mouth of the Red Sea. At the end of the sixth day we cast anchor at the Peninsula of Aden, a rocky, isolated spot held by English troops, and very properly called the Gibraltar of the Indian Ocean. Like that famous promontory, it was originally little more than a barren rock, which has been improved into a picturesque and habitable place, bristling with British cannon of heavy calibre. It is a spot much dreaded by sailors, the straits being half closed by sunken rocks, besides which the shore is considered to be the most unhealthy spot yet selected by civilized man as a residence. The Arabs call the strait Babelmandeb, that is, the "Gate of Tears," because of the number of vessels which have been wrecked here in the endeavor to enter from the open sea. Aden lies within the rainless zone, so that sometimes the inhabitants see no rainfall for three years together. The remains of an ancient and magnificent system of reservoirs hewn out of the solid rock, are seen here, the construction of which is placed at a date previous to the Christian era, and which have been adapted to modern use.

As we lie at anchor here, there come about the ship a score of young natives, from ten to fifteen years of age. By eloquent gestures, and the use of a few English words, they beg of us to throw small silver coin into the sea, for which they will dive in water that is at least seven fathoms deep. The instant a piece of money is thrown overboard, every canoe becomes emptied, and twenty human beings disappear from sight like a flash. Down, down go the divers, and in the depths struggle together for the trifle, some one of the throng being sure to rise to the surface with the coin displayed between his teeth. Nothing but otters and seals could be keener sighted or more expert in the water.

The general aspect of Aden from the sea, though picturesque, is not inviting, giving one an idea of great barrenness. The mountains and rocks have a peaked appearance, like a spear pointed at one, as much as to say, "better keep off." People who land, however, for the first time, are agreeably disappointed by finding that every opportunity for encouraging the growth of vegetation and imparting its cheerful effect to the hard rocky soil has been carefully improved.

Our course after leaving Aden is nearly north; the headlands of Abyssinia are long visible on our port side, while on the other we have a distant view of Arabia. Jeddah, the seaport of Mecca, with its bright minarets, is to be seen in the distance. In coasting along the shores of Nubia, the dense air from off the land is like a sirocco, suffocatingly hot. Suez is reached at last, a place which is all waste and barrenness, so we hasten on by railway to Cairo, a distance of two hundred miles.

A WELL IN THE DESERT BETWEEN SUEZ AND CAIRO.

Long after leaving Suez we see only a sandy desert, the yellow soil quivering in the heated atmosphere. It is a picture of desolation. Not a blade of grass, not a shrub or tree, until by and by we come upon gently undulating and fertile soil, enriched by the annual deposits from the Nile, where intelligent cultivation produces its natural results. Small herds of brown buffaloes or Eastern oxen are seen, and peasants plying the irrigating-buckets. The pastures become alive with sheep and goats and dromedaries. While we are approaching Cairo, and are yet two or three leagues away, the dim outlines of the everlasting pyramids are seen through the shimmering haze, softly outlined against the evening sky. It is impossible not to recall the words of the Humpback, in the Thousand and One Nights, as we see the pyramids and glistening minarets of the Oriental city coming into view; "He who hath not seen Cairo hath not seen the world; its soil is golden; its Nile is a wonder; its women are like the black-eyed virgins of Paradise; its houses are palaces; and its air is soft, — its odor surpassing that of aloes-wood and cheering the heart, — and how can Cairo be otherwise, when it is the Mother of the world?"

This ideal city of the Arabian Nights is very Oriental, very original, very curious. Its four hundred thousand souls form a strange conglomerate of humanity. In its narrow, picturesque streets one is jostled by gayly dressed Greeks and cunning Jews, by overladen donkeys and by sober, mournful-looking camels. One half expects to meet Ali Baba and the Forty Thieves, as we still look for Antonio and the Jew on the Rialto at Venice. Like Paris, Cairo is a city of cafés. During the evening and far into the night crowds of individuals of every nationality are seen seated in groups before them in the open air, drinking every sort of known liquid, but coffee takes precedence of all others. In picturesqueness of costume the Turk leads the world. His graceful turban and flowing robes are worthy of the classic antique, while the rich contrast of colors which he wears adds to the striking effect. As he sits cross-legged before his open bazaar, or shop, smoking a long pipe, he looks very wise, very learned, though in point of fact there is no doubt more intelligence under the straw hat of a Yankee peddler than under three average turbans. The dark, narrow lanes and endless zigzag alleys have an indescribable interest, with their accumulated dirt of neglect and the dust of a land where rain is so seldom known. One looks up in passing at those overhanging balconies, imagining the fate of the harem-secluded women behind them, occasionally catching stolen glances from curious eyes peering between the lattices.

Egyptian porters, bent half double, are seen carrying on their backs loads that would stagger a brewer's horse. Women, who ride their horses and mules astride, are very careful to cover their faces from view, while their eyes gleam out of peep-holes. Other women, of a humbler class, jostle us in the streets, with little naked children straddling one shoulder, and holding on to the mother's head with both hands. People who ride upon donkeys require a boy to follow behind them with a stick to belabor the poor overladen creatures, without which they will not move forward, being so trained. Those who drive through the streets in carriages are preceded by a gorgeously draped runner bearing a white wand, and who constantly cries to clear the way. These runners go as fast as a horse usually trots, and seem never to tire. The common people lie down on the sidewalk, beside the road, in any nook or corner, to sleep off fatigue, just as a dog might do. Every public square has its fountain, and there are two hundred in Cairo.

The bazaars present a novel aspect. Here an old bearded Turk offers for sale odors, curious pastes and essences, with kohl for shading about the eyes, and henna dye for the fingers. Another has various ornaments of sandal wood, delicately wrought fans, and other trifles. His next-door neighbor, whose quarters are only a degree more dingy, offers pipes, curiously made, with carved amber mouthpieces, and others with long, flexible, silken tubes. Turbaned crowds stroll leisurely about. Now a strong and wiry Bedouin passes, leading his horse and taking count of everything with his sharp, black eyes, and now a Nile boatman. Yonder is an Abyssinian slave, and beyond is an Egyptian trader, with here and there a Greek or a Maltese. Amid it all one feels curious as to where Aladdin's uncle may be just now, with his new lamps to exchange for old ones. We will ascend the loftiest point of this Arabian city to obtain a more comprehensive view.

The mosque of Mehemet Ali, with its tapering minarets, overlooks Cairo, and is itself a very remarkable and beautiful edifice. This spacious building is lined throughout with Oriental alabaster, the exterior being covered with the same costly material. It contains the sarcophagus of Mehemet Ali, the most enlightened of modern rulers, before which lamps are burning perpetually. The interior of this mosque is the most effective, architecturally, of any temple in the East. There is a height and breadth, and a solemn dignity in its aspect, which cannot fail to impress every visitor. The exterior is much less striking, yet it is admirably balanced and harmonized. The situation of the mosque commands one of the most interesting views that can be conceived of. The city, with its countless minarets and domed mosques, its public buildings, and tree-adorned squares, its section of mud-colored houses and terraced roofs, lies in the form of a crescent at the visitor's feet; while the plains of Lower Egypt stretch far away in all directions. The tombs of the Mamelukes (a body of mounted soldiery of Egypt massacred by Mehemet Ali) lie close at hand, full of historic suggestiveness, and just beyond stands the lonely column of Heliopolis, four thousand years old, marking the site of the famous "City of the Sun." Towards the sea is the land of Goshen, where the sons of Jacob fed their flocks. A little more westerly, in the mysterious Nile, is seen the well-wooded island of Roda, quietly nestling in the broad bosom of the river. Here is the place where the infant Moses was found. The grand Aqueduct, with its high-reaching arches, reminds us of the ruins outside of Rome; while ten miles away are seen the time-defying Pyramids, the horizon ending at the borders of the great Libyan Desert. Far away to the southwest a forest of palms dimly marks the site of dead and buried Memphis, where Joseph interpreted a monarch's dream. It is the twilight hour as we stand in the open area of the mosque, and view the scene. The half-suppressed hum of a dense Eastern population comes up to us from the busy, low-lying city, and a strange, sensuous flavor of sandal wood, musk, and attar of roses floats on the golden haze of the sunset, indelibly fixing the scene upon the memory.

The Pyramids of Gizeh are situated about three leagues

Page 132.
A LADY OF CAIRO AS SEEN IN PUBLIC.

from Cairo, and, after crossing the Nile by an iron bridge, guarded at either end by two bronze lions, they are reached by a straight, level road, lined with well-trimmed trees. This road terminates at a rocky plateau, which serves to give these wonderful structures an elevated site, as well as to form a firm, natural foundation for the enormous weight of solid stone to be supported. There is always an importuning group of Arabs here, who live upon the gratuities obtained from visitors. They help people to ascend and descend the Pyramids for a fixed sum, or, for a few shillings, will run up and down them like monkeys. On the way between Cairo and the Pyramids, through the long alley of acacias, we pass hundreds of camels bound to the city, laden with green fodder and newly cut clover for stable use in town. Carts are not employed; the backs of camels and donkeys supersede the use of wheels.

Nothing new can be said about the Pyramids, — monuments hoary with age; the statistics relating to them are familiar. They simply show, standing there upon the border of the desert, a vast aggregate of labor performed by compulsion, and only exhibit the supreme folly of the monarchs, who thus vainly strove to erect monuments which should defy all time and perpetuate their fame. To-day not even the names of their founders are surely known. There are plausible suppositions enough about them, each writer upon the subject having plenty of arguments to support his special convictions; but their history rests, after all is said, amid a confusion of very thin speculation. There is little genius evinced in the design or execution of the Pyramids. Neither art, taste, nor religion is in any way subserved by these unequalled follies. There is no architectural excellence in them, though great skill is evinced in their construction, they are merely enormous piles of stone. Some pronounce them marvellous as evidences of ancient greatness and power. True; but if it were desirable, we could build loftier and larger ones in our day. As they are doubtless over four thousand years old, we admit that they are venerable, and that they are entitled to a certain degree of consideration on that account. In the religious instinct which led the Buddhists to build, at such enormous expense of time and money, the cave-temples of Elephanta, Ellora, and Carlee; in the idolatrous Hindoo temples of Madura and Tanjore, the shrines of Ceylon, the pagodas of China, and the temples of Japan, one detects an underlying and elevating sentiment, a grand and reverential idea, in which there may be more of acceptable veneration than we can fully appreciate; but in the Pyramids we have no expression of devotion, only an embodiment of personal vanity, which hesitated at nothing for its gratification, and which proved a total failure.

The immensity of the desert landscape, and the absence of any object for comparison, make these three pyramids seem smaller than they really are; but the actual height of the largest, that of Cheops, is nearly five hundred feet. The theory that they are royal tombs is generally accepted. Bunsen claims for Egypt nearly seven thousand years of civilization and prosperity before the building of these monuments. We do not often pause to realize how little of reliable history there is extant. Conjecture is not history. If contemporary record so often belies itself, what ought we to consider veracious of that which comes to us through the shadowy distance of thousands of years? Not many hundred feet from the nearest pyramid, and on a somewhat lower plane, stands that colossal mystery, the

Sphinx. The Arabs call it "The Father of Terror," and it certainly has a weird and unworldly look. Its body and most of the head is hewn out of the solid rock where it stands, the upper portion forming the head and bust of a human being, to which is added the body with the paws of an animal. The great size of the figure will be realized when we mention the fact that the face alone is thirty feet long and half as wide. The body is in a sitting posture, with the paws extended forward some fifty feet or more. This strange figure is believed to be of much greater antiquity than the Pyramids, but no one can say how old it really is. Notwithstanding its mutilated condition, showing the furrows of time, the features have still a sad, tranquil expression, telling of the original dignity of the design.

From Cairo we take the railway to Ismailia, the little town situated midway on the Suez Canal, between the two seas, at the Bitter Lakes, through which the course of the canal runs. It is a pretty and attractive place, containing four or five thousand inhabitants, and is a creation of the last few years. Here we observe gardens filled with choice flowers and fruit-trees, vegetation being in its most verdant dress, promoted by irrigation from the neighboring freshwater canal. The place has broad, neat streets, and a capacious central square, ornamented with large and thrifty trees. It was here that the representatives of all nations met on the occasion of the inaugurating ceremony on the completion of De Lesseps's canal. We take a small mail steamer at Ismailia, through the western half of the canal to Port Said, the Mediterranean terminus of the great artificial river. It is a fact worthy of remembrance that, with all our modern improvements and progressive ideas, the Egyptians were centuries before us in this plan of shortening the path of commerce between the East and the West; or, in other words, of connecting the Red Sea with that of the Mediterranean across the Isthmus and through the Gulf of Suez. The purpose was probably never thoroughly carried out until De Lesseps's consummation of it as it now exists.

Port Said, like Suez, derives its only interest and importance from the canal. It contains some seven thousand inhabitants, with a floating population of two thousand. The region round about it is perfectly barren, like Egypt nearly everywhere away from the valley of the Nile. Through that part of the desert which we pass in coming from Suez, one looks in vain for any continuous sign of vegetation. The entire absence of trees and forests accounts for the lack also of wild beasts, excepting the hyena and jackal, which are occasionally met with. Here and there, at long intervals, an oasis of green is seen, like a smile breaking over the arid face of nature. Once or twice we see a cluster of palms beside a rude well, hedged in by a little patch of green earth, about which a few camels or goats are quenching their thirst or cropping the scanty herbage. Some Arabs, in picturesque costumes, linger hard by. The tents pitched in the background are of the same low, flat-topped, camel's-hair construction as have been used by these desert tribes for many thousands of years.

Egypt has only her ruins, her antiquity, her Bible associations to give her interest with the world at large. Japan is infinitely to be preferred; China even rivals her in natural advantages; and India is much more inviting. In looking at Egypt we must forget her present and recall her past. The real Egypt is not the vast territory which we find laid down by geographers, reaching to the Indian Ocean, the Red Sea, and embracing equatorial regions; it is and was, even in the days of the Pharaohs and Ptolemies, the valley of the Nile, from the First Cataract to the Mediterranean Sea, hemmed in by the Libyan and Arabian deserts, whence there came to the rest of the world so much of art, science, and philosophy. The fellah or peasant, he who tills the soil, is of a fine and industrious race, well built, broad chested, and lithe of frame. He is the same figure that his ancestors were of old, as represented on the tombs and temples of Thebes, and on the slabs one sees from Gizeh, in the museum of Cairo. He still performs his work in the nineteenth century just as he did before the days of Moses, scattering the seed and irrigating by hand. He is little seen in the cities, — his place is in the field, where he lives and thrives. Though his native land has found such various masters in Greek and Roman, Arab and Turk, he has never lost his individuality; he has ever been, and is to-day, the same historic Egyptian.

The next point to which our course will take us is the Island of Malta, which involves a sail of a thousand miles from Port Said. The city of Valetta is the capital, having a population of a hundred and fifty thousand. The island is an English outpost, similar to Gibraltar, and, in a military point of view, is about as important. It is twenty miles long and sixteen wide, and has held a conspicuous place in historical records for nearly three thousand years. The houses of the city are mostly large stone structures, and many have notable architectural merit, fronting thoroughfares of good width, well paved, and lighted with gas. An aspect of cleanliness and freshness pervades everything. Many of the streets run up the steep hillside on which the town stands, and are flanked by broad stone steps for foot-passengers, the roadway of such streets being quite inaccessible for vehicles. The principal thoroughfare is the Strada Reale, nearly a mile long, lined with attractive stores and dwelling-houses, forming a busy and pleasant boulevard. The houses over the stores are ornamented by convenient iron balconies, where the citizens can sit and enjoy the cool evening breezes after the hot days that linger about Malta nearly all the year round.

At the upper end of the Strada Reale we observe a large and imposing stone opera-house, presenting a fine architectural aspect, being ornamented with lofty Corinthian columns, a side portico and broad stone steps leading up to the vestibule. A visit to the Church of St. John will afford much enjoyment. It was built a little over three hundred years since by the Knights of the Order of St. John, who lavished fabulous sums of money upon its erection and its elaborate ornamentation. Statuary and paintings of rare merit abound within its walls, and gold and silver ornaments render the work of great aggregate value. The entire roof of the church, which is divided into zones, is admirably painted in figures of such proportions as to look life-size from the floor, representing prominent Scriptural scenes. In this church the Knights seem to have vied with each other in adding to its ornaments and its treasures, so that the rich marbles, bas-reliefs, and mosaics are almost confusing in their abundance. The floor is formed of inlaid marble slabs, which cover the last resting-places of the most distinguished Knights of the famous Order of St. John.

Snow is not known in Malta, but ice sometimes forms

during the coldest nights of winter, though only in very thin layers, the climate being much like that of Southern Italy. Fruit and ornamental trees abound, and flowers attract the eye in nearly every domestic window. There must be a prevailing refinement of taste in this island city, otherwise the abundance of flowers offered for sale in the Strada Reale would not find purchasers. There is a section near the harbor named Casal Attand; that is, the "Village of Roses." *Casal* in Maltese signifies village. There is also Casal Luca, the "Village of Poplars," and still another, Casal Zebbug, the "Village of Olives," a natural and appropriate system of nomenclature. It is extremely interesting to visit the armory of the Knights of St. John, to see the rusty lances, dimmed sword-blades, and tattered battle-flags which were borne by the Crusaders in the days of Saladin and Cœur de Lion. A visit to Fort St. Angelo, perched upon the summit of the island, enables us to look far away over the blue Mediterranean, dotted by the picturesque maritime rig of these waters. It is pleasant to stroll about the bright, cleanly streets of Valetta, to chat with the smiling flower-girls who occupy the little kiosks (flower-stands) on the corners of the Strada Reale, and to enjoy a cooling ice in the gardens of the café adjoining the Knights' Palace. But we must not linger here, whence we sail for Gibraltar, a thousand miles away, at the other end of this great inland sea.

Arrived at the famous Rock, we are at once impressed upon landing with its military importance. Every other person one meets is in uniform, and cannon are as plenty as at Woolwich or West Point. The Signal Station is fifteen hundred feet in height. The zigzag path leading to the summit is lined with wild-flowers, though we come now and again upon embrasures, whence protrude grim-muzzled guns. Further up we stoop to gather some daphnes and disclose a battery screened by fragrant and blooming flowers. From the top the view is magnificent; the white wings of commerce which sprinkle the sea look like sea-gulls, and steamships are only discernible by the long line of smoke trailing behind them. Far below us, on the Spanish side, lies the town, a thick mass of yellow, white, and brown houses; and nestling in the bay is the shipping, looking like toy-boats. The mountain ranges of Ceuta and Andalusia, on opposite continents, mingle with soft, over-shadowing clouds, while over our heads is a glorious dome of turquoise blue, such as no temple raised by the hand of man can imitate.

We find that England has thus established and maintains a line of outposts from the Mediterranean to the far East, beginning at Gibraltar, thence to Malta, Aden, Ceylon, Penang, Singapore, and Hong Kong, completely dominating the South of Asia, and giving her a clear route to her extensive possessions in India.

CHAPTER X.

WE embark at Gibraltar for Tangier in a small coasting steamer, crossing the straits which separate Europe from Africa, a distance of less than a hundred miles. As we draw away from the Spanish shore, the long range of Andalusian mountains stands out compact and clear, the snow-white summits sparkling in the sunshine. On the lowlands, sloping to the water's edge, the fields are robed in a soft green attire, dotted with herds of goats and cattle. Old stone watch-towers line the shore at regular intervals, and coast-guard houses sheltering squads of soldiers, for this region is famous as the resort of smugglers and lawless bands of rovers. On the opposite coast of Africa, the Ceuta range grows every moment more distinct, the loftiest peaks mantled with snow, like the bleached, flowing drapery of the Bedouins. Still further on, dazzling white hamlets enliven the Morocco shore, with deep green, tropical verdure in the background. Ceuta attracts our interest, being a Spanish penal colony, which is surrounded by jealous, warlike Moors, slave-traders, and smugglers.

Tangier stands on the western shore of a shallow bay, upon a sloping hillside, but it is not at all impressive as one approaches it. The windowless houses rise like cubical blocks of masonry one above another, dominated by a few square towers which crown the several mosques; while here and there a consular flag floats lazily upon the air from a lofty pole. The rude, irregular wall which surrounds the city is seen stretching about it, pierced with arched Moorish gates.

Oriental as Cairo is, Tangier strikes us as even more so. In coming from Gibraltar, one seems, by a single step as it were, to have passed from civilization to barbarism. There is no European quarter here. Every evidence of the proximity of the opposite continent disappears: the distance might be immeasurable. The city has narrow, dirty, twisted streets, through which no vehicle can pass, and which are scarcely accessible for donkeys, camels, and foot-passengers. There is not a straight or level street in all Tangier. Veiled women, clad in white, move about the lanes like uneasy spirits; men in scarlet turbans and striped robes lounge carelessly about, with their bare heels sticking out of yellow slippers. Now we meet a tawny Arab, a straggling son of the desert, his striped abba or white bournous (robe-like garments) hanging in graceful folds about his tall, straight figure; and now a Nubian, with only a waistcloth about his body. The scene is constantly changing. There are Jews, with dark blue vests and red sashes; Jewesses, in bright purple silks, and with uncovered, handsome faces. Here and there is seen a Maltese or Portuguese sailor hiding from punishment for some crime committed on the opposite continent. The variety of races one meets in these contracted passage-ways is indeed curious, represented by faces yellow, bronze, white, and black. Add to all, the crowd of donkey-boys, camels, goats, and street pedlers, crying, bleating, blustering, and braying, and we get an idea of the sights and sounds that constantly greet one in this Moorish capital.

The slave market is situated just outside of the city

walls, where the sales take place on the Sabbath, which is regarded as a sort of holiday. The average price of the women and girls is from fifty to sixty dollars, according to age and good looks; the men vary much in price, according to the demand for labor. About the large open space of the market is a group of Bedouins, just arrived from the interior with dried fruits, dates, and the like. Camels and men, weary after the long tramp, are reclining upon the ground, forming a picture only to be seen on the border of the desert, and beneath the glow and shimmer of an African sun.

We ascend the heights, which form a background to the city. The sloping hillside is mostly occupied by a few European merchants and the consuls of the several nations. Their villas are very picturesque, half buried in foliage, and located in an atmosphere redolent with fruits and flowers. From the fronts of their dwellings the view is superb: the broad piazzas are hung here and there with hammocks, telling of luxurious out-door life; family groups are seen taking their morning coffee on the verandas, and the voices of many children ring out, clear and bird-like, floating up to the eyrie where we are perched; down towards the shore lies brown, dingy, dirty Tangier, with its mud-colored groups of tiled roofs, its teeming population, its mouldy old walls, its Moorish arched gates, and its minarets, square and dominant. On our way back we again pass through the slave market, where a bevy of dancing-girls with tambourines and castanets look wistfully at us, hoping for an audience.

Nearly the last sound that greets our ears, as we walk over the irregular pavements and through the narrow lanes toward the pier whence we are to embark, is the rude music of the snake-charmer; and the last sight is that of a public story-teller in one of the little squares, earnestly gesticulating before a score of eager listeners while he recites a chapter from the "Thousand and One Nights."

The sultan of Morocco is supreme, and holds the lives and fortunes of his subjects at his will. He is judge and executioner of the laws, which emanate from himself. Taxation is so heavy as to amount to prohibition, in many departments of enterprise; exportation is hampered, agriculture so heavily loaded with taxes that it is only pursued so far as to supply the bare necessities of life; manufacture is just where it was centuries ago, and is performed with the same primitive tools; the printing-press is unknown; there are no books, save the Koran; and the language is such a mixture of tongues, and is so corrupted, as to hardly have a distinctive existence. The people obey the local sheikhs (pronounced *shāk*); above them are the cadis, who control provinces; and still higher, are the pashas, who are accountable only to the sultan.

Returning to Gibraltar we take a coasting steamer along the shore of Spain eastward to Malaga, the city of raisins and sweet wine. It is commercially one of the most important cities of the country, and was once the capital of an independent state. It was a large and prosperous Phœnician metropolis centuries before the time of Christ upon earth. The older portions of the city have all the Moorish peculiarities of construction,—narrow streets, crooked passages, small barred windows, and heavy doors; but the modern part of Malaga is characterized by broad, straight thoroughfares and elegantly built houses of stone. This is especially the case with the Alameda, which has a central walk ornamented by flowers and shrubs, and which is bordered with handsome almond-trees. On either side of this broad promenade is a good roadway, flanked by houses of pleasing architectural effect, lofty and well relieved.

There are several fine open squares in Malaga, some of which contain statues and ornamental trees, together with well-kept flower-beds. The discovery not long since of Roman antiquities in the environs has created a warm interest among archæologists. The trade of the city in wine and dried fruits is large. Four-fifths of the forty thousand butts of sweet wine shipped from here are exported to the United States. The present population is about a hundred and twenty-five thousand, made up of a community of more than average respectability, though beggars are found to be very annoying in the public streets. The old Moorish castle crowning the seaward heights has been converted into a modern fortress, affording a charming view from its battlements. In the squares and streets, as well as in the market-place, women sit each morning weaving fresh-cut flowers of rose-buds, mignonette, pansies, violets, and geraniums into pretty little clusters, of which they sell many as button-hole bouquets. One may be sure there is always a refined element in the locality, whether otherwise visible or not, where such an appreciation is manifested. The bull-fight may thrive, the populace may be riotous, education at a very low ebb, and art almost entirely neglected; but when a love of nature is evinced in the appreciation of beautiful flowers, there is still extant on the popular heart the half-effaced image of its Maker.

It is an interesting fact that Spain, in the time of Julius Cæsar, contained nearly eighty million inhabitants, but to-day it has less than eighteen million. By glancing at the map it will be perceived that Spain is a large country, comprising nearly the whole of the southern peninsula of Europe, Portugal being confined to a very small space. It is about double the size of Great Britain, and is rich in every known mineral, though poor enough in the necessary energy and enterprise requisite to improve such possibilities. In many sections of the country great natural fertility is apparent, but nature has to perform the lion's share of the work in producing crops. In the environs of Malaga, and the southern provinces generally, there are orange, lemon, and olive groves miles in extent. The Moors had a poetical saying that this favored region was dropped from paradise, but there is more of poetry than truth in the legend. What is really required is good cultivation and skilled agricultural enterprise. These would develop a very different condition of affairs and give to legitimate effort a rich reward. The sugar-cane, the grape-vine, the fig-tree, and the productive olive, mingling with the myrtle and the laurel, gratify the eye in and about the district of Malaga; but as one advances inland, the products become natural or wild, cultivation primitive and only partial, grain-fields being scarce and universal neglect the prominent feature.

Granada is situated about seventy miles north of Malaga, where set the sun of Moorish glory, but where still exists that embodiment of romance, the Alhambra. This palace-fortress is the one attraction of the district. It is difficult to realize that the Moors possessed such architectural skill, and that they produced such splendid palaces centuries ago. It is also quite as remarkable that Time, the great destroyer, should have spared for our admiration such minute, lace-like carvings, and such brilliant mosaics. The marvel of the architecture is its perfect harmony; there

GENERAL VIEW OF THE ALHAMBRA.

Page 146.

A RECEPTION HALL IN THE ALHAMBRA.

are no jarring elements in this superb structure, no false notes in the grand anthem which it articulates. In visiting the Alhambra one must be assisted by both history and the imagination; he must know something of the people who built and beautified it; he must be able to summon back the brave warriors and beautiful ladies from the dim past to people again these glorious halls. He must call to life the orange, the myrtle, and the myriads of fragrant flowers that bloomed of old in these now silent marble courts. As we pass from one section to another, from hall to hall, chamber to chamber, lingering with busy thoughts amid the faded glory, the very atmosphere teems with historical reminiscences of that most romantic period, the mediæval days, when the Moors held regal court in Andalusia. A lurking sympathy steals over us for that exiled people who could create and give life to such a terrestrial paradise.

Alhambra signifies "Red Castle," and the vermilion-tinted structure, with its outlying towers, was thus appropriately named. In the days of its glory it was half palace, half fortress; indeed, a city in itself, capable of accommodating quite an army, and containing within its walls an immense cistern as a water supply, besides armories, storehouses, foundry, and every appliance of a large citadel. A considerable portion of the far-reaching walls is still extant. Under good generalship, and properly manned, the place must have been nearly impregnable to attack with such arms as were in use at the period. For a long time after the expulsion of the Moors, the Castilian monarchs made it their royal residence, and revelled within its splendid walls; but they finally deserted it. The place was next infested by a lawless community of smugglers and banditti, who made it their headquarters, whence to sally forth and lay the neighboring plains under contribution. Then came the French as conquerors, who expelled the lawless intruders, themselves, perhaps, quite as deserving of the title; but they did good work in clearing what had become an Augean stable of its worst filth and partially restoring the choicest work of the Moorish builders. To-day the Spanish government guards with jealous care a monumental treasure which cannot be equalled in the kingdom.

A day's journey northward brings us to Cordova, which was the capital of Moorish Spain ten centuries ago, when the city could boast a million inhabitants. Now it has thirty thousand. One of the most prominent objects is the ancient stone bridge, supported by broad, irregular arches. For two thousand years that old bridge has battled with the elements; Romans, Moors, and Spaniards have fiercely contended at its entrances; the tides of victory and of defeat have swept again and again across its roadway. Leaning over its stone barriers we watch the river pursue its rapid course just as it has done for twenty centuries. Palaces, temples, shrines, may crumble, nations rise and fall, but the Guadalquiver still flows on.

The one great interest of Cordova is its cathedral, erected sixteen centuries ago. Beautiful are its still remaining hundreds of interior columns, composed of porphyry, jasper, granite, alabaster, verd-antique, and marble of various colors. Each of the columns upholds a small pilaster, and between them is a horseshoe arch, no two of the columns being alike. They came from Greece, Rome, Constantinople, Damascus, and the Temple of Jerusalem. All the then known world was put under contribution to furnish the twelve hundred columns of this wonderful temple. The great mosque was changed into a cathedral after the expulsion of the Arabs, but a large portion of the interior is untouched and remains as it was when the caliphs worshipped here. Inside and out it is gloomy, massive, and frowning, forming one of the most remarkable links still existing in Spain between the remote past and the present. It appears to be nearly as large upon the ground as St. Peter's at Rome, and contains fifty separate chapels within its capacious walls. It has, in its passage through the several dynasties of Roman, Moorish, and Spanish rule, received distinctive architectural marks from each. Its large, cool court of orange-trees, centuries old, its battlemented walls and huge gateway, its famous fountains and its mingled palms and tall cypresses, all combine to perfect an impressive picture of the dead and buried thousands connected with its history.

We still pursue a northerly course. From Cordova to Madrid is about three hundred miles by railway, carrying us through some very interesting and typical scenery. Occasionally a gypsy camp is passed, pitched near our route, presenting the usual domestic groups, mingled with animals, covered carts, lazy men stretched on the greensward, and busy women cooking the evening meal. Long strings of mules, with widespread panniers, are seen winding across the plain, sometimes in charge of a woman clad in gaudy colors, while her lazy husband thrums a guitar as he lies across one of the mules. Towards evening groups of peasants, male and female, with farming tools in their hands, are seen winding their steps towards some hamlet after the day's labor. Arched stone bridges, old and moss-grown, come into view, spanning small watercourses on their way from the mountains to join more pretentious streams. Elevated spots show us the ruins of old stone towers, once a part of some feudal stronghold, but the eye seeks in vain for well-wooded slopes, thrifty groves, or cultivated fields with promising crops. While the more practical traveller realizes a sense of disappointment at the paucity of thrift and vegetation, the poet and the artist will find enough to delight the eye and to fire the imagination in Spain. The ever-transparent atmosphere, and the lovely cloud-effects that prevail, are accompaniments which will hallow the desolate regions for the artist at all seasons. The poet has only to wander among the former haunts of the Moors and view the crumbling monuments of their gorgeous, luxurious, and artistic taste, to be equally absorbed and inspired.

When we arrive at Madrid, the first query which suggests itself is, why Charles V. should have made his capital on this spot. True, it is in about the geographical centre of Spain, but it is hemmed in on all sides by arid plains, and has an adjacent river, so-called, but which in America would be known as a dry gulch. It is difficult to see what possible benefit can be derived from a waterless river. Like the Arno at Florence, it seems troubled with a chronic thirst. In short, the Manzanares has the form of a river without the circulation. In the days of Charles II. its dry bed was turned into a sort of racecourse and drive-way, but since the completion of the magnificent Prado it has been abandoned even for this purpose. Eight or nine hundred years ago Madrid was a fortified outpost of Toledo — "imperial" Toledo. Though it is situated between two and three thousand feet above sea-level, it does not seem to possess the advantages usually following such position, the climate being scorchingly hot in summer and piercingly cold in winter. So that one comes to the conclusion that in point of climate, as well as in location, the Spanish capital is a mistake.

Having been established when the furor for cathedral-building had passed, the city has none within its borders, though there is no lack of modern churches. Notwithstanding these criticisms, Madrid is a large and fine city, with some four hundred thousand inhabitants; not noticeable, like Genoa, Rome, or Florence, for palaces and ancient monuments, but it is well laid out, the streets broad and nicely paved, while numerous open squares ornament the several sections. Some of these are filled with attractive shrubbery and ornamental trees, as well as statuary. Among the latter are representations of Murillo, Philip III., Cervantes, Lope de Vega, Philip V., Calderon, and others. The finest statue in the city is that of Philip IV., representing that monarch on horseback, the animal in a prancing position. This is a wonderfully life-like bronze, designed by Velasquez. It forms the centre of the Plaza del Oriente, or square in front of the royal palace, from which it is separated, however, by a broad thoroughfare. According to history, Galileo showed the artist how the horse could be sustained in its remarkable position, the whole weight of the rider and the animal resting on the hind legs.

On the Prado, the grand public drive of the citizens, there are fine marble statues, and groups combined with very elegant fountains. The Puerto del Sol, that is, the "Gate of the Sun," is situated in the heart of the city, and is always full of busy life. A dozen large streets and boulevards radiate from this area, where the lines of street-cars also meet and diverge. The fashionable idlers of the town hold high carnival in the Puerto del Sol, day and night. One is half dazed by the whirl of carriages, the rush of pedestrians, the passing of military bands with marching regiments, and the clatter of horses' feet caused by dashing equestrians. This plaza or square is a scene of incessant movement from early morn until midnight. Like Paris and Vienna, Madrid does not seem to thoroughly awaken until evening, the tide of life becoming most active under the glare of gas-light. The Prado, just referred to, is to Madrid what the Champs Elysées and the Bois de Boulogne are to Paris, a splendid avenue, through the centre of which runs a walk and garden similar to the Unter den Linden of Berlin, or Commonwealth Avenue, Boston, save that it is more extensive than either of these last named. The Prado nearly joins the Public Garden of Madrid, on the borders of the city proper, in which there are also fine carriage-drives, roadways for equestrians, many delightful shaded walks, and paths lined with choice flowers. On Sundays and holidays these grounds are thronged with citizens and their families for out-of-door enjoyment; several military bands distributed about the grounds add to the attraction.

The royal palace is located upon a slightly elevated site, and is so isolated as to give full effect to its appearance. It is the only building of a remarkable character, architecturally speaking, in the city; being the largest, and one of the finest, royal palaces in Europe. It belongs to the Tuscan style, and cost between five and six million dollars a hundred years ago. The base is of granite; but the upper portion is built of a fine white stone, very closely resembling marble.

In its splendid art collection of the Museo, the city has

a treasure only equalled by the Louvre at Paris and the galleries of Florence. To artists it is the one attraction of Madrid, and is principally composed of works by Spanish masters, though also containing many other fine works of art. Here we may see forty examples by the hand of Murillo, sixty-four from Velasquez, sixty by Rubens, twenty-five from Paul Veronese, thirty-four by Tintoretto, and many by Andrea del Sarto, Titian, Vandyke, and others of similar artistic fame. It is believed that Murillo appears at his best in this collection. Being a native of Seville, he is seen, as it were, at home; and artists declare that his works here show more power and expression than anywhere else. So we go to Antwerp to appreciate Rubens, though we find him so fully represented elsewhere. The same may be said of Velasquez as of Murillo; he also was at home here, and cannot be fairly, or rather fully, judged outside of the Madrid gallery.

When the French were masters in Spain, they proved to be terrible agents of destruction; leaving marks of their devastation everywhere. Not content with stealing many unequalled works of art, they often wantonly destroyed what they could not conveniently take away with them. In the tomb of Ferdinand and Isabella, at Grenada, they pried open the royal coffins, in search of treasure; at Seville they broke open the coffin of Murillo, and scattered his ashes to the wind; Marshal Soult treated the ashes of Cervantes in a similar manner. War desecrates all things, human and divine, but sometimes becomes a Nemesis (goddess of retribution), dispensing poetical justice; as when Waterloo caused the return to Spain of a portion of her despoiled art-treasures.

The bull-ring of the capital will seat eighteen thousand

spectators. Here, on each Sunday of the season, exhibitions are given to enthusiastic crowds, the entertainments always being honored by the presence of the state dignitaries, and members of the royal family. The worst result of such cruelty is that it infects the beholders with a like spirit. We all know how cruel the English became during the reign of Henry the Eighth. Sunday is always a gala-day in Madrid, though the attendance upon early mass is very general, at least among the women. It is here, as at Paris and other European capitals, the chosen day for military parades, horse races, and the bull fight. Most of the shops are open, and do a profitable business; especially is this the case with the liquor and cigar stores and the cafés. The lottery-ticket vendor makes double the usual day's sales on this occasion, and the itinerant gamblers, with their little tables, have crowds about them wherever they locate. The gayly dressed flower-girls, with dainty little baskets rich in color and captivating in fragrance, press button-hole bouquets on the pedestrians, while men perambulate the streets with cakes and candies displayed in open wooden boxes hung about their necks. In short, Sunday is made a holiday, when grandees and beggars come forth like marching regiments into the Puerto del Sol. The Prado and public gardens are crowded with gayly dressed people, children, and nurses, the costumes of the latter being of the most theatrical character. No one who can walk stays within doors on Sunday at Madrid.

The cars will take us forty miles hence to Toledo, where the rule of the Moor is seen in foot-prints which time has not yet obliterated. It seems like realizing a mediæval dream to walk the narrow, sombre streets of this famous old capital. Strangely steep, winding, and irregular, they are! The reason for constructing them thus was doubtless that they might be the more easily defended when attacked by an enemy. In the days of her prime, Toledo saw many battles, both inside and outside of her gates. One can touch the houses of these streets, in many instances, on both sides at the same time by extending the arms. There are scores of deserted buildings, securely locked up, the heavy gates studded with great iron nails, while the lower windows are closely iron-grated. Some of them are open and unguarded, having paved entrances or court-yards, with galleries around them, upon which the rooms open. Everything bespeaks their Moorish origin. Some of these houses, which were palaces once, are now used as storehouses, some as carpenter-shops, some occupied as manufactories, while the appearance of all shows them to have been designed for a very different use.

The whole valley which Toledo overlooks, now lying so dead and silent, once teemed with a dense population, and sent forth armies, and fought great battles, in the days of the Goths. The cathedral of this old city is visited by architects from all parts of Europe and America, solely for the purpose of professional study, it being one of the finest examples of the Gothic order in existence, while the richness of its ornamentation and its artistic wealth, not to mention in detail its gold and silver plate, make it the rival of most cathedrals in the world, with the possible exception of that at Burgos. Its size is vast, with a tower reaching three hundred feet heavenward, the interior having five great aisles, divided by over eighty aspiring columns. It is said to contain more stained-glass windows than any other cathedral that was ever built. The high altar, a marvel of splendid workmanship and minute detail, is yet a little confusing from the myriads of single statues, groups, columns, and ornaments generally.

Toledo stands upon the boldest promontory of the Tagus, a dead and virtually deserted city. Coveted by various conquerors, she has been besieged more than twenty times; so that the river beneath her walls has often flowed red with human gore where it is spanned by the graceful bridge of Alcantara. Phœnicians, Romans, Goths, Moors, and Christians have all fought for, and at different times have possessed the place. Only the skeleton of a once great and thriving capital remains. It has no commerce, and but one industry, the manufacture of arms and sword-blades, which gives occupation to a couple of hundred souls — hardly more. The coming and going of visitors from other lands gives it a little flutter of daily life, — like a fitful candle, blazing up for a moment, and then dying down in the socket, making darkness only the more intense by the contrast. The one sword factory is found to be of little interest, though we are told that better blades are manufactured here to-day than of old.

In looking at the present condition of this once famous seat of industry and power, recalling her arts, manufactures, and commerce, it must be remembered that outside of the immediate walls, which formed the citadel of a large and extended population, were over forty thriving towns and villages in the valley of the Tagus, under the shadow of her wing. These communities and their homes have all disappeared, pastures and fields of grain covering their dust from the eyes of the curious traveller. The narrow, silent, doleful streets of the old city, with its overhanging roofs and yawning arches, leave a sad memory on the brain as we turn thoughtfully away from its crumbling walls and picturesque, antique Moorish gates.

Thirty-five miles from Madrid by rail will bring us to the Escurial, which the Spaniards call the eighth wonder of the world. This vast pile of stone buildings is more than three hundred years in age, and nearly a mile in circumference, — tomb, palace, cathedral, monastery, all in one. It was the royal home of that bigoted monarch Philip II., but is now only a show place, so to speak, of no present use except as an historical link and a royal tomb. One hall, over two hundred feet long and sixty wide, contains nearly seventy thousand bound volumes, all arranged with their backs to the wall so that the titles cannot be read, a plan which one would say was the device of some madman. The shelves, divided into sections and ornamental cases, are made of ebony, cedar, orange, and other choice woods. What possible historic wealth may here lie concealed, what noble thoughts and minds embalmed! In the domestic or dwelling portion of the Escurial, the apartments are very finely inlaid with various woods, besides containing some delicate and antique furniture of great beauty. A few cabinet pictures are seen upon the walls, and one or two large apartments are hung with tapestry, which, though centuries old, is as fresh as when it was first made. It might have come from the manufactory during this present year; for it certainly could not look brighter or more perfect.

The grounds surrounding the structure are laid out in pleasant gardens, where fountains, flowers, and a few inferior marble statues serve for external finish. On the outside, high up above the broadest portion of the dome, was placed the famous plate of gold, an inch thick and containing some ten square feet of surface, forming a monument of the bravado and extravagance of Philip II., who put it there in reply to the assertion of his enemies that he had financially ruined himself in building so costly a palace as the Escurial.

Burgos is situated about two hundred miles north of Madrid, and is reached by railway. Here the first impression upon the stranger is that of quaintness. It is a damp, cold, dead-and-alive place, with but three monuments worthy of our attention. These are its unrivalled cathedral, its Carthusian monastery, and its convent of Huelgas; and yet there is a tinge of the romantic Castilian period about its musty old streets and archways scarcely equalled elsewhere in Spain, and which one would not like to miss. It is very amusing, on arriving in such a place, to start off in the early morning without any fixed purpose as to destination, and wander through unknown streets, lanes, and archways, coming out upon a broad square, — the Plaza Mayor, for instance, which contains a bronze statue of Charles III.; thence to another with a tall stone fountain in its centre, where a motley group of women and young girls are filling their jars with water; and again, through a dull dark lane, coming upon the lofty gate of Santa Maria, erected by Charles V., and ornamented with statues of the Cid (a noted knight and warrior), Fernando Gonzales (famous Spanish general), and the emperor. Strolling on, we presently come to another open square, full of busy groups of women and donkeys, gathered about piles of produce. It is the vegetable market, always a favorite morning resort in every new locality. How animated are the eager sellers and buyers! What a study is afforded by their bright, expressive faces; how gay the varied colors of dress and of vegetables; how ringing the Babel of tongues and the braying of donkeys!

The cathedral, which the Emperor Charles V. said ought

to be placed under glass, renders the town a famous resort of travellers, being one of the largest, finest, and most richly endowed of all the Spanish churches. This lofty structure, like that at Antwerp, is situated behind a cluster of inferior buildings, so as greatly to detract from its external effect, though from the opposite side of the river Arlanzon a favorable view is obtained of its open-work spires and its tall corrugated roof. The columns and high arches of the interior are a maze of architectural beauty in pure Gothic. In all these Spanish churches the choir completely blocks up the centre of the interior, so that no comprehensive view can be had. Above the space between the altar and the choir rises a cupola, which, in elaborate ornamentation of bas-reliefs, statues, small columns, arches, and sculptured figures, exceeds anything of the sort in this country so famous for its cathedrals. The hundred and more carved seats of the choir are in choice walnut, and form a great curiosity as an example of artistic wood-carving, presenting human figures, vines, fantastic animals, and foliage. The several chapels are as large as ordinary churches, while in the centre of each lies buried a bishop or a prince. The great number of statues and paintings scattered through the interior of the cathedral are almost as confusing as the pinnacled and statue-covered roof of the Milan cathedral, whose beauty disappears amid accumulation. In a side apartment the attendant will show us many curious relics, among them the well-known effigy of Christ on the Cross, which devout believers say was carved by Nicodemus just after he had buried the Saviour.

Our course is still northward. From Burgos to San Sebastian by rail is a hundred and fifty miles. As we leave the ancient town, memory is busy for a moment recalling its legends and history. We remember that centuries ago a knight of Castile, Diego Porcelos, had a lovely daughter named Sulla Bella, whom he gave as a bride to a German cavalier, and together they founded this place and fortified it. They called it Burg, a fortified place, hence Burgos. We recall the Cid and his gallant war-horse, Baveica, we think of the richly endowed cathedral, and the old monastery, where rest Juan II. and Isabella of Portugal in their elaborately carved alabaster tomb. But gradually these memories fade away as we awaken to new and present surroundings while rushing along at railway speed. Sparkling watercourses, with here and there a fall, give power to some rickety old stone mill and add variety to the scene. On the not far-off hills are castles, border fortresses in ruins, whose gray towers have borne witness to the conflicts of armor-clad warriors in the days of Castilian knighthood and glory. What interest hangs about these rude battlements! In looking back upon the ancient days it is fortunate that the mellowing influence of time dims the vision, and we see as through a softening twilight; otherwise we should behold such harshness as would embitter all. The olden time, like the landscape, appears best in the purple distance.

The general aspect of the country since we left Malaga in the south has been rather disappointing, and the rural appearance on this beautiful trip from Burgos to San Sebastian is therefore the more heartily appreciated. It should be called the garden of Spain, the well-watered valleys and plains being spread with a carpet of exquisite verdure. In the far distance one detects snow-clad mountains, which in fact are not out of sight during the entire journey. Thousands of acres are covered by the vine from the product of which comes our sherry wine. It is impossible not to feel a sense of elation amid the delightful scenery and while breathing the genial air. Nature seems to be in her merriest mood, clothing everything in poetic attire, rendering more than beautiful the gray hamlets on the hillsides, over which rise square bell-towers, about which the red-tiled cottages cluster. Outside of these are seen family groups, some sewing, some spinning, while children gleefully tumble about and play in the inviting grass.

San Sebastian is a somewhat famous watering-place, situated on the boisterous Bay of Biscay, and drawing its patronage largely from Madrid, though of late many English people have resorted thither. It is a small city, but the thriftiest and most business-like, when its size is considered, to be found in the borders of Spain. The place was entirely destroyed by fire when captured from the French by the English, a piece of sanguinary work which cost the latter five thousand lives! It was on this occasion that Wellington is reported to have said, "The next most dreadful thing to a battle lost is a battle won."

After leaving San Sebastian our first stopping-place is Bayonne; that is, "Good Port." It is a city of some thirty thousand inhabitants, situated at the junction of the Adour and Nive rivers, in the Lower Pyrenees. Here again the cathedral forms the principal attraction to travellers. Though very plain and with little architectural merit, still it is very old, gray and crumbling, plainly telling the story of its age. The city has considerable commerce by the river, both in steam and sailing vessels, and exports a very respectable amount of domestic produce. Here we see the palace where Catharine de Medici and the Duke of Alva planned the terrible massacre of the Huguenots of France. A large, well-arranged public garden begins just at the city gate and extends along the left bank of the Adour, and there are many pleasant drives in the environs.

From here we take the cars for Bordeaux, France, a distance of over a hundred miles, the road running mostly through what seems to be an interminable pine forest.

In leaving Spain we pause for a moment to contrast her past and her present. In the sixteenth century she was the most powerful nation in the world. In art she held the foremost position. Murillo, Velasquez, and Ribiéra were her honored sons; in literature she was represented by Cervantes, Lope de Vega, and Calderon; while of discoverers and conquerors she sent forth Columbus, Cortez, and Pizarro. The banners of Castile and Aragon floated alike on the Pacific and the Indian oceans. Her warriors were brave and adventurous, her soldiers inherited the gallantry of the followers of Charles V. She was the court of Europe, the acknowledged leader of chivalry. How rapid has been her decadence! As in the plenitude of her power she was ambitious, cruel, and perfidious, so has the measure which she meted to others been in turn accorded to herself, until to-day there are none so lowly as to do her homage.

Bordeaux is reckoned the third city in France as to its commercial importance. The form of the town is that of a crescent extending along the shore of the Garonne, which here forms a broad and navigable harbor, always well filled with foreign and domestic shipping, though it is sixty miles from the sea. There are many interesting Roman antiquities and monuments to be seen in and about the city, venerable with the wear and tear of eighteen centuries. The public buildings are commanding in their architectural effect, and are many of them adorned with sculpture. The most ancient part of the town, like nearly all others we visit in Europe, has narrow and crooked streets, but the modern portion is open, airy, and well arranged for business and domestic comfort. The Grand Theatre is a remarkable piece of effective architecture, with its noble Ionic columns, and was built a little more than a century since by Louis XVI.

The distance from Bordeaux to Paris is about four hundred miles. The route passes all the way through a charming and highly cultivated country. The well-prepared fields are green with varied crops, showing a high state of cultivation. Flocks of sheep, tended by shepherdesses with tall Norman caps of white linen and picturesque bright colored dresses, enliven the landscape. These industrious women are seen knitting as they watch their charge. Others are driving oxen while men hold the plow. Gangs of men and women together in long rows are preparing the ground for the seed, and all seem cheerful and happy. The small railroad stations recall those of India between Tuticorin and Madras, where the surroundings are beautified by fragrant flower-gardens, their bland, odorous breath acting like a charm upon the senses amid the noise and bustle of arrival and departure. Now and again as we progress the pointed architecture of some picturesque château presents itself among the clustering trees, with its bright verdant lawn and neat outlying buildings, and so we speed swiftly on until by and by we glide into the large station at Paris.

CHAPTER XI.

IN passing through Paris we shall pause to present a few sketches representative of the great French capital. It is the gayest metropolis of Europe, the spot where the traveller is most inclined to linger, and whose siren voice is most dangerous to the inexperienced. Its attractions are innumerable, combining unequalled educational advantages in art, literature, and the learned professions, together with unlimited temptations to frivolity. Here are offered daily, without money and without price, lectures upon all themes known to science, free schools in all departments of learning, free art museums and free art galleries, such as can hardly be excelled in the world.

The finest view to be had in the city may be enjoyed by taking one's stand in the Tuileries Garden and looking straight across the Place de la Concorde to the far-away Arc de Triomphe. Here is a clear view, in the very heart of Paris, two miles long, over the entire length of the Champs Elysées. The only thing to impede the sight in the least degree is the grand old column of Luxor, which stands in the middle of the Place de la Concorde, but which is of only needle-like proportions in so comprehensive a view as we speak of. This is the finest square of the city, and indeed we may go further and say the finest in all Europe. It is bounded on the north by the spacious buildings occupied by the Ministry of the Marine, on the south by the Seine, here crossed by the Pont des Invalides, and having the Tuileries on the east and the Champs Elysées on the west. As this is the first square in Europe, so is the Champs Elysées, which opens out of it, the grandest boulevard in the world. It is divided into three alleys, liberally planted with trees, the principal entrance being marked by the celebrated sculptures known as the "Horses of Marly," standing like sentinels, one on each side of the broad carriage-way. This is the road leading to the Bois de Boulogne, the favorite pleasure-drive of the Parisians, where also may be found the fine race-grounds and the Jardin d'Acclimation, with its superb and unrivalled collection of wild animals and rare birds.

Sunday is a weekly recurring carnival here, on which occasions the races and the military reviews take place, and all Paris seeks to amuse itself by open air pleasures. Fifty thousand people and more throng the Champs Elysées; the toy and refreshment booths drive a lucrative business; the numerous goat and pony wagons for children are in constant use. One little turn-out is particularly noticeable, consisting of four well-trained Newfoundland dogs, elegantly harnessed and attended by a couple of servants in livery, a boy of ten or twelve years holding the lines from his seat in the light and graceful little vehicle. Merry young misses drive their ribbon-decked hoops with special relish, and roguish boys spin their tops with equal zeal. Clouds of toy-balloons, of various colors and sizes, flash high above the heads of itinerant vendors, while the sparkling fountains throw up softly musical jets everywhere. Soldiers off duty, strolling idly about, dot the scene with their various uniforms, their shining helmets, and elaborate gold lace. The busy road-way is crowded by a thousand turnouts, drawn by high-stepping horses.

Delighted youths, of both sexes, mount wooden horses in the merry-go-rounds and enjoy their ride at a cost of a couple of cents. Lofty aerial cars, upon huge revolving wheels, afford as much delight and more risk to other youths. Punch and Judy, and the man with the air-gun and conspicuous mark, are also present. A performing monkey divides the honors and pennies with the rest of the entertainers. Not far away an acrobat, in flesh-colored tights, lies upon the carpeted ground and tosses a lad, dressed in spangled thin clothes, into the air, catching him upon his foot again as he comes down, and twirling him so rapidly that the boy becomes invisible. Such is a glimpse of the Champs Elysées on Sunday.

Strangers in Paris do not forget to visit the Expiatory Chapel, erected by Louis the Eighteenth to the memory of Louis the Sixteenth, Marie Antoinette, and other victims of the Revolution, which took place about a century since. Historic recollections crowd upon us as we stand within this small but beautiful chapel. Time has softened the sternness of judgment relating to the king and queen; and we all pause to admire their bearing in adversity, but are forced to the conclusion "that nothing in their life so well became them as the manner of their leaving it." The queen was remarkable for her dignity of person, which she loved to increase by the accessories of ornament, until, as a writer of that period tells us, covered with diamonds and precious stones, she was literally a thing of light. But Marie Antoinette, in the dungeons of the Conciergerie, in her widow's cap and patched black dress, was worthier of love and veneration than when she blazed as the royal star of Versailles.

The flower market of this large capital is ever suggestive and interesting. The women, of all ages, who bring these floral gems to the city, exhibit a taste in their arrangement which would be of value to a professional artist. One may detect a living poem in each little department. The principal square devoted to this purpose is situated just over the Pont Neuf and borders the Seine. The market is changed so as to be held for two days of each week under the shadow of the Madeleine, in the Place de la Madeleine, the noblest of modern Christian temples in its chaste architecture. As we come down from the Rue Scribe, in the early part of the day, we see vehicles, with liveried attendants, pause while the fair occupants purchase a cluster of favorite flowers; dainty beauties on foot come hither to go away laden with fragrant gems, while well-dressed men deck their button-holes with a bit of color and fragrance combined. Here is a white-frocked butcher selecting a full-blown pot of pansies, and here a sad-faced woman, in widow's weeds, takes away a wreath of immortelles — to-night it will deck a tomb in the cemetery of Père la Chaise. This giddy and nervous fellow, who is full of smiles, takes away a wedding wreath — price is no object to him. Yonder is a pale-faced shop-girl — what sunny yet half-sad features she has! She must perhaps forego her dinner in order to possess that pot of mignonette, but she trips lightly away with it in a happy mood.

The most interesting church here is that of Notre Dame, whose massive towers greet the eye in every comprehensive view of the city. The present structure is probably not over seven hundred years old, but it stands upon a site successively occupied by a Pagan temple and a Christian church of the time of the early kings. The present building presents one of the most perfect examples of Gothic architecture extant. It contains about forty separate chapels. Here the late Emperor and Empress were married, in January, 1853, just fifty-two years after the coronation of the first Napoleon in the same place.

A little way from Notre Dame, upon a street situated behind it and near the Pont St. Louis, is the Morgue, or dead-house of Paris, at all times open to the public, where are exposed the corpses of unknown persons who have met their death in the streets or the Seine by violence or drowning. These bodies remain here three days for the purpose of identification. If not recognized and claimed by friends, they are then buried at the expense of the city, or consigned to the dissecting-tables. There are brought here during the year, the officer in charge will tell us, over three hundred bodies, two-thirds of whom are men, and about one-third women. A large number of the latter are known to be suicides, and are recovered from the waters of the Seine, close at hand.

The daily scenes occurring in the gardens of the Tuileries, which open from the Place de la Concorde, are characteristic. The spacious grounds, adorned with stately trees, fountains, tiny lakes, statues, and flowers, the latter kept fresh and green by artificial means nearly all the year round, form an ever-varying attraction. Hundreds of merry children enliven every nook and corner by their careless, happy voices. The gayest of promenaders of both sexes throng the broad, smooth paths in the after part of the day. Round the fountains the sparrows, as tame as the pigeons of St. Mark at Venice, light upon one's arms and shoulders, convinced that the only legitimate business of the world is to supply them with cake and biscuit. Now there break upon the ear the strains of a full military band posted among the trees, and brilliant music adds its charm to the attractive scene. This is one side of the picture; we may perhaps with profit to ourselves turn to the other. The same bell that rings out the marriage peal, tolls forth the funeral knell; sweet flowers that deck the bridal altar, are also brought to lay upon the tomb. We have not far to go in seeking for the shadow of the Tuileries gardens. Misery in all its varied forms is to be found in the Faubourg St. Antoine, partially hidden by almost transparent screens from the naked eye. Crime, sickness, starvation, death, all are within no great distance of these beautiful resorts. Dark streets where thieves and outcasts slink away from the light of day like hunted animals; where one reads hunger and want in silent human faces; where men are met whose villanous expression only too plainly betrays their criminal nature.

All strangers make a visit to Père la Chaise, the historic burial-ground of the French capital. Its two hundred acres of monuments, tombs, and costly sepulchres present only a sad and sombre aspect to the eye, as unlike to Greenwood, Mount Auburn, or Forest Hills, as narrow streets and brick houses are unlike the green and open fields of the country. One reads upon the tombs, however, the familiar historic names with vivid interest, such as Rossini, Molière, Scribe, Alfred de Musset, Talma, Arago, and others. One remarkable tomb attracts us; it is that of Abélard and Héloise, upon which some hand has just placed *fresh* flowers. One cannot but respect the sentiment which would perpetuate the memory of this hero and heroine of seven hundred years ago. There are sixty thousand tombs, mausoleums, and memorial stones within these grounds, but none equal this one tomb for interest.

We must not forget to visit the Cluny Museum, situated on the Rue des Mathurins, near the Boulevard St. Michel. The remarkable collection of historic relics of the Middle Ages and subsequent period, consisting of glass, porcelain, tapestry, carvings, weapons, and domestic utensils, are tangible history of great interest. The building itself in which these treasures are exhibited is a curiosity five or six hundred years in age, near the very extensive remains of Julian's palace. With one exception this is the only visible structure of the Roman period that still exists in the city of Paris. The other is the Roman Amphitheatre, situated in the Rue Monge. Here, not long since, coins were found, bearing the date of the time of Adrian.

On the Rue Rivoli, opposite the Tuileries gardens, stands a bronze equestrian statue, erected within the last few years, representing Joan of Arc. As we look upon it, the mind reverts to the romantic story of the maid of Domremy, which this tardy act of justice commemorates. A conclave of bishops sent her to the stake at Rouen —an act as unwarrantable as the hanging of innocent women for witches in the early days of New England. History repeats itself, and the victims of one generation become the idols of the next. We like best to believe that this simple maid was inspired to do the work which she so well performed. At the age of thirteen she began to devote herself to liberate her country from the English invaders, selling the very bed she slept upon to aid in the equipment of soldiers for the field. Joan was but eighteen years old when she appeared before Charles VII. and told him that she was impelled by Heaven to raise the siege of Orleans, and to conduct him to Rheims to be crowned. She was young and beautiful; the king believed in her; the soldiers thought she was inspired, and so followed her to victory. City after city surrendered to her, battle after battle was won under her leadership, until Charles was indeed crowned at Rheims; but, through the influence of her English enemies, the brave and modest maid was condemned as a sorceress and burned at the stake!

It is foreigners, not Parisians, who support the splendid jewelry and other fancy stores of the boulevards, as well as the thousand extravagant hotels of the metropolis. Paris is the mart of the world for fancy goods. It is the policy of the government to establish and freely maintain such attractions as shall draw to the city strangers from all parts of the world, who come and empty their well-filled purses into the pockets of French merchants. But let us not forget that the best means of education are free to all, the poorest scholar being welcome to the unrivalled libraries and archives, as well as to the splendid advantages of the art galleries. Scientific lectures and the rarest books upon special themes are free to him, while every facility which the government can control is liberally offered to the humble but ambitious student of science and of art.

We start for Lyons by the way of Fontainebleau, which is situated about forty miles from Paris. The Palace was founded over seven hundred years ago, and has been kept during all these years in perfect condition, each new monarch adding to its embellishments, until it forms to-day a magnificent museum of art. There are over eight hundred apartments, all of which are sumptuously decorated and furnished. Here was signed the revocation Edict of Nantes; from here was announced the divorce of Josephine; and here Napoleon the First signed his abdication. The Palace is surrounded by beautiful and extensive gardens, small lakes, and fountains. The famous forest of Fontainebleau is of more than passing interest; there is no such wooded and shady drive elsewhere in the world as is afforded by the admirably kept roads that intersect the sixty-four square miles covered by this forest, and in the midst of which is the town. The inhabitants number twelve thousand, added to which there is here a military station with barracks for about a thousand men. Until within a few years the forest was the resort of persons from the capital who had affairs to settle with sword or pistol, but police arrangements have put an end to this business.

Lyons has a population of half a million, and ranks as the second city of France in that respect. The manufacture of silk is the great industry here, and everybody seems to be in some way interested in forwarding this business. There are between forty and fifty thousand silk-looms actively employed. In the extent of its silk trade it is the first city in the world. Being located at the confluence of two important rivers, the Rhone and the Saône, the city has almost the advantage of a maritime port, besides which it has ample railroad connections. After a day's rest at Lyons, we will proceed on our journey by rail to the city of Marseilles, the first commercial port of the Mediterranean.

The importance of Marseilles as a business centre can hardly be overestimated, its harbor having safe accommodations for over a thousand ships at the same time. The flags of Italy, Portugal, England, and America mingle with those of the far East at her quays. In the breezy streets of the town surrounding the harbor, we meet Turks, Italians, Spaniards, British tars, and the queerly dressed sailors of the Grecian Archipelago, while a Babel of tongues rings upon the ear. This is the principal port for embarkation to reach Corsica, Genoa, Leghorn, Constantinople, and Smyrna, the harbor being the finest in France, and it has been prominent in its commercial connections for fully two thousand years. Marseilles, with a population of four hundred thousand, is remarkable for the number and excellence of its public institutions, among which is a royal exchange, a national observatory, an academy of sciences, a public library, a school of design, a deaf and dumb institute, a museum of paintings and antiquities, etc. The Palace of Longchamps, standing upon one of the most prominent spots in the city, is a museum, geological school, library, and picture gallery combined. It is a superb structure architecturally, and cost over seven millions of dollars.

Overlooking the city of Marseilles is the hill of Notre Dame de la Garde, a lofty eminence, which seen from the town appears to be hung in the very clouds. Skilful engineering has made a winding road to the apex accessible for vehicles. Once reached, this lofty spot affords one of the most delightful and comprehensive views on the continent, embracing a wide extent of sea and land. Immediately beneath the visitor's feet lies the city, nearly encircled by vine-clad hills, interspersed by châteaux, Swiss and English cottages, all assuming Lilliputian proportions. The winding cliff-road looks like a silver thread, and the blue Mediterranean, dotted here and there with sails and steamships, glistens in the warm, soft sunshine. But the bird's-eye view of the city is a marvel in its perfection and comprehensiveness. This hill is named after the singular Roman Catholic chapel upon its cloud-capped summit. It is visible for many leagues at sea, and is the subject of mysterious veneration to sailors who navigate these inland waters. A large number of curious articles from all parts of the world contributed by believing sailors are to be seen within its walls, in the form of rich samples of ores, shells, corals, and savage weapons from the far-away South Sea Islands, forming a kind of religious museum.

From Marseilles we take the railway route to Nice, a distance of one hundred and forty miles. This world-renowned sanitary resort is most delightfully situated at the base of an amphitheatre of hills, which are decked with villas, gardens, orange and olive groves. Roses bloom out of doors all the year round, and fruit ripens on the trees in January. Nice has a population of about sixty-five thousand. The foot-hills of the Alpine range come so close to the town as to cut off all the view inland, but the opposite side is open to the far-reaching Mediterranean, which curves gracefully in crescent form to make the beautiful bay of Nice. Lying so very close to the Italian frontier, the people are as much of that nationality as of France, and both languages are spoken. The old portion of the town is Roman in many of its characteristics, and here those former masters of the world had an important naval station in the days of Augustus. Dirty as this portion of Nice is, one lingers here a little to study the quaint architecture, and the aspects of humble life. The peculiarities of dress, habits, and general appearance of the people differ materially from other continental towns. Half-clad, bare-footed boys and girls of twelve or fourteen years of age abound, many of them with such beauty of face and form as to make us sigh for the possibilities of their young lives probably never to be fulfilled. Under favorable auspices what a happy future might fall to their share! A year or two more of wretched associations, idle habits, and want of proper food and clothing will age them terribly. What a serious social problem is presented by such lives!

All strangers who come hither visit Cimies, about three miles from Nice, upon a lofty hillside, where there are some remarkable Roman ruins, among which is a spacious amphitheatre, once capable of seating eight or ten thousand spectators. This place, like the neighboring Convent of Cinieres, is more than a thousand years old, and so well built that the intervening centuries have not been able to disintegrate its masonry to any great extent. It is upon a Sunday afternoon that we visit the amphitheatre and convent. The Franciscan monks, who alone inhabit the terrace, seem to be rather a jolly set of men, notwithstanding their coarse dress, shaven heads, and bare feet. The Sabbath does not interfere with their game of tennis, which a group of them pursue with great earnestness in the pleasant old garden of the monastery, now and then disputing a little rudely as to the conduct of the game. One of the brethren is our guide; he explains intelligently what we desire to understand, and gives us a drink of water out of the old well from which the Romans drank so many hundred years ago, and which he assures us has never been known to fail of yielding pure water.

Mentone, the border town between France and Italy, is situated fifteen miles from Nice. We pass through it on the route to Genoa. A deep ravine forms the dividing line between the two countries, spanned by the bridge of St.

Louis. Mentone is a favorite resort for persons suffering with pulmonary affections, and has about ten thousand inhabitants. It is characterized by very beautiful scenery bordering the great classic sea, and lying at the base of the Maritime Alps. Adjoining the town is the principality of Monaco, an independent state covering an area of less than fifty square miles. It is a curious fact that the independence of this spot has been respected by Europe for so many years, and that it is to-day ruled over by a descendant of the house of Grimaldi, by whom the principality was founded in the tenth century. The castle, which forms also the palace of the Prince of Monaco, is situated on a rocky promontory overlooking the sea and the wonderful coast scenery between Nice and Mentone. Here the prince maintains a battalion of soldiers who perform guard duty and keep up the semblance of military authority. His subjects are supposed to number about three thousand. To sustain his princely state he must have a revenue other than could be derived from taxation of so small a population, and the main source of his income is very well known. The dominion of the prince is now the only legalized gambling spot in Europe, and from the permit thus granted he receives an annual payment of half a million dollars.

Monte Carlo, the headquarters of the gambling fraternity, lies within a mile of the palace on the shore line. The beautiful spot where the "Casino" (gambling saloon) is situated is one of the most picturesque which can be conceived of, overlooking from a considerable height the Mediterranean Sea. To the extraordinary beauties accorded by nature man has added his best efforts, lavishing money to produce unequalled attractions. There is here an elegant hotel, brilliant café, attractive saloons, delightful gardens, floral bowers, shooting-galleries, in short, nearly every possible device to fascinate and occupy the visitor. The roads over which we drive in this vicinity are full of interest, besides the delightful views which greet us on every hand. Wayside shrines to the Virgin are seen at every cross-road, and upon every hillside we meet scores of priests; the little church-bells are ringing incessantly; the roads are thronged with beggars; the beautiful-faced but ragged children attract us by their bright eyes and dark complexions, just touched with a soft rose-tint. We are surprised at the multiplicity of donkeys, their bodies hidden by big loads of merchandise; we observe with interest those handsome milk-white oxen, with wide-spreading horns; we inhale the fragrance of the orange groves, and remember that we are in Italy.

About a hundred miles from St. Mauro, the border town after crossing the bridge of St. Louis, will take us by the Corniche road to Genoa. This ancient capital rises in terrace form, presenting the aspect of an amphitheatre whose base is the water's edge, while the city is situated between the two lofty hills of Carignano on the east and St. Benigno on the west. The harbor of Genoa is semi-circular in form, nearly a mile across, and is protected by two substantial piers, on one of which is a lighthouse three hundred feet in height. From the seaward end of the lighthouse pier we have a fine view of the town, the slope being covered with palaces, churches, hotels, gardens, forts, and public buildings. The arsenal, the prison, the custom-house, and government warehouses all cluster about the wharves, where great business activity centres at all times. The older part of the city consists of narrow and confusing lanes, accessible only to foot-passengers. In the olden days, when this city was first laid out after the fashion of the times, it was crowded with fortified lines, and perched upon elevations to aid in resisting the attack of an invading enemy. The newer portions present broad, accessible thoroughfares, with one or two elegant boulevards.

The number of marble palaces in Genoa is really surprising, but they are built in streets so narrow that their elaborate fronts lose architectural effect. These were not all occupied by the class termed the nobility, but were often the homes of merchant princes. Many of these structures are now vacant or occupied for business purposes. Splendid marble corridors and mosaic floors, with halls opening from grand marble staircases, seem ill-adapted to the purposes of common trade. A few of these structures belong to people whose condition enables them to retain them as dwellings; others have been purchased by the government and are occupied as public offices; and still others are hotels. This city was the birthplace of Columbus, the "Great Genoese Pilot," who first showed the way across the then trackless ocean to a western world. Almost the first object to attract the attention of the traveller on emerging from the railroad depot is the statue of Columbus in a broad open space. It was erected so late as 1862, and stands upon a pedestal ornamented with ships' prows. At the feet of the statue kneels the figure of America, the whole monument being of white marble, and surrounded by allegorical figures in a sitting posture, representing Religion, Geography, Force, and Wisdom.

There are many noble public institutions in Genoa, noticeable among which is the general hospital and the asylum for the poor, as it is called, capable of sheltering sixteen hundred people. The Deaf and Dumb Asylum and the Hospital for the Insane are the best organized in Italy. The Public Library contains some hundred and twenty thousand bound volumes, and is open for free use at all suitable hours. There is also an Academy of Fine Arts, with an admirable collection of paintings and sculpture: many of the examples are from the hands of the old masters.

The Cathedral of St. Lorenzo is richly worthy of our attention. Among the curiosities to be seen within its walls are the two urns said to contain the ashes of St. John the Baptist, which are paraded with religious pomp through the streets of the city once a year. They are said to have been brought from the city of Myrrha in Lycia, in the year 1097. There is also exhibited here an emerald dish, which is an object of great veneration with the Genoese, and which is said to have held the Paschal Lamb at the Last Supper. It was captured from the Saracens, in the year 1101, at the storming of Cesarea.

From elevated points in and about Genoa most charming and extended views of the Mediterranean are enjoyed. It is not the tranquil and lake-like expanse which inexperience would believe it to be, but is capable of nearly as fierce commotion as the angry waves of the Atlantic itself. It is still navigated very much as it was of old by the Greeks, the Phœnicians, and the Romans. The mariners still hug the shore, and at every unfavorable change of weather run into the nearest safe anchorage. Thus most of the coasting-vessels are under one hundred tons' measurement, and are of a model which will permit of their being beached upon the shelving shore in an emergency. It seems to be generally believed that this sea is tideless, but it is not the case; it feels the same lunar influence which affects the ocean, though in a less degree. These waters are warmer than the Atlantic, owing probably to the absence of polar currents. The Mediterranean is almost entirely enclosed by the continents of Europe, Asia, and Africa, and covers a space of a million of square miles, being over two thousand miles long and, in one place, more than a thousand wide. The tide is most noticeable in the Gulf of Venice, where the rise and fall is from three to four feet.

Before leaving Genoa we will drive out to the Campo Santo, or public burial ground. It is a remarkable place laid out in terraces, containing many monuments, and having in its centre a large circular chapel with Doric columns, the vestibule walls also containing tombs, bearing an inscription on the face of each. Seeing in many instances small baskets partially wrapped in paper or linen laid beside or on the graves about the Campo Santo, one is apt to inquire what their significance can be, and he will be told that food is thus placed from time to time, for the sustenance of the departed!

CHAPTER XII.

WE embark at Genoa for Leghorn by a coasting-steamer. On arriving at the latter port the first thing which strikes the traveller is the mixed character of the population, composed of Greeks, Armenians, Turks, Moors, and Italians, whose strongly individualized costumes give picturesqueness and color to the public ways. Until within the last two centuries Leghorn was a very small village, and therefore presents comparatively a modern aspect, with its present population of about a hundred and twenty thousand. The streets are wide, well laid out, and regularly paved, the northern section of the city being intersected by canals, enabling the merchants to float their goods to the doors of their warehouses. Its fine situation upon the Mediterranean shore is its one recommendation, forming an entry port connected with Rome, Pisa, and other inland cities of Italy. There are pointed out to us here three special hospitals, an observatory, a poorhouse and a public library, but there is not much of local interest.

An excursion of fifteen miles by railway will take us to Pisa, one of the oldest cities of Italy, and formerly the capital of the grand duchy of Tuscany, being finely situated on the banks of the Arno, which divides the city into two parts, and is crossed by three noble bridges. The population is about fifty thousand, and it has broad, handsome streets, with a number of spacious squares, fine churches, and public edifices. The most attractive part of the city is that lining the Arno, where there are several palaces of some architectural pretensions. The great attraction of Pisa lies just outside of the city proper, consisting of a group of edifices which are celebrated all over the world. These are the Cathedral, the Baptistery, and the Belfry, or, as it is more generally known, the Leaning Tower. Each of these is separated from the others by several rods. The Cathedral is the oldest structure, and has an existence covering a thousand years. The isolation of these buildings from the town, and their complete separation from each other, add very much to their general effect. The Cathedral, built entirely of white marble, is crowned by a noble dome, which is supported by over seventy pillars, while it is gorgeously furnished with almost innumerable art treasures, paintings, variegated marbles, panels, superb colored glass windows, and statues. The altar and the pulpit rest upon pillars of porphyry. The roof is not arched, but is of wood, divided into sections and elaborately gilded, — a very ancient style of finish found only in the oldest churches upon the continent. The doors are of bronze finely sculptured. In the nave the guide will call our attention to a large bronze hanging-lamp, the oscillations of which are said to have suggested to Galileo the theory of the pendulum. The Baptistery, or Church of St. John, is situated nearly opposite the Cathedral, a most beautifully shaped church, which is noted for a marvellous echo.

The Leaning Tower of Pisa is one of the famous structures of the world. It is seven stories high, the summit measuring one hundred and eight feet from the ground. Each story is divided by rows of columns, so that architecturally it has a resemblance to the other buildings near

LEANING TOWER OF PISA, CATHEDRAL AND BAPTISTRY.

at hand. There are many theories as to the leaning position of this tower, but no two persons seem to quite agree upon the matter. A plummet and line depending from the top would strike the ground some ten feet from the base of the structure. It has stood here for more than six hundred years, and does not appear to be in any danger of falling. A view from the upper gallery, over which hangs a chime of heavy bells, is very fine, embracing the fertile plains of Tuscany.

Near at hand is the Campo Santo, a cloistered cemetery constructed many centuries ago. It is a large rectangular enclosure surrounded by arcades. After the loss of the Holy Land the Pisans caused some fifty shiploads of soil to be brought hither from Mt. Calvary, in order that the dead might rest in what was conceived to be holy ground. It was in this Campo Santo that the earliest Tuscan artists were taught to emulate each other, and here the walls are covered with remarkable representations of Scriptural and historical subjects. The originals of many pictures made familiar to us by engravings, are still to be found here, such as "Noah Inebriated," "Building of the Tower of Babel," "The Last Judgment," etc. The tombstones of those whose remains rest here, form the pavement of the arcades. The sculptures, monuments, and bas-reliefs in the Campo Santo are almost innumerable, forming a strange and varied collection.

The history of Pisa is of great antiquity, having been one of the famous twelve towns of Etruria. It maintained its municipal government and almost unlimited freedom while nominally under Roman protection, but on the decline of the imperial power it was compelled to submit in turn to the various transalpine nations who overran Northern Italy. Early in the eleventh century it had risen to the rank of a powerful republic and to this period belong most of the splendid monuments on which it now justly prides itself. Its soldiers were conspicuous in the crusades, and at that time its fleets were the most powerful that navigated the Mediterranean Sea.

Returning to Leghorn we embark for Naples by steamer. As we glide slowly into the lovely bay just as the morning light is breaking in the east, we feel that no more propitious hour for arrival could be devised, and are glad that the view of the city is presented to us for the first time from the sea rather than from the shore. How impressive is the historic scene which gradually spreads out before us as we steam slowly in by the islands of Procida and Cape Miseno, while we behold what an imaginative writer has termed "a fragment of heaven to earth vouchsafed"; it certainly seems more like a picture than like reality. Few cities on the globe are so famous for their advantageous site as is Naples. It lies in amphitheatre form on the shore of the classic bay, which is shut in from the sea by the island of Capri, extending in part across its entrance to the southeast, while to the northwest loom up the beautiful islands of Procida and Ischia, so full of sad and historic associations. It will be remembered that many of the population were engulfed at Ischia by an earthquake within a few years past. On the eastern side of this panoramic view rises Vesuvius, with its bold and isolated pinnacle, while its dusky sides are dotted up to within half the distance of the summit by villages, hamlets, villas, and vineyards, awaiting the destruction which it would seem must come sooner or later. Along the base of the volcano lie the towns of Portici, Annunziata, and Torre del Greco, everything glittering in the light of the rising sun. The eyes cannot rest upon a spot which has not its classic association, turn which way we will. In the distance eastward is seen Castellamare and Sorrento on the right curve of the crescent-shaped shore, while on the left lie Solfatara and Pozzuoli. What a shore to look upon, where Cicero, Horace, Virgil, Tasso, Pliny, and Macænas lived! How thrillingly beautiful it is, as we creep slowly up to our moorings in the soft, dewy freshness of the morning!

In direct contrast to all this beauty of nature and picturesqueness of scenery, as soon as we land there comes before our eyes so much of dirt, poverty, and beggary, as to cause us to shudder. How humanity outrages the loveliness of nature! Begging is reduced to a profession here; thousands of both sexes and of all ages have no other employment or seeming ambition than to beg at every opportunity, to fill their stomachs with food, and then, like the inferior animals, to stretch themselves in the sun until again aroused by hunger. There is no quarter of the city exempt from this pest of beggary. The palace and the hovel join each other in strange incongruity; starvation and abundance are close together; elegance and rags are in juxtaposition; the city has nearly half a million population, and this condition applies to all its streets. There are many fine public buildings, and yet they can lay no special claim to architectural excellence. The old streets are narrow, crooked, and in some places ascended by steps, on an angle of forty-five degrees; but the modern part of the city is well laid out. The Strada di Roma is the Broadway of Naples, a fine, busy street, more than a mile in length and lined with elegant business stores, cafés, hotels, and public offices. The famous Riviera di Chiaja, or Quay, is also a noble street running along the shore of the bay, lined on one side by an almost endless array of palaces, and on the other by the long park separating it from the sea.

This Chiaja is the famous drive-way of Naples, and is a broad and beautiful street by which we enter the city from the west. Just about sunset this thoroughfare presents daily a scene more peculiar and quite as gay as the Bois de Boulogne, or the Prater of Vienna, being crowded at that hour by the beauty and fashion of the town enjoying an afternoon drive or horseback ride. Here may be seen gigs driven by young Neapolitans in dashing style, and some smart brushes in the way of racing take place. The small Italian horses are real flyers, and are driven only too recklessly over the crowded course. Mingling with the throng are long lines of donkeys laden with merchandise, keeping close to the side of the way in order to avoid the fast drivers; pedestrians of both sexes dodging out and in among the vehicles; cavalry officers cantering on showy horses; and the inevitable army of beggars with outstretched hands pleading for alms, among whom is an occasional mendicant friar also soliciting a few pennies.

It is not alone the common classes who live so much in the streets. It is not alone the palace windows that are filled with spectators all along the drive-way of the Chiaja during the carnival hour of the day, but before each residence are gathered a domestic group sitting contentedly in the open air, bareheaded and in gauze-like costume. Some of the ladies employ their hands with dainty needlework, some are crocheting, others are engaged in simple domestic games, and all are chatting, laughing, and enjoying themselves heartily. The ladies wear the gayest colors, these adding vividness to the whole picture. To complete the strongly individualized scene, there are the graceful palms, orange-trees, and fountains of the park, amid abundant marble statuary, and flowering shrubs, with the sea, Capri, and Vesuvius for a background, which together make up the view of the Chiaja at twilight.

Naples is very peculiar in the aspect of its out-of-door life; we see the public letter-writer at his post in the open square; the common people are conducting most of their domestic affairs outside of their dwellings. Sellers of macaroni, oranges, grapes, fish, vegetables, flowers, and hawkers of every sort fill the air with their shrill cries. Common-looking men fling thin, greasy, tattered cloaks over their shoulders, with a proud air and inimitable grace; groups of half-clad children play in the dirt; whole families cook and eat in the street; while liveried turn-outs are dashing hither and thither. No matter in which direction one may go in or around the city, there looms up heavenward the sky-piercing summit of Vesuvius, shrouding the blue ether all day long with its slowly-rising column of smoke, and the sulphuric breathing of its unknown depths. The burning mountain is about three leagues from the city, but is so lofty as to seem closer at hand. It is quite solitary, rising in a majestic manner from the plain, but having a base thirty miles in circumference and a height of about four thousand feet. When emitting fire as well as smoke, the scene is brilliant indeed as a night picture, mirrored in the clear surface of the beautiful bay.

We find ourselves asking, What is the real life of Italy to-day? The sceptre of Commerce has passed from her; Venice is no longer the abode of merchant princes; Genoa is but the shadow of what she once was. What causes a foreign population to circulate through its cities, constantly on the wing, scattering gold right and left among her needy population? It is the rich, unique possession which she enjoys in her monuments of art, her museums, her libraries, her glorious picture-galleries, public and private, but all of which are freely thrown open to the traveller, and to all comers. The liberality of her nobles and merchant princes in the days of her great prosperity has left her now a resource which nothing can rob her of. Where could money purchase such attractions as crowd the museum of Naples? The marble groups and statues, mostly originals, number more than a thousand, including the Dying Gladiator, the famous group of Ganymede and the Eagle, and that of Bacchus and the Laocoön. Here also we have Psyche, Venus Callipyge, — this last dug up from Nero's golden home at Rome, — and hundreds of others of worldwide fame, and of which we have so many fine copies in America. Rome lies but a hundred and sixty miles north of Naples, and the " Eternal City " has largely contributed to the art treasures of the institution of which we are now speaking, and which secures to the city a floating population annually of several thousands.

One of the greatest attractions of Naples is the partially exhumed city of Pompeii, three leagues more or less away. The drive thither skirts the Mediterranean shore, with its beautiful villas, private residences, convents, and churches, while the destructive mountain is always close at hand. The place in its present aspect is simply that of the remains of an entire city, destroyed and buried by volcanic action nearly two thousand years ago. The movable objects found here from time to time, as the slow work of

A STREET IN POMPEII.

Page 188.

excavation has progressed, have been removed to the museum at Naples. Quite enough, however, is left upon the spot to form tangible history, and to help the antiquarian to read the story of Pompeii, which was a populous city four or five centuries before the coming of Christ, and which lay entirely buried for some seventeen hundred years. It is about a century since the first effort was made towards uncovering the dwelling-houses, streets, and public edifices, but the progress which has been made clearly proves that the inhabitants were suffocated by a shower of hot ashes, and not destroyed by a sudden avalanche of lava and stones. The dwelling of Diomedes, who was the Crœsus of Pompeii, was the first house disentombed. Its owner was found with a key in one hand and a bag of gold in the other. Behind him was a slave with his arms full of silver vessels, evidently trying to escape from the coming devastation when they were suddenly overwhelmed, and must have been instantly suffocated.

In the house of Diomedes, glass windows, six or eight inches square, are found; showing that this article is not of such modern invention as had previously been supposed. The luxurious public baths are yet perfect; while the house where Cicero lived and wrote his speeches, besides a hundred other well-preserved historic objects, are pointed out by the guides. We are shown the Temple of Hercules, the theatres, the open courts, etc. The excavated portion represents about one-third of the whole city; but enough is clearly discovered to show that between thirty-five and forty thousand people here made their homes, and that the place contained all the fine public monuments and resorts that indicate a refined and luxurious community.

An excursion of ten miles along the coast to the eastward

will take us to Baiæ, where the luxurious Romans were wont to resort for their summer seasons. Here are still to be seen the remains of the villas where once dwelt Julius Cæsar, Pompey, Marius, and such other notables as they would naturally draw about them. The eyes can be turned in no direction without our being charmed by a view of exceptional beauty, to say nothing of the unequalled historic interest that attaches to every square mile of territory and to the broad bay close at hand. Horace declared it to be the loveliest spot on earth, and Seneca warned every one who desired to maintain dominion over himself to avoid this fascinating watering-place. It is here that Virgil laid many of his poetic scenes.

A day's journey by railway takes us to Rome, the "Eternal City," which is built on both sides of the Tiber, three or four leagues from its influx to the Mediterranean. We know that this city must at one time have been nearly as populous as London is to-day, but the present number cannot much exceed four hundred thousand. The ruins of Rome — for it is a city of ruins, notwithstanding its many fine modern structures — can give but a faint idea of what the great capital was in the days of its glory. At the zenith of her fame the city was filled with grand squares, temples, amphitheatres, circuses, baths, and public and private palaces, scarcely more than the ruins of which now remain — eloquent, however, in their grim silence. In the days of the Cæsars, fourteen grand aqueducts, supported by immense arches, hundreds of which still remain, conducted whole rivers into Rome from a distance of many leagues, supplying one hundred and fifty public fountains, with over a hundred public baths. In those marvellous days, over a hundred thousand marble and bronze statues ornamented the public squares, streets, and fountains, together with ninety colossal statues on lofty pedestals, and over forty Egyptian obelisks were in place. What an enumeration! Yet it falls far short of the facts as illustrated in the text of history and proven by the tangible evidence of numberless ruins.

The Piazza del Popolo is a famous square in Roman history, in the centre of which is one of those curious obelisks transported from Egypt eighteen centuries ago, where it stood before the Temple of the Sun, at Heliopolis, thousands of years since. On one side of the square there are twin churches, far enough apart to permit the Corso, or Broadway of Rome, to enter the square between them. The Corso has an average width of fifty feet, and is a mile long. It is on this central street that the horse-races take place during the Carnival; and it is here that the finest shops, cafés, and palaces are to be found.

The Piazza di Spagna is another interesting square, about a quarter of a mile from that just described. It covers five or six acres of land, and has a curious old fountain in its centre. From one side of the square a grand, broad flight of stone steps leads up to the elevated ground where stands the church of Trinita de Monti. Lingering on and about these steps the artists' models are seen at all hours of the day, both sexes and all ages being represented among them. Old men of seventy years, with noble heads and flowing snowy beards, bent forms and tattered garments, sit patiently awaiting a demand upon them. Perhaps they could afford better clothing; but they have an eye for artistic effect, and a true sense of the fitness of things. The children, waiting here for the same purpose, captivate our attention by their large black eyes and gypsy complexions. How graceful and kitten-like they are, in their lazy, lolling motions! The young girls are such as are not seen out of Italy, with large, beautifully expressive eyes, gypsy complexions touched with the rose color of health, and forms which would establish a sculptor's reputation could he reproduce them. All of these persons are here for a legitimate purpose; that is, to sit as models, for a given sum per hour, and to this object they honestly adhere.

The favorite promenade of the Romans of to-day is the Pincio ("the hill of gardens"), situated near and overlooking the Piazza del Popolo. It probably derives its name from the Pincii family, whose estate it belonged to in the period of the Empire. Hereabouts, of old, were the celebrated gardens of Lucullus; and here Messalina, wife of Claudius, indulged in revelries. Two afternoons of each week, as well as on all holidays, the king's military band gives a public concert in the Pincio gardens. The walks are kept in scrupulous neatness and order, shaded by groups of trees, and adorned by beautiful beds of flowers. At prominent points, fine marble statues of ancient Romans are conspicuously placed. The paths and drives about these gardens present a gay picture at the closing hours of each day, being the assembling-point of the social life of modern Rome.

The Vatican, which is the Pope's palace, is one of the first and most remarkable attractions for the traveller. We say the palace, but it is actually a succession of palaces. This elegant stone structure, close to the Cathedral of St. Peter's, is three stories in height, and contains a vast number of saloons, galleries, chapels, and corridors, embracing a comprehensive library and a re-

THE COLISEUM AT ROME.

markable museum, the whole surrounded by spacious and elegantly kept gardens. Twenty courts, eight grand staircases, and two hundred ordinary ones, are all contained within its walls. It is connected by a covered gallery with the castle of St. Angelo, a quarter of a mile away, and with St. Peter's, which it nearly adjoins. Probably no other building, or series of buildings, in the world contains so much wealth of art and riches generally as does the Vatican at Rome. Its treasures in gold, silver, precious stones, books, priceless manuscripts, and relics, are almost beyond enumeration. All the world — ancient and modern, savage and Christian — has contributed to swell this remarkable accumulation. The two most celebrated paintings, and esteemed to be the two most valuable in existence, are to be seen here; namely, "The Transfiguration," by Raphael, and "The Communion of St. Jerome," by Domenichino. So incomparable are these works of art that no critic of note has ventured to say which deserves to be named first; but all agree that they are the two greatest paintings, as to real merit, in the world. They are colossal in size, and have both made the journey to Paris. Napoleon I. had them both transferred to the Louvre; but they are back again, forming the great attraction of the Vatican. The "Last Judgment," by Michael Angelo, covers one whole side of the Sistine Chapel, one of the very best of this great master's works, requiring hours of study to enable one to form a just conception of its design and merits. Raphael has a series of fifty other paintings within the walls of the Pope's palace.

The most notable ruin in this ancient city is the Coliseum, the largest amphitheatre, and still one of the most imposing structures, in the world; broken in every part, but still showing, by what remains of its massive walls, what it must once have been. History tells us, that, upon its completion, it was inaugurated by gladiatorial combats continued for one hundred days; during which time five thousand wild beasts were killed in contests with Christian slaves, who acted as gladiators. The Coliseum was begun by Vespasian, on his return from his war with the Jews, but was dedicated by his son Titus, and completed by Domitian over eighteen hundred years ago. Ten thousand captives are said to have been slain at the time of its dedication, and it was designed to accommodate one hundred thousand spectators. The present circumference of the structure is about one-third of a mile. From the arena rise the tiers of seats, one above another, indicated by partially preserved steps and passage-ways. In its prime it was doubtless elegantly ornamented; and some evidences of fine art still remain upon the crumbling and lofty walls. The material is a kind of freestone. The style of architecture embraces four orders, imposed one upon another: the lower one is Tuscan or Doric; the second, Roman-Ionic; and the third and fourth, Corinthian or Composite.

The Pantheon is the only entirely preserved edifice of Greek architecture in Rome. This grand and marvellous structure was originally dedicated to the Pagan gods, but is now a Christian church. It is the largest building of ancient times, and whose splendid Corinthian columns fill the eye with pleasure at the first glance. The diameter of the structure is one hundred and fifty feet, and the summit of the upper cornice over one hundred feet from the base, the entire height being one hundred and fifty feet. The interior effect is one of true majesty, and that of the combined whole is deemed the acme of architectural perfection of the ancient buildings of Rome. The plates of gilded bronze which once covered the roof, the bronze ornaments of the pediment, and the silver that adorned the interior of the dome, it is said, were carried off by Constans II. more than a thousand years ago.

St. Peter's is considered to be the most magnificent church of Italian or classical architecture in the world. Its extreme length within the walls is a trifle over six hundred feet, while its greatest width is about four hundred and fifty feet. The height, from the pavement to the cross at the apex, is four hundred and fifty-eight feet. By comparing these dimensions with familiar objects, we can gain some general idea of the immensity of this structure, the largest ever reared by Christians in honor of the Supreme Being; but only by frequent and long-continued visits do we finally come fully to realize its unequalled beauty and grandeur.

As Florence only dates from three or four hundred years before Christ, it is not considered very ancient in the Old World. It sprang, undoubtedly, from Fiesole, at the foot of which it now lies. The Fiesole of the ancients was perched upon an almost inaccessible height, in accordance with the style in which they used to build in those days of constant warfare; but as civilization advanced, the city of Florence began to grow up on the banks of the Arno and to cover the valley at the base of the paternal settlement, until, to-day, it has a population of about a hundred and fifty thousand. It did not assume any importance until the time of Charlemagne, from which period it grew rapidly in numbers and in prosperity of trade, its early and long-continued specialty being the manufacture of Etruscan jewelry and mosaics; the latter business, especially, having descended from father to son until it has reached the present time. One may now purchase in the Florentine shops the finest specimens of the art to be found in all Europe.

The square of St. Croce receives its name from the remarkable church of Santa Croce which is located here, and which is the Italian Pantheon or Westminster Abbey, where rest the ashes of Alfieri, Machiavelli, Galileo, and a score of equally historic names. What a galaxy of great poets, artists, statesmen, and philosophers are here sleeping in their winding-sheets. Another fine square is that of the Piazza della Annunziata, in which is situated the church of the same name, a foundling hospital, and an equestrian statue of Ferdinand I. by John of Bologna. The Piazza della Signoria is the busiest place in Florence, containing also some remarkable buildings, as well as statues, fountains, and colonnades. The fine tower of one of the Boston city churches is copied from the lofty campanile, or bell-tower, of the Vecchio Palace, now occupied as the city hall, and which forms the most striking object in this interesting centre.

The hills which overlook Florence are indeed classic ground. Here Catiline conspired, and Milton wrote; here Michael Angelo occupied his studio, and Galileo conducted his discoveries, while here, also, Boccaccio wrote his famous love tales. These hillsides are dotted with beautiful villas, mostly owned by foreigners drawn hither in search of health, or the study of art. No other city in the world, not excepting Rome, affords such extended facilities for the latter purpose. Those great depositories of art, the Uffizi Gallery and the Pitti Palace, are perhaps unequalled, having within their walls over a thousand paintings, each one of which is meritorious, and many of which are hardly surpassed, if they are equalled. Raphael, Murillo, Titian, Michael Angelo, Paul Veronese, Velasquez, and like masters of art are here fully represented. To stand before canvas which the world has crowned with undivided approval, to realize that the finest copies which we have seen are but faint shadows of the originals, is a privilege which makes us forget all petty annoyances, all cost of time and money in the accomplishment. One pauses with more than ordinary curiosity before the Madonna della Seggiola, one of the most famous pictures of Raphael, and indeed of all art. We fancy that we have seen it faithfully reproduced, but a glance at the original convinces us that, like the Beatrice Cenci, it cannot be copied, but only imitated.

The Uffizi and Pitti Palaces are connected, and really form but one great gallery of art. In the Uffizi division is what is known as the Tribune,—the throne room of art, where stands "the statue that enchants the world,"— the Venus de Medici,—dividing its homage with that equally exquisite painting, Titian's recumbent Venus, declared to be the masterpiece of color. These two works are surrounded by others almost as perfect, and which in the eyes of trained artists share their loyalty. No wonder the student of art selects Florence as a place of residence, where he can visit as often as he pleases such models, without cost, works which cannot fail to inspire artistic genius in whomsoever the germs exist. But not alone those who wield the pencil and the chisel come hither to seek a congenial home. The soft beauty of the scenery, the delightful climate, and the poetic associations have tempted artists and literary people in other lines to pitch their tents here abouts. Mario, the great tenor, once lived yonder; in that villa on the sloping hillside, Taglioni once made her home; Walter Savage Landor sheltered his gray hairs in this cottage home overlooking the valley of the Arno, and died here. This old church not far away is that of St. Miniato al Monte, nearly ten centuries in age, famous for its carved work and paintings.

The common people of Florence seem actuated by a universal spirit of industry; and as to beggars, we see none upon its streets — a fact worthy of note in Italy. The women fruit-dealers on the corners of the streets are busy with their needles, while awaiting customers; the flower-girls are equally industrious, sitting beside their fragrant wares; the girl who opens the gate for us and guides us to the tombs of Mrs. Browning and Theodore Parker, in the city burial grounds, knits steadily as she walks. The public park is called the Cascine, and lies along the banks of the Arno; in some respects it is more attractive than most of such resorts in Europe, being finely wooded, and consequently presenting shady drives, and quiet rural retreats for pedestrians. It is the favorite resort of all classes who have leisure in the after part of the day, and is enlivened three or four times each week by the presence of a military band, which discourses the choicest music to ears ever ready for this sort of entertainment: no people are more fond of music than the Italians.

The Arno, which divides the city into two unequal parts, is only a very small stream during half the year; but when the snow melts upon the mountains, or the rainy season sets in, it then becomes a broad, swift river, conveying a great volume of water. It is crossed by six bridges, not far apart, besides two suspension bridges at the extremities of the city. The Ponte Vecchio is nearest the Pitti and Uffizi galleries, and is covered by curious little shops. We must not fail to visit the house where Dante was born, and also the house of Michael Angelo. In this latter are shown many of the personal belongings of the great artist and master, and the room where he studied and painted, containing numerous articles of which he made daily use. The last representative of his family bequeathed the whole priceless treasure to the city of Florence.

There is a lovely and celebrated park situated back of the Palazzo Pitti which is open to the public, and known as the Boboli Gardens. The grounds are quite spacious, being over a mile in circumference, divided into shady walks invitingly retired, shaded by thrifty laurels and cypresses, being also ornamented with some fine marble statues, and many gracefully carved vases. Among the statues are four by Michael Angelo, upon which he is said to have been at work when he died.

CHAPTER XIII.

VENICE is a genuine surprise to the stranger. No matter what idea he may have formed concerning it, he can hardly have approximated to the truth. It is unique, mystical, poetic, constantly appealing in some new form to the imagination, and often more than fulfilling expectation. The people, institutions, buildings, history — all are peculiar. Her statesmen, artisans, merchants, and sailors have been the first in Europe, while for over twelve hundred years she has gone on creating a history as remarkable as is her physical formation. No city fills a more prominent page in the records of the Middle Ages, or is more enshrined in romance and poetry. It is a city of a hundred thousand inhabitants, and yet what comparative stillness reigns over all, solemn and strange especially to the newly arrived traveller. There is no rattling of wheels, no tramp of horses' feet upon the streets; wheels and horses are unknown; only the gondola serves as a mode of conveyance, and the noiseless canals take the place of streets. The gondola is nowhere else seen save on these canals and lagoons (shallow bays). It is of all modes of transportation the most luxurious. The soft cushions, the gliding motion, the graceful oarsmen, who row in a standing position, the marble palaces between which we float in a dreamy state, harmonize so admirably, that the sense of completeness is perfect. The Grand Canal, two hundred feet wide, is the Broadway, or popular boulevard, of Venice, and over this glide the innumerable gondolas and boats of light traffic, with a quiet panoramic effect, which we watch curiously from our overhanging balcony. This main artery of the city is lined with palaces and noble marble edifices nearly the whole of its length of two miles. Some of these, to be sure, are crumbling and deserted, with the word decay written in their aspect, but even in their moss-grown and neglected condition they are intensely interesting.

The city is built upon one hundred and seventeen islands, separated by a hundred and fifty canals, and as the local guides will tell us, has three hundred and sixty-five bridges, mostly of stone,—"that is; one for every day in the year;" but there are, in fact, twenty more bridges to add to this aggregate. Most of the dwellings rise immediately out of the water, and one passes out of the gondolas on to marble steps to enter them. Altogether Venice is a little over seven miles in circumference.

As we sit floating in our gondola just off the Piazzetta of St. Mark, the moon comes up above the waters of the Adriatic and hangs serenely over the lagoons. No pen can justly describe such a sight — only a Claude Lorraine could paint it. Glancing gondolas on their noiseless track cut the silvery ripples; a sweet contralto voice, with guitar accompaniment, salutes the ear; stately palaces cast long, mysterious shadows upon the water; the Bridge of Sighs arches the canal between the palace and prison close at hand; oddly-rigged craft from the far East float lazily at anchor in the open harbor; the domes of lofty churches are outlined against the dark blue sky; while the proud columns of St. Mark and St. Theodore stand like sentinels at the water's edge. It seems, altogether, like some well-prepared theatrical scene upon the stage, on which the curtain will presently fall, shutting out everything from view.

The broad outline of the history of this long-lived republic is familiar to most of us. Many of its details have been enshrined by Byron, who, without assuming the dignity of historical record, has taught us in poetic form. The names of Dandolo, Faliero, and the two Foscari are familiar to all cultured people. The close of the fifteenth century may be designated as the culminating point of the glory of Venice, it being then the grand focus of European commerce, and twice as populous as it is to-day. At that time it possessed three hundred sea-going vessels and forty-five naval galleys, with which it maintained sway over the Mediterranean Sea. With the commencement of the sixteenth century her glory began gradually to fade until she ceased to maintain a prominent position among the powers. In art, Venice always occupied a first position, and was celebrated for the brilliancy of the coloring which characterizes the Venetian school.

Though fallen in commercial glory, Venice still stands without a rival. Where else can be found a city composed of over seventy islands? Is there another city where architects, sculptors, painters, and workers in mosaic devoted their lives to the purpose of decorating and beautifying their native place? No capital, even in Italy, is richer in splendid and antique churches, in superbly decorated palaces, and with the exception of Rome and Florence, no city has more invaluable art treasures. Here the works of Guido, Paul Veronese, Titian, Bonifacio, Giordano, and Tintoretto especially abound. The Venetian school of painting maintains precedence even in our day. In the Doge's Palace, built many hundred years ago, the visitor

SCENE ON THE GRAND CANAL, VENICE.

will find paintings and sculpture which he can never forget, and among them Tintoretto's Paradise, said to be the largest oil painting extant by a great master. It contains an army of figures, and would seem to have required a lifetime to produce.

The Piazza of St. Mark is the centre of attraction. How strange, and yet how familiar everything seems to us here! We require no guide to point out the remarkable monuments. We do not fail to recognize at a glance the tall masts from which the banners of the republic floated in triumph, when the carrier pigeons brought news that "blind old Dandolo had captured Constantinople!" We recognize the lofty Campanile, the sumptuous palace of the Doges, and the gorgeous front of the Cathedral over-topped by its graceful domes, bristling with innumerable pinnacles. Above the portals of St. Mark we gaze upon the celebrated bronze horses which Napoleon I. stole and transported to Paris, but which the Emperor Francis restored to Venice. It is not the first time these historic horses of Lysippus have been stolen, these monuments of the departed glory of Chios and Constantinople — of Venice and Napoleon.

In many respects the Cathedral of San Marco is the most remarkable church in existence, while its ornamentation is rich to excess. For good architectural effect it stands too low, the present grade of the surrounding square being some fifteen inches or more above its mosaic pavement. The pillars and ornaments are too crowded; having been brought hither from other and historic lands, there is a want of harmony in the aggregation. Nearly a thousand years old, it has an indescribable aspect of faded and tarnished splendor, and yet it presents an attractive whole quite unequalled. It combines Saracenic profusion with

Christian emblems, weaving in porphyries from Egypt, pillars from St. Sophia, altar pieces from Acre, and a forest of Grecian columns. Especially is this church rich in mosaics — those colors that never fade. There is a sense of solemn gloom pervading the place, the dim light struggling through the painted windows being only sufficient to give the whole a weird aspect, in its over-decorated aisles. Some idea may be formed of the elaborate ornamentation of the Cathedral from the fact that it contains over forty thousand square feet of mosaic work! The vaulting consists entirely of mosaic, representing scenes in the Old Testament, beginning with the story of the creation, and followed by scenes from the New Testament. As we walk about the church, the floor beneath our feet is found quite uneven from the slow settlement of ages. Inside and out the structure is ornamented by over five hundred columns of marble, the capitals of which present a fantastic variety of styles true to no country or order, but the whole is, nevertheless, a grand example of barbaric splendor.

Just opposite the entrance to the Church of San Marco stands the lofty Campanile, reaching to a height of three hundred feet, and which was over two hundred years in building. A view from its summit is one of the sights not to be missed in this city, as it affords not only a splendid picture of Venice itself, but the city and lagoons lie mapped out before the eye in perfection of detail, while in the distance are seen the Adriatic, the Alpine ranges, and the Istrian Mountains. The Campanile is ascended by a winding way in place of steps, and there is a legend that Napoleon rode his horse to the top, a feat which is certainly possible. In this lofty tower Galileo prosecuted his scientific experiments.

Petrarch wrote that Venice was the home of justice and equity, refuge of the good; rich in gold, but richer in renown; built on marble, but founded on the surer foundation of a city worthy of veneration and glory. But this is no longer the Venice he described; no longer the city of grasping and successful ambition, of proud and boastful princes. It has become what pride, ostentation, and luxury in time must always lead to. It presents to-day a fallen aspect — one of grandeur in rags. No argosies are bound to foreign ports, no princely merchants meet on the Rialto; that famous bridge is now occupied on either side by Jews' shops of a very humble character; and yet do not let us seem to detract from the great interest that overlies all drawbacks as regards the Venice even of the present hour.

The Academy of Fine Arts is reached by crossing the Grand Canal, over the modern iron bridge, which, with that of the Rialto, a noble span of a single arch, built of white marble, forms the only means of crossing the great water-way, except by gondola. This remarkable gallery contains almost exclusively works by Venetian artists. Here we find a remarkable representation of the "Supper of Cana," which is nearly as large as the "Paradise." It is considered by competent critics, to be one of the finest pieces of coloring in existence. Here we have some of Titian's best productions, and those of many Italian artists whose pictures are not to be found elsewhere. The gallery, like all of the famous ones of Europe, is free to every one, either for simple study, or for copying. This is the collection which Napoleon I. said he would give a nation's ransom to possess. On the way to the Academy the guide points out the Barberigo Palace, in which Titian lived and died.

The Doge's Palace is full of historic interest. We wander with mingled feelings through its various apartments, visiting the halls of the Council of Ten, and the still more tragic chambers of the Council of Three. Many secret passages are threaded; we cross the Bridge of Sighs, and descend into the dungeons in which Faliero, Foscari, and other famous prisoners are said to have been incarcerated. These mediæval dungeons are wretched beyond belief, and how human beings could live and breathe in such places is the marvel of every one who visits them in our day. Here we are shown the apartment where the condemned prisoners were secretly strangled, and the arched windows by which their bodies were launched into boats on the canal, to be borne away, and sunk in the distant lagoons. Trial, sentence, fate,—all in secret, and this was done under the semblance of justice and a republican form of government.

The church of the Frari, whither we will next turn our steps, is in an American's estimation quite as much of a museum as a church. It is the Westminster Abbey of Venice, and is crowded with the monuments of doges, statesmen, artists, philosophers, and more especially is ornamented in a most striking manner by the tombs of Titian and Canova. These elaborate marble structures face each other from opposite sides of the church — monuments raised in memory of rarest genius, and which for richness of design and completeness of finish exceed anything of the sort in Italy.

In the square of St. Mark we have an opportunity for studying the masses, the well-to-do classes, but not the refined and cultured; these maintain a certain dignified exclusiveness. The uniforms of the police, each one of whom is bedizened equal to a militia general, are a standing caricature. One notes the many Jews among the throng; here a turbaned Turk sits before a café smoking his pipe, and near by a handsome Greek, with his red fez, smokes a cigar. There are Orientals of all types, with jaunty Englishmen, and gay parties of Americans.

We will now pass on to Milan, once considered the second city of Italy in importance, but it was totally destroyed in 1162 by Barbarossa, and we therefore see a comparatively modern capital. In the olden time it was filled with temples, baths, amphitheatres, circuses, and all the monuments common to great Italian cities. Seven hundred years and more have elapsed since its destruction, during which it rapidly sprang into life again as the capital of Lombardy, and is still a growing metropolis. True, it can offer no such attractions to the traveller as abound in Naples, Rome, and Florence, though there are some art treasures here which are unique. Were it not that the city is so near to Lakes Como and Maggiore, and in possession of half a hundred remarkable pictures, with a score of choice original pieces of sculpture, together with its wonderful cathedral, the traveller would hardly care to pass more than a day in Milan. The present population is about two hundred and forty thousand. It is thrifty and devoted more to successful branches of business than are the cities of Southern Italy.

The Milan Cathedral is regarded as one of the wonders of the world, being also next to the cathedral at Seville and St. Peter's at Rome, the largest church in Europe, though this matter of size is of insignificant consideration compared with its other marvels. The interior is nearly five hundred feet in length and but a fraction less than two hundred in width, while the dome is over two hundred feet in height. Its loftiest tower is over three hundred and sixty feet above the ground; there are a hundred pinnacles in all, and no less than four thousand five hundred marble statues ornament the exterior. The interior consists of a nave with double aisles, and is supported by fifty-two pillars, each fifteen feet in diameter, the summits of which are decked with canopied niches presenting statues in place of the customary capitals. The pavement is finished in marble and mosaic. The edifice was in course of construction for five hundred years, and to look at it one would hardly suppose there was white marble enough in Europe to furnish the raw material of which it is built. The principal part of the work has been performed during the last hundred years.

One mounts nearly five hundred stone steps to reach the summit of the cathedral, where we stand in the highest pinnacle, nearly four hundred feet from the street. Far below lies the city, the dwellings and churches resembling toy-houses, while the people moving about in the thoroughfares assume pigmy proportions, horses looking like exaggerated insects. We gaze about in dizzy wonder, and are half inclined to believe it all a trick of the imagination. After the first surprise is over, the true aspect gradually dawns upon the stranger, and the labor of ascending those tedious steps is forgotten. The distant view is particularly fine; the green and fertile plains of Lombardy stretching away from the city walls in all directions until they meet the foot-hills of the Alpine range, or mingle with the horizon towards the shores of the Adriatic. Mont Blanc, Mont Cenis, Mont St. Bernard, the Simplon Pass, the Bernese Oberland range, and further to the northeast the long range of the Tyrolean Alps, are recognized with their white snow-caps glittering in the bright sunlight. The forest of pinnacles beneath our feet, mingled with a labyrinth of ornamented spires, statues, flying buttresses, and Gothic fretwork, piled all about the roof, is seen through a gauze-like veil of golden mist.

Milan has several other churches more or less interesting, but the visitor rarely passes much time in examining them. No traveller should fail, however, to visit the Brera Palace, the one gallery of art in this city. It was formerly a Jesuit college, but is now used for a public school, with the title of Palace of Arts and Sciences, forming a most extensive academy, containing paintings, statuary, and a comprehensive library of nearly two hundred thousand volumes. There is also attached a fine botanical garden, exhibiting many rare and beautiful exotics as well as native plants. In the gallery of paintings the visitor is sure to single out for appreciation a canvas, by Guercino, representing Abraham banishing Hagar and her child. The tearful face of the deserted one, with its wonderful expression, tells the whole story of her misery. This picture is worthy of all the enthusiastic praise so liberally bestowed by competent critics.

No picture is better known than Leonardo da Vinci's "Last Supper," millions of copies of which have been circulated in engravings, oil paintings, and by photography. We find the original in the Dominican monastery, where the artist painted it upon the bare wall or masonry of a lofty dining-hall. It is still perfect and distinct, though not so bright as it would have been had it been executed upon canvas. Da Vinci was years in perfecting it, and justly considered it to be the best work of his artistic life. The moment chosen for delineation is that when Christ utters the words, "One of you shall betray me!" The artist said that he meditated for two years how best to portray upon a human face the workings of the perfidious heart of Judas, and ended at last by taking for his model the prior of this very monastery, who was well known to be his bitterest enemy! The likeness at the period of its production was unmistakable, and thus perpetuated the scandal.

We must not fail to make an excursion from Milan to Pavia, one of the oldest of Italian cities. It lies on the left bank of the Ticino River, and was in the olden times the residence of the Lombard kings, who did not fail to beautify and improve it in their day to such an extent that it was known all over Europe as the "City of a Hundred Towers," many of which are extant and in excellent preservation. Though the finger of time has pressed heavily upon it, and its ancient glory has departed, still Pavia has a population of over thirty thousand, and lays claim to no inconsiderable importance. If it were not a little off the usual track of travellers, we should hear much more of its associations. The university founded here by Charlemagne, over a thousand years ago, is still prosperous; and the famous church of San Michael, erected at even an earlier period, is still an object of profound interest. As we wander about the quaint streets the impress of antiquity is upon everything that meets the eye. Just north of the city, about a league from the walls, is the Certosa, one of the most splendid monasteries in Europe, founded about five hundred years since. It is absolutely crowded with fine paintings, statuary, mosaics, and rich art ornamentation. Private palaces abound, though now largely diverted from their original purposes. There are also theatres, libraries, museums, gymnasiums, still thriving after a moderate fashion. Pavia looks backward to her past glories rather than forward to new hopes. Sacked by Hannibal, burned by the Huns, conquered and possessed by the Romans, won by the Goths and Lombards, it was long the capital of what was then known as the kingdom of Italy. Then came a period of fierce civil wars, when its history merged in that of the conquerors of Lombardy. Taken and lost by the French so late as 1796, it was stormed and pillaged by Napoleon, but once more came into the possession of Austria, until it finally found refuge in the bosom of United Italy. The famous battle of Pavia, which occurred in 1525, when Francis I. was taken prisoner, was fought close to the Certosa.

Our next objective point is Vienna, and we take the route through Innspruck, the capital of the Tyrol, which is most charmingly situated in the valley of the Inn just where it joins the Sill. The town is about two thousand feet above sea-level, and is surrounded by mountains six and eight thousand feet in height. It derives its name from the bridge which here crosses the river — Inn's Brücke (that is, the Inn's Bridge). We enter Austria through the Brenner Pass, and after a long Alpine journey of three or four hundred miles are very glad to pause here both for rest and observation. There must be about twenty thousand inhabitants, but the town seems almost solemnly silent. At certain periods of the year, known as "the season," doubtless its two or three large hotels are plentifully supplied with guests. Historical associations are not wanting; among them is the Franciscan church of Innspruck, containing the elaborate and costly monument to the Emperor Maximilian I., which, though constructed by order of the monarch himself, does not contain his remains. The structure consists of a marble sarcophagus supporting the emperor's effigy in bronze in a kneeling position, while on the other side of the aisle are rows of monumental bronze figures, twenty-eight in number, representing various historic characters. The mention of this unique group in the old church of Innspruck, by the poet Longfellow, will be remembered.

The Schloss Ambras is of considerable interest, having been the favorite home of the Archduke Ferdinand II. The view from its battlements is worthy of a pilgrimage to enjoy. Innspruck looks like a toy-village, so far below, upon the plain. The broad streets of the new portion of the town lie spread out as upon a map. The three handsome bridges give variety to the scene. The central one, as the guide will tell us, was the scene of a fierce battle, in 1809, between the Bavarians and the Tyrolese. The former could not withstand the superior marksmanship of these chamois-hunters, who picked off the men at the cannon as fast as they came into action, until the Bavarians fled in despair, abandoning their guns.

On resuming our journey towards Vienna, we pass up the constantly narrowing valley of the Inn, through a range of mountain scenery, covered with snow, and grand beyond description, where Alp is piled upon Alp, until all distinctive outline is lost in the clouds which envelop them. Now and then we see a rude but picturesque chamois huntsman struggling up the mountain side in search of the special game which is growing annually scarcer and scarcer. There is a wild interest which actuates the chamois-hunter, amounting to fanaticism. The country is very sparsely inhabited, but we occasionally come upon a cluster of picturesque habitations, quite theatrical in effect, the counterpart of the familiar pictures and photographs we see in America. By and by, after a long day of travel, we reach Salzburg, in the Noric Alps.

Salzburg was the birthplace of Mozart, and is still a musical place, that branch of the fine arts being universally cultivated among the more refined class of inhabitants. There are several public monuments commemorative of the great composer, who played his own compositions before the public here at the age of five years! The massive wall which once surrounded the place is now mostly dismantled, and could only have been of use in the Middle Ages, at which time Salzburg was probably in its greatest state of prosperity. The manufacture of Majolica ware has been a specialty here for a couple of centuries or more, and it has a reputation for the production of fine fancy leather goods. Its connection by rail with Vienna, Munich, and Innspruck insures it considerable trade, but still there is a sleepiness about the place which is almost contagious. It was probably different when the archbishops held court here, at a period when those high functionaries combined the dignity of princes of the Empire with their ecclesiastical rank. It was at this period that the town received its few public ornaments, and the half-dozen fine public edifices, still to be seen, were erected.

In the absence of statistics one would say there was a population of fifteen thousand. Some of the street scenes are peculiar. We see single cows and oxen harnessed and worked like horses, not in shafts, but beside a long pole. The entire absence of donkeys, so numerous elsewhere in

Europe, is quite noticeable. The women surprise us by their large size and apparent physical strength — quite a necessary possession, since they seem to perform the larger portion of the heavy work, while their lazy husbands are engaged in pipe-smoking and beer-drinking. We see girls and dogs harnessed together into milk and vegetable carts, which they draw through the streets at early morning, to deliver the required articles to the consumers. When the little team arrives before a customer's door, the girl drops her harness, measures out and delivers the milk or vegetables, while the dog waits patiently.

There is no special beauty observable among the female population. The dark eyes and hair with the lovely faces of the South are left behind, as well as the soft, musical cadence of voice which so charms the ear in Italy. German is not a musical tongue. It is a vigorous language, but not a harmonious one in speech. Doubtless there are pretty blonde Marguerites — like Goethe's heroine — hidden away somewhere among the domestic circles of Salzburg, but their long golden braids of hair and their fair, rose-tinted complexions are not often seen in public.

CHAPTER XIV.

UNDOUBTEDLY Vienna is the finest city on the European continent next to Paris, and it is often called the Northern Paris. It resembles the French capital both in its social life and its architecture. The style of the modern buildings is very attractive, displaying great richness and beauty of outline, while the charming perfection of detail is by no means neglected. At least one-quarter of Vienna is new, presenting broad streets lined with noble edifices. The Ring Strasse is a notable example of this, being an elegant avenue, which takes the place of the old city wall that once surrounded the town, but which it has long since outgrown. This metropolis now contains considerably over a million inhabitants. It is situated upon an arm of the Danube where it is joined by the two small streams known as the Wien and the Alster, from the former of which the city takes its name. Vienna is not lacking in antiquity. It was renowned in Roman times two thousand years ago, and there is an ancient aspect quite unmistakable about its western portion in the vicinity of the Emperor's palace. This imperial assemblage of buildings, with the broad court about which they stand, presents no claim whatever to architectural beauty, being exceedingly heavy and substantial.

One of the principal attractions of the city is its numerous parks, squares, and breathing-spots. Above all else in this regard is the Prater, situated on the verge of the city, forming one of the most extensive pleasure drives or parks connected with any European capital. It was in this park that the famous exhibition buildings were erected, covering twelve or fifteen acres of ground; but the Prater could afford room for fifty such structures. All the fashionable citizens, including the royal family, come here for the enjoyment of their afternoon drive or horseback ride. The sight presented on these occasions is one of the very gayest conceivable, recalling the brilliancy of the Chiaja of Naples, the Maiden of Calcutta, or the Champs Elysées of Paris. One does not see even in Hyde Park, London, more elegant vehicles and horses, or more striking liveries than on the Prater at Vienna. Equestrianism is the favorite mode of exercise here, both with ladies and gentlemen, and the Austrians are better horsemen and horsewomen than the English. Cavalry officers in uniform, as well as representatives of other arms of the service, add much to the brilliancy of this park during the popular hour. It is divided into a broad driveway, a well-kept equestrian track, and smooth walks devoted exclusively to pedestrians. For spaciousness as well as attractive gayety, the Prater is scarcely equalled — certainly not surpassed — by any other European driveway.

There are two noble palaces at Vienna which must not be forgotten; namely, the Upper and Lower Belvedere. They are intimately connected, though divided by a large and splendid garden, and together form an art collection and museum combined, only second to the Uffizi and Pitti palaces at Florence, and the galleries of Paris and Rome. A simple list of the pictures to be found here would cover many pages in print, embracing the names of such artists as Salvator Rosa, Giorgone, Bassano, Perugino, Carlo

Dolce, Guido Reni, Rembrandt, Andrea del Sarto, Van Dyck, etc. All of these paintings are high in artistic merit; many of them are admirable, and all are beyond price in money. Various schools are represented in the galleries, and there are among the rest a hundred or so of modern pictures; but the majority are by the old masters or their immediate pupils. The Flemish, Dutch, and Spanish schools are especially well represented. The visitor will find in the Lower Belvedere a marvellous collection of antiquities, perhaps the most curious to be seen in Europe. Among other departments of interest is one in which there are over a hundred warriors of life size clad in complete armor, most of whom are mounted on mail-clad horses, all confronting the visitor, with visor down and lance in rest. All of these effigies are designed to be likenesses, and each is labelled with the name of the warrior-king, emperor, or great general he represents, while we have before us the real armor and weapons which he bore in actual life. Here hangs the tattered banner which was carried through the Crusades, and returned by the hand of the Archduke Ferdinand, beside hundreds of similar tokens.

The Cathedral of St. Stephens, between five and six hundred years of age, is of very great interest, and forms a rare example of pure Gothic. The Imperial Library contains over three hundred thousand volumes. Vienna has all the usual Christian charitable institutions, schools, and progressive organizations of a great city of the nineteenth century.

From Vienna we continue our journey to Prague, the capital of Bohemia, a quaint old city, founded in 1722 by the Duchess Libussa, and which has to-day nearly sixty thousand inhabitants. It is crowded with historical monuments, ancient churches, and queer old chapels, some of which are ornamented by frescoes hardly rivalled by the finest at Rome and Florence. One is here shown underground dungeons as terrible as those of Venice, and to which historic associations lend their special interest. It would seem that human beings could hardly exist in such holes for a month, and yet in some of these, prisoners are known to have lingered miserably for years. Prague was remarkable for its institutions of learning and its scientific societies. The university, founded by Charles IV. in 1348, had at one time a hundred professors and three thousand students. This university enjoyed a world-wide reputation, but all this has passed away. There are two or three large libraries, a museum of natural history, a school for the blind, and several public hospitals. We find here some beautiful specimens of glass manufacture, for which Bohemia has long been celebrated, though she is now rivalled in this line by both England and America.

Prague has had more than its share of the calamities of war, having been besieged and taken six times before the year 1249. In the war of the Hussites it was taken, burned, plundered, and sacked with barbarous ferocity. The Thirty Years' War began and ended within its walls, and during its progress the city was three times in possession of the enemy. In 1620 the battle was fought just outside of the city in which Frederick V. was conquered, and after which he was deposed. During the Seven Years' War it fell into the hands of different victors, and in 1744 capitulated to Frederick the Great of Prussia. Indeed, until within the last half-century Prague and its environs may be said to have been little better than a constant battle-field. Seen from an elevated position the city presents

BRIDGE CROSSING THE MOLDAU.

To face p. 219.

a very picturesque aspect. A fine view may be had of it from either of the bridges which cross the Moldau, but a more satisfactory one is to be had from the Belvedere, a large public garden situated on an eminence just outside the city proper. This garden forms a beautiful park and is a favorite drive with the citizens. One of the bridges is called the Karlsbrücke (Charles Bridge); the other is the Suspension Bridge, also known as Emperor Francis's Bridge. At the end of the latter is the memorial which commemorates the five hundreth anniversary of the founding of the university. The niches on either side are filled with statues representing the several sciences, added to which are statues of two archbishops. The Charles Bridge, built of stone over five hundred years ago, is the most interesting of the two bridges, and has its two extremities protected by lofty towers. The arches of the bridge are ornamented with groups of saints numbering thirty life-size figures. It is not surprising that Prague appears in decay; but as it is a sort of half-way place between Dresden and Vienna, it is insured a certain amount of business from travellers of all nations.

One prominent feature of Dresden, the capital of Saxony, which strikes the stranger, is that the military appear in such large numbers everywhere, in the streets, the hotels, in the shops and parks. The expense and waste of supporting such large numbers of soldiers is enormous. The student of art, music, and history finds a rich field for educational purposes here, where there are so many choice collections of antiquities, museums, and remarkable paintings. The Zwinger Museum contains among other treasures a collection of three hundred and sixty thousand engraved plates, all of great value. Art treasures and libraries are freely open to the public, as in all parts of Europe. Dresden is a busy city, commanding a large trade, and containing over a quarter of a million inhabitants. Gold and silver manufactures form a large share of the industry; artificial flowers, china ware, and paper hangings also, constitute a large portion of its extensive exports. The Royal Public Library contains four hundred thousand volumes, and is particularly rich in the several departments of literature, history, and classical antiquity. There are many volumes in this Dresden library which are not to be found elsewhere in Europe, and learned men come thousands of miles to consult them.

The Green Vaults, so called from the style of the original decorations, are a portion of the Royal Palace, and contain an extraordinarily valuable collection, belonging to the State, consisting of works of art, jewels, royal regalia, etc., classified in eight connected saloons. One sees here a certain green stone, a most brilliant gem, esteemed of great value. Whether it be really a diamond or an emerald, it is intrinsically of equal worth. The weight of this rare gem is forty carets. The Grosse Garten is the favorite public park of the city, containing about three hundred acres of land. It is very beautifully laid out in ornamental sections, drives, walks, and groves. The historical associations about this park are interesting, it being the spot where the French and Prussians more than once encountered each other in battle, the last time in 1813.

The most attractive portion of this really fine city is the Theatre Platz, about which lie the principal objects of interest to the traveller. Here are situated the Royal Palace, the Zwinger with its choice collections, and the theatre. The old bridge over the Elbe is a substantial stone structure. The palace forms a large square of spacious edifices surmounted by a tower nearly four hundred feet high. The principal picture-gallery of Dresden is the finest in Germany, and contains between three and four thousand admirable examples of high art, — the work of such artists as Raphael, Holbein, Corregio, Albert Dürer, Rubens, Giotto, Van Dyck, and other masters already named in these pages. Among them all the favorite, as generally conceded, is Raphael's Madonna di San Sisto, believed to be one of the last and best examples produced by this great master. We are sure to find a goodly number of Americans residing in this European capital, gathered here for educational purposes in art, literature, and music.

Berlin, the capital of Prussia, contains about a million inhabitants, and is one of the finest cities of Europe. The principal street is the Unter den Linden, and most of the objects of interest centre here between the Royal Palace and the Brandenburg Gate. This thoroughfare is planted in its centre with four rows of trees, having a capacious pedestrian section, an equestrian road, and two driveways, one on each side of the broad street. It resembles Commonwealth Avenue, Boston, both in size and design, though the architecture of the American street is far superior to the German. The Unter den Linden is a hundred and ninety-six feet wide, and receives its name from the double avenue of linden trees extending through the centre. The street is flanked with fine buildings, a few hotels, three palaces, a museum, a school of art, public library, etc. At one end is the famous bronze statue of Frederick the Great. The Brandenburg Gate, where the Linden commences, forms the entrance to the city from the Thiergarten, and is a sort of triumphal arch, erected in 1789. It is seventy feet in height, and two hundred in width, being modelled after the entrance in the gateway of the temple of the Parthenon at Athens. It affords five passage-ways through its great width.

This proud capital, six hundred years ago, was only of small importance, since when it has grown to its present mammoth proportions. Frederick William made it his home and started its most important structures. Frederick I. added to it, and so it has been improved by one ruler after another until it has become one of the most important political and commercial centres in Europe. It is divided by the river Spree, which at this point is about two hundred feet in width, and communicates with the Oder and the Baltic by canal. No continental city except Vienna has grown so rapidly during the last half-century. The late emperor did little or nothing to beautify the capital, whose growth has been mostly of a normal character, greatly retarded by a devotion to military purposes.

The Unter den Linden is the charm of Berlin, so bright, shaded, and retired, as it were, in the very midst of outer noise and bustle. At nearly all hours of the day the long lines of benches are crowded by laughing, flaxen-haired children, attended by gayly dressed nurses, the groups they form contrasting with the rude struggle of business life going on so close at hand. A regiment of soldiers is passing as we gaze upon the scene, accompanied by a full band, their helmets and bright arms glittering in the sunlight; the vehicles rattle past on both sides of the mall; here and there is seen an open official carriage with liveried servants and outriders; well-mounted army officers pass at a hand-gallop on the equestrian division of the street, saluting right and left; dogs and women harnessed together to small carts wind in and out among the throng, while girls and boys with huge baskets strapped to their backs, containing merchandise, mingle in the scene.

The Thiergarten is the grand park of Berlin, situated along the banks of the Spree; it is two miles long by a mile in width, with an abundance of noble trees, well-kept drives, and clear, picturesque lakes. The ponds and canals intersecting this park afford a choice resort for the lovers of skating in winter. In the southwest corner of the Thiergarten is the famous zoölogical garden of Berlin, established nearly fifty years since.

The Royal Palace is an imposing structure six hundred and forty feet long by about half that width, and is over a hundred feet in height. It was originally a fortress, but has been altered by successive monarchs until it is now a very perfect royal residence, containing six hundred rooms and state departments.

We still pursue our course northward, bearing a little to the west, until we reach Hamburg, which contains some three hundred thousand inhabitants, and is one of the most important commercial cities on the continent. It is not only situated on a navigable river, the Elbe, — seventy miles from its mouth, — but is connected by railway with every part of Europe. Hamburg was founded by Charlemagne a thousand years ago, the older portions being dark and dirty; but the modern section of the city is very fine in the size of its streets and its architectural aspect. Its commercial connections with America exceed that of any other northern port, and form its main features of business importance. Vessels drawing eighteen feet of water can ascend the Elbe to the wharves at high tide.

The city is intersected by canals and branches of the Alster River, and was once surrounded by a series of ramparts, but these have been converted into attractive, tree-planted promenades. The public library of Hamburg contains over two hundred thousand volumes, and there is no lack in the city of hospitals, schools, colleges, churches, charitable institutions, museums, and theatres. The botanical gardens and the zoölogical exhibition are remarkable for excellence and completeness. It would be difficult to conceive of a more attractive sight than that afforded by the broad sheet of water in the centre of the town known as the Alster Basin, a mile in circumference, bounded on three sides by streets ornamented liberally with trees, while its surface is dotted with little omnibus steamers and pleasure boats darting hither and thither like swallows on the wing. Snow-white swans, tame and graceful, are constantly seen floating over the surface of this attractive city-lake. The environs of Hamburg are rendered very charming by pleasant villas and numberless flower-gardens, with an abundance of ornamental trees.

Our journey northward continues by railway and steamboat *via* Kiel, crossing an arm of the Baltic to Copenhagen, the capital of Denmark, situated on the island of Zeeland. This city, which now contains a population of about two hundred and fifty thousand, was a large commercial port centuries ago, and has several times been partially destroyed by war and conflagration. The houses are mostly of brick, some of the better class being built of Norwegian granite, while the newer portion of the town presents many examples of fine modern architecture. The streets are of good width, laid out with an eye to regularity, besides which there are sixteen public squares.

Taken as a whole, the first impression of the place and its surroundings is remarkably pleasing and attractive. As one approaches the city the scene is enlivened by the many windmills in the environs, whose wide-spread arms are generally in motion, appearing like the broad wings of enormous birds hovering over the land. Perhaps the earliest association in its modern history which the stranger is likely to remember as he looks about him in Copenhagen, is that of the dastardly attack upon the city, and the shelling of it for three consecutive days, by the British fleet in 1807, during which reckless onslaught an immense destruction of human life and property was inflicted upon the place. Over three hundred important buildings were laid in ashes on that occasion, because Denmark refused permission for the domiciling of English troops upon her soil, or to withdraw from her connection with the neutral powers in the Napoleonic wars.

As in the Mediterranean, so in the Baltic, tidal influence is felt only to a small degree, the difference in the rise and fall of the water at this point being scarcely more than one foot. Owing to the comparatively fresh character of this sea its ports are ice-bound for a third of each year, and in the extreme seasons the whole expanse is frozen across from the coast of Denmark to that of Sweden. In 1658 Charles X. of the latter country marched his army across the Belts, dictating to the Danes a treaty of peace; and so late as 1809 a Russian army passed from Finland to Sweden, across the Gulf of Bothnia.

The territory of Denmark upon the mainland is quite limited, consisting of Jutland only; but she has a number of islands far and near, Zeeland being the most populous, and containing, as we have shown, the capital. As a state she may be said to occupy a much larger space in history than upon the map of Europe. The surface of the island of Zeeland is uniformly low, in this resembling Holland, the highest point reaching an elevation of about two hundred and fifty feet. To be precise in the matter of her dominions, the colonial possessions of Denmark may be thus enumerated: Greenland, Iceland, the Faroe group of islands, between the Shetlands and Iceland; adding St. Croix, St. Thomas, and St. John in the West Indies. Greenland is nearly as large as Germany and France combined; but owing to its ice-clothed character in most parts, its inhabitants do not quite reach an aggregate of ten thousand. Iceland is nearly the size of our New England States, and has a population of seventy-five thousand. The Faroes contain ten thousand inhabitants, and the three West Indian islands united have a population of a little over forty thousand.

In the year 1880 the Danish monarchy reached the thousandth anniversary of its foundation under Gorm the Old, whose reign bridges over the interval between mere legend and the dawn of recorded history. Gorm is supposed to have been a direct descendant of the famous Regnar Lodbrog, who was a daring and imperious ruler of the early Northmen. The common origin of the three Baltic nationalities which constitute Scandinavia is clearly apparent to the traveller who has visited Denmark, Sweden, and Norway. The race has been steadily modified, generation after generation, in its more important characteristics by the progressive force of civilization. These Northmen are no longer the haughty and reckless warriors who revelled in wine drunk from the skulls of their enemies, and who deemed death respectable only when encountered upon the battle-field. Clearer intelligence and culture have substituted the duties of peaceful citizens for the occupation of marauders, and the enterprises of civilized life for the exaggerated romance of sea-rovers. Reading and writing, which were once looked upon by them as allied to the black art, are now the accomplishment of nearly all classes, and nowhere on the globe do we find people more cheerful, intelligent, frank, and hospitable than in the three kingdoms of the far North.

The Denmark of to-day, typified by Copenhagen, its capital, is a great centre of science and art. The spirit of Thorwaldsen, the contemporary and brother-sculptor of Canova, permeates everything, and in making his native city his heir, he also bequeathed to her an appreciation of art which her eminent scientists have ably supplemented in their several departments of knowledge. The Thorwaldsen Museum contains over forty apartments, ample space being afforded for the best display of each figure and each group designed by the great master. The ceilings are elaborately and very beautifully decorated with emblematical designs by the best Danish artists. This enduring monument is also Thorwaldsen's appropriate mausoleum, being fashioned externally after an Etruscan tomb. It contains only this master's own works, and a few pictures which he brought with him from Rome. He revelled in the representation of tenderness, of youth, beauty, and childhood. Nothing of the repulsive or terrible ever came from his hand. The sculptor's fancy found expression most fully, perhaps, in the works which are gathered here, illustrating the delightful legends of the Greek mythology. No one can be surprised at the universal homage accorded to his memory by his countrymen.

The Ethnological Museum of the city, better known as the Museum of Northern Antiquities, is considered to be the most remarkable institution of the sort in Europe. Students in this department of science come from all parts of the civilized world to seek knowledge from its countless treasures. One is here enabled to follow the progress of our race from its primitive stages to its highest civilization. The national government liberally aids all purposes akin to science and art; consequently this museum is a favored object of the state. Each of the three distinctive periods of stone, bronze, and iron forms an elaborate division in the spacious halls of the institution.

This government was the first in Europe to furnish the means of education to the people at large on a liberal scale; to establish schoolhouses in every parish, and to provide suitable dwellings and income for the teachers. The incipient steps towards this object began as far back as the time of Christian II., more than three centuries ago, while many of the European states were clouded in ignorance. Copenhagen has two public libraries: the Royal, containing over six hundred thousand books; and the University, which has between two hundred and fifty and three hundred thousand volumes.

Though Denmark is a small kingdom containing scarcely three million people, yet it has produced many eminent men of science, art, and literature. The names of Hans Christian Andersen, Rasmus Rask, the philologist, Oersted, the discoverer of electro-magnetism, Forchhammer, the chemist, and Eschricht, the physiologist, occur to us in this connection. It is a country of legend and romance, of historic and prehistoric monuments, besides being the very fatherland of fairy tales. The Vikings of old have left their footprints all over the country in mounds. It is not therefore surprising that the cultured portion of the community is stimulated to antiquarian research.

The Palace of Rosenborg, situated near the centre of the city, was built by Christian IV., in 1604. It is no longer used for its original purpose, but is devoted to the preservation of a chronological collection of the belongings of the Danish kings, spacious apartments being devoted to souvenirs of each, decorated in the style of the period, and containing a portion of the original furniture from the several royal residences, as well as the family portraits, gala costumes, jewelry, plate, and weapons of war. Altogether it is a collection of priceless value and of remarkable historic interest, covering a period of over four hundred years. One is forcibly reminded of the Green Vaults of Dresden while passing through the several sections of Rosenborg Castle. Many of the royal regalias are profusely inlaid with diamonds, sapphires, emeralds, rubies, and other precious stones, forming all together a value too large for us to venture an estimate. The toilet sets which have belonged to and been in daily use by various queens are numerous, each set embracing a dozen pieces more or less, made of solid gold, superbly inlaid with many precious stones. Among them one is especially interested in the jewelled casket of Queen Sophia Amalie, wife of Frederick III., a relic inlaid with scores of diamonds. Here, too, we see the costly and beautiful bridal dresses of several royal personages, all chronologically arranged, so that the intelligent visitor clearly reads veritable history in these domestic treasures.

The Round Tower of Copenhagen is a most singular structure, formerly used as an observatory. It consists of two hollow cylinders between which is a spiral, gradually inclined foot-way leading from base to top. It is quite safe for a horse to ascend, and the Empress Catharine is said to have reached the summit on horseback. From the top of the Round Tower, the red-tiled roofs of the city lie spread out beneath the eye of the visitor, mingled with green parks, open squares, tall steeples, broad canals, wide thoroughfares and palaces. To this aspect is added the multitude of shipping lying along the piers and grouped in the harbor, backed by a view of the open sea. The Swedish coast across the Baltic is represented by a low range of coast-line losing itself upon the distant horizon. The ramparts which formerly surrounded Copenhagen have been demolished, the ground being now improved for fine garden-walks, planted with ornamental trees and bright-hued flowers, which add greatly to the attractive aspect of the Danish capital. The former moats have assumed the shape of tiny lakes, upon which swans and other aquatic birds are seen at all hours; and where death-dealing cannon were formerly planted, lindens, rose-bushes, and tall white lilies now bloom in peaceful beauty.

No finer scenery is to be found in Europe than is presented by the country lying between Copenhagen and Elsinore, composed of a succession of forests, lawns, villas, cottages, and gardens, for a distance of twenty-five miles. Elsinore is a small seaport, looking rather deserted, bleak, and silent, with less than ten thousand inhabitants. From out of the uniformity of its red brick buildings there looms up but one noticeable edifice; namely, the Town Hall, with a square tower flanked by an octagonal one built of red granite. The charm of the place is its remarkable situation, commanding a view of the Baltic, with Sweden in the distance, while the Sound which divides the two shores is always dotted with myriads of steamers and sailing-vessels. The position of Elsinore recalls that of Gibraltar and the Dardanelles as surely as its name reminds us of the play of Hamlet, and Shakespeare. North of the town, on the extreme point of the land, stands the famous castle of Kronborg, with its three tall towers, the central one overtopping the others to the extent of some forty or fifty feet. The tower, upon the most seaward corner, is devoted to the purposes of a lighthouse. The castle is about three centuries old, having been built by Frederick II. for the purpose of commanding the Sound, and of enforcing the marine tolls which were exacted from all foreign nations for a period of two hundred years and more.

If you visit Elsinore, the guide will show you what is called Hamlet's grave, situated in a small grove of trees, where some cunning hands long ago erected a rude mound of stones. Shakespeare, who had a most royal way of disregarding dates, made Hamlet live in this place after the introduction of gunpowder, whereas if any such person ever did exist, it was centuries earlier and hundreds of miles farther north upon the mainland, in what is now called Jutland. However, that is not important. Do not leave Elsinore without visiting Ophelia's fatal brook! To be sure, this rivulet is not large enough for a duck to swim in, but a little stretch of the imagination will overcome all local discrepancies.

Far back in Danish legendary story, a time when history fades into fable, it is said there was a Hamlet in Northern Denmark, but it was long before the birth of Christ. His father was not a king, but a famous pirate chief who governed Jutland in conjunction with his brother. Hamlet's father married the daughter of a Danish king, the issue being Hamlet. His uncle, according to the ancient story, murdered Hamlet's father and afterwards married his mother. Herein we have the foundation of one of Shakespeare's grandest productions.

The Sound, which at Copenhagen is about twenty miles wide, here narrows to two, the old fort of Helsingborg on the Swedish coast being in full view, the passage between the two shores forming the natural gate to the Baltic. There are delightful drives in the environs of Elsinore presenting land and sea views of exquisite loveliness, the water-side bristling with reefs, rocks, and lighthouses, while that of the land is charmingly picturesque with many villas, groves, and broad, cultivated meads.

CHAPTER XV.

ONE day's sail due north from Copenhagen, through the Sound, — Strait of Katte, — brings us to Gottenburg, the metropolis of Southwestern Sweden. The Strait, which is about a hundred miles in width, is nearly twice as long, and contains many small islands. Gottenburg is situated on the Gotha River, about five miles from its mouth. Though less populous, it is commercially almost as important as Stockholm. The deep, broad watercourse which runs through the town to the harbor is a portion of the famous Gotha Canal, which joins fjord (inlet from the sea; pronounced *feord*), river, lakes and locks together, thus connecting the North Sea and the Baltic. The two cities are also joined by railroad, the distance between them being over three hundred miles. The country through which the canal passes is not unlike many inland sections of New England, presenting pleasant views of thrifty farms and well-cultivated lands. There are some sharp hills and abrupt valleys to be encountered which are often marked by grand and picturesque waterfalls, wild, foaming rivers, and fierce surging rapids.

Gottenburg is divided into an upper and lower town, the latter being a plain cut up by canals, and the former spread over the adjoining hills. The town is composed of two or three principal streets, very broad, and intersecting one another at right angles, with a canal in the centre. These water-ways are lined by substantial granite borders, with here and there convenient stone steps connecting them with the water. The spacious harbor admits of vessels drawing seventeen feet. The citizens feel a just pride in a well-endowed college, a large public library, an exchange, two orphan asylums, a flourishing society of arts and sciences, a large theatre, and two public parks. In front of the theatre is an admirable reproduction of the Swedish sculptor Molin's famous group of two figures representing "the girdle-duellists" [these duellists, bound together, fought with knives], the original of which stands in front of the National Museum at Stockholm. Gottenburg is not without a cathedral and numerous fine churches, nor let us forget to speak of its excellent schools, attendance upon which is compulsory throughout Sweden. English is regularly taught in her public schools, and is very generally spoken by the intelligent people. Education is more general, and culture is of a higher grade in Sweden than is common with the people of Southern Europe, while music is nearly as universal an acquirement here as it is in Italy. The population is frugal, honest, self-helping, and in many respects resembles that of Switzerland.

The system of inland communication by means of the Gotha Canal is one of the most remarkable ever achieved by man, when the obstacles which have been overcome and the advantages accomplished are considered. Steam-vessels, limited to one hundred and six feet in length on account of the size of the locks, are carried hundreds of miles by it across and over the highlands of Southern Sweden from sea to sea. When we see a well-freighted steamboat climb a mountain side, float through lock after lock, and after reaching the summit of the hills, descend with equal facility towards the coast and sea-level, this great triumph of engineering skill is fully appreciated. The vessels navigating the canal rise in all, three hundred and eighty feet above the level of the Baltic during the passage across country. At the little town of Berg the locks are sixteen in number, and form a gigantic staircase by means of which vessels are raised at this point one hundred and twenty feet.

On the line of the Gotha Canal is situated the famous Trollhatta Falls, which are so remarkable as to attract visitors from all parts of Europe. These falls consist of a series of tremendous rapids extending over a distance of about two hundred yards, and producing an uproar almost equal to the ceaseless oratorio of Niagara. This angry water-way is interspersed by some well-wooded islands, on either side of which the waters rush with a wild, resistless power, tossed here and there by the many under-currents. The whole forms a succession of falls of which the first is called Gullöfallet, where on both sides of an inaccessible little island the waters make a leap of twenty-six feet in height, the rebound creating a constant cloud of feathery spray. Then follows the highest of the falls, the Toppö-fallet, forty-four feet in height, which is likewise divided by a cliff into two parts, against which the frantic waters chafe angrily. The next fall measures less than ten feet in height, followed a little way down the rapids by what is called the Flottbergström, all together making a fall of foaming eddies and whirls equal to about one hundred and twelve feet.

The marine shells which are found in the bottom of some of the inland lakes of both Norway and Sweden, show that the land which forms their bed was once covered by the sea. This is clearly apparent in Lake Wener and Lake Welter, which are situated nearly three hundred feet above the present ocean level. Complete skeletons of whales have been found inland at considerable elevations during the present century. The oldest shell-banks discovered by scientists in Scandinavia are situated five hundred feet above the level of the sea.

Sweden has comparatively few mountains, but many ranges of hills. Norway monopolizes almost entirely the mountain system of the great northern peninsula, but the large forests of pine, fir, and birch, which cover so much of the country, are common to both. Though iron is found in large deposits in Norway, it is still more abundant in Sweden, where it is chiefly of the magnetic kind, yielding when properly smelted the best ore for the manufacture of steel. It is believed that there is sufficient malleable iron in the soil of Sweden to supply the whole world with this necessary article for centuries. Mount Gellivare, which is over eighteen hundred feet in height, is said to be almost wholly formed of an ore containing eighty per cent of iron.

In approaching Christiania, the capital of Norway, by sea from Gottenburg, we ascend the fjord of the same name a distance of seventy miles. The city, which is built upon a gradual slope facing the south, is seen to good advantage from the harbor. No more appropriate spot could have been selected for the national capital by Christian IV., who founded it, and after whom it is named, than the head of this beautiful elongated bay. It is the seat of the Storthing, or Parliament, and the king, whose permanent residence is at Stockholm, is expected to reside here, attended by the court, at least three months of the year. With its immediate suburbs, the population of the city is a hundred and twenty-five thousand. It should be remembered that Norway is practically a free and independent state though it is under the crown of Sweden, and that the people are thoroughly democratic, having abolished all titles of nobility by enactment of the Storthing so early as 1821, at which time a law was also passed forbidding the king to create a new nobility. Nevertheless, the thought occurs to us that these are the descendants of those Northmen of whom one branch, under the name of Normans, conquered the British Isles, and founded the very nobility there which is the present boast and pride of England.

We find some problems solved in Norway which have created political strife elsewhere. Though its Church is identical with the State, unlimited toleration exists. There is a perfect system of political representation, and while justice is open to all, litigation is earnestly discouraged. The meetings of the Storthing are independent of the king, not even requiring a writ of assemblage from him. Thus it will be seen that although nominally under monarchial rule, Norway is in reality self-governed.

The legal code of Norway is worthy of study, both on account of its antiquity and its admirable provisions. The old sea-kings or free-booters, as we have been accustomed to consider them, had a more advanced and civilized code than any of the people whose shores they devastated. Before the year of our Lord 885, the power of the law was established over all persons of every rank, while, in the other countries of Europe, the independent jurisdiction of the feudal lords defied the laws. Before the eleventh century, the law of Scandinavia provided for equal justice to all, established a system of weights and measures, also one for the maintenance of roads and bridges, and for the protection of women and animals from abuse; subjects which few other European legal systems at that time embraced. These laws were collected into one code by Magnus VII., about the year 1260. They were revised by Christian IV. in 1604, and in 1687 the present system was drawn up. So simple and compact is it, that the whole is contained in a pocket volume, a copy of which is in the possession of every Norwegian family. Each law occupies but a single paragraph, and all is simple and intelligible.

The commerce of Christiania is growing rapidly. Over one thousand vessels enter and depart from its harbor annually, which, however, is closed by ice three months in the year, though that of Hammerfest, situated a thousand miles further north on the same coast, is never frozen, owing to the genial influence of the Gulf Stream, — an agent so potent as to modify the temperature of the entire coast of Scandinavia on its western border.

The university founded here by Frederick VI. in 1811, is a plain but massive structure; the front ornamented by Corinthian pillars of polished granite. It accommodates some nine hundred students, the tuition being free to all native applicants suitably prepared. It contains a noble library of over two hundred thousand volumes, which is freely open even to strangers under very simple restrictions. Beneath the same roof is an extensive museum of zoölogy and geology. The city has a naval and military school, a lunatic asylum, an astronomical observatory, and various charitable institutions. Its botanical garden is situated about a mile from the town, and contains among other interesting and finely arranged specimens, a collection of Alpine plants from Spitzbergen and Iceland.

The parliament house is an imposing building of original design, very pleasing in general effect and style, facing the Carl Johannes Square, the largest open area in the city. It was finished in 1866. The market-place is adorned with a marble statue of Christian IV. Another fine square is the Eidsvolds Plads, planted with choice trees and carpeted with intensely bright greensward. The chief street is the Carl Johannes Gade, a broad thoroughfare extending from the railroad station to the king's palace, halfway between which stands the university. In a large wooden building behind the university is kept that unrivalled curiosity, the "Viking Ship," a souvenir of nine hundred years ago. The blue clay of the district, where it was exhumed in 1880, a few miles south of Christiania, has preserved it all these years. The men who built the graceful lines of this now crumbling vessel, "in some remote and dateless day," knew quite as much of true marine architecture as do our modern shipwrights. This interesting relic, doubtless the oldest ship in the world, once served the Vikings, its masters, as a sea-craft. It is eighty feet long by sixteen wide, and is about six feet deep from the gunwale. Seventy shields, as many spears, and other war equipments recovered with the hull, show that it carried that number of fighting-men.

In such vessels as this the dauntless Northmen made voyages to every country in Europe a thousand years ago, and, as is confidently believed by many, they crossed the Atlantic, discovering North America centuries before the name of Columbus was known. Ignoring the halo of romance and chivalry which the poets have thrown about the valiant Vikings and their followers, one thing we are compelled to admit — they were superb marine architects. Ten centuries of progressive civilization have served to produce none better. Most of the arts and sciences may, and do, exhibit great progress in excellence, but ship-building is not among them. We build bigger, but not finer, vessels.

The burial of this ship so many centuries ago was simply in accordance with the custom of those days. When any great sea-king perished, he was enclosed in the cabin of his galley, and either sunk in the ocean or buried with his vessel and all of its warlike equipments upon the nearest suitable spot of land. We are told that when a chieftain died in battle, not only were his war-horse, his gold and silver plate, and his portable personal effects buried or burned with his body, but a guard of honor from among his followers slew themselves that he might enter the sacred halls of Odin (the Scandinavian Deity) properly attended. The more elevated in rank the chief might be, the larger the number who must sacrifice themselves as his escort to the land of bliss. So entire was the reliance of these Heathens in the demands of their peculiar faith, that they freely acted up to its extreme requirements while singing songs of joy.

A general aspect of good order, thrift, industry, and prosperity prevails at Christiania. The simplicity of dress and the gentle manners, especially among the female portion of the community, are marked features. No stranger can fail to notice the low, sympathetic tones in which the women always speak; but though decorous and worthy, it must be admitted that the Norwegian ladies, as a rule, are not handsome. One sees here none of the rush and fever of living which so wearies the observer in many parts of Southern Europe. The common people evince more solidity of character with less of the frivolities of life.

They may be said to be a trifle slow and phlegmatic, but by no means stupid. The most careless schoolboy, when addressed by a stranger, removes his hat and remains uncovered until he has responded to the inquiry made of him.

Upon visiting a new city in any part of the world, one learns much of the national characteristics of the people, and of other matters worth knowing, by mingling unconventionally with the throng, watching their every-day habits and by observing the stream of busy life pouring through its great thoroughfares. More valuable information is thus acquired than from visiting grand cathedrals, art galleries, or consulting guide-books. Years of travel fatigue us with the latter, but never with Nature in her varying moods, with the peculiarities of races, or with the manners and customs of each new locality and country. The delight in natural objects grows by experience in every cultivated and receptive mind. The rugged architecture of lofty mountains, the aspect of tumbling waterfalls, noble rivers, glowing sunsets, broad land and sea-views — each of these has a special, never-tiring and impressive individuality.

While enjoying a bird's-eye view of Christiania, from the heights of Egeberg, a well-wooded hill in the southern suburb, it is difficult to believe one's self in Icelandic Scandinavia, — the precise latitude of the Shetland Islands. A drowsy hum like the drone of bees seems to float up from the busy city below. The beautiful fjord, with its graceful promontories, its picturesque and leafy isles, might be Lake Maggiore or Como, so placid and calm is its pale blue surface. Turning the eyes inland, one sees clustered in lovely combinations fields of ripening grain, gardens, lawns, cottages, and handsome villas, like a scene upon the sunny shores of the Maritime Alps. An abundance of trees enliven the view, — plane, sycamore, ash, and elm, in luxurious condition. Warmer skies during the summer period are not to be found in Italy, nor elsewhere outside of Egypt. As we stand upon the height of Egeberg on a delicious sunny afternoon, there hangs over and about the Norwegian capital a soft golden haze such as lingers in August above the Venetian lagoons.

The summer is so short here as to give the fruits and flowers barely time to blossom, ripen, and fade, and the husbandman a chance to gather his crops. Vegetation is rapid in its growth, the sunshine being so nearly constant during the ten weeks which intervene between seed-time and harvest. Barley grows two inches, and pease three, in twenty-four hours at certain stages of development. It is an interesting fact that if the barley-seed be brought from a warmer climate, it has to become acclimated, and does not yield a good crop until after two or three years.

The flowers of the torrid and temperate zones, as a rule, close their eyes like human beings, and sleep a third or half of the twenty-four hours, but in Arctic regions, life to those lovely children of Nature is one long sunny period, and sleep comes only with death and decay. It will also be observed that the flowers assume more vivid colors and emit more fragrance during their brief lives than they do in the south. The long, delightful period of twilight during the summer season is seen here in perfection, full of roseate loveliness. There is no dew to be encountered or avoided, no dampness; all is crystal clearness.

In the rural districts women are generally employed in

out-of-door work, as they are in Germany and Italy, and there is quite a preponderance of the sex in Norway and Sweden. As many women as men are seen engaged in mowing, reaping, loading heavy carts, and getting in the harvest generally. What would our American farmers think to see a woman swing a scythe all day in the hay-fields, cutting as broad and even a swath as a man can do, and apparently with as little fatigue? Labor is very poorly paid. Forty cents per day is considered to be liberal wages for a man, except in the cities, where a small increase upon this amount is obtained.

Norway has been appropriately called the country of mountains and fjords, of cascades and lakes. Among the largest of the latter is Lake Mjösen, which is about sixty miles long and has an average width of twelve. It receives in its bosom one important river, the Longen, after it has run a course of nearly a hundred and fifty miles. At its southern extremity is the port of Eidsvol, and at the northern is Lillehammer. These are situated in the direct route between Christiania and Tröndhjem. But the most singular fact attached to the lake is that it measures about fifteen hundred feet in depth while its surface is only four hundred feet above the level of the ocean. Its bottom is known to be nearly a thousand feet below that of the adjacent North Sea, which would seem to show that the lake must be the mouth of some long-extinct volcano.

As to the animals of Norway, the reindeer, the bear, the wolf, the fox, and the lynx about complete the list. The ubiquitous crow abounds, and fine specimens of the golden eagle, that dignified monarch of the upper regions, may often be seen sailing through the air from cliff to cliff, across the fjords and valleys. At certain seasons of the year this bird proves destructive to domestic fowl and young lambs. Magpies appear to be as much of a nuisance in Norway as crows are in India or Ceylon, and quite as unmolested by the people. What are called the wild birds of Scandinavia are in fact quite tame, and they are in large variety. As the traveller passes through the country, he will observe sheaves of unthreshed grain elevated upon poles beside the farm-houses and barns, which are placed there to furnish the feathered visitors with food. These sheaves are frequently renewed throughout the long winters; otherwise the birds would starve. The confiding little creatures know their friends, and often enter the houses for protection from the severity of the weather. Neither man, woman, nor child would think of disturbing them, for they are considered to bring good luck to the premises.

In a journey from the capital to Tröndhjem, where the coasting steamer is usually taken for the North Cape, we cross the Dovrefjeld, or mountain table-land. The famous elevation called the Sneehaetta — "Snow Hat" — forms a part of this Alpine range, and it is one of the loftiest in Norway. It should be remembered that one-eighth of the country lies within the region of perpetual snow, and that these lofty and nearly inaccessible heights are robed in a constant garb of bridal whiteness. No known portions of the globe have more extensive glaciers or snowfields, unless, possibly, it be some portions of Alaska or Greenland. There are glaciers in Norway which cover from four to five hundred square miles, descending from plateaus three and four thousand feet in height, down to very near sea-level.

Though the highest point in the peninsula is only about

eight thousand five hundred feet above the sea,—an elevation which is reached only by Jotunfjeld, or Giant Mountain,—still no highlands in Europe surpass those of Scandinavia in terrific grandeur. Mont Blanc (Switzerland) is nearly twice as high as this Giant Mountain, but being less abrupt is hardly so striking.

The elevations of Norway are intersected by deep, dark gorges and threatening chasms, roaring with impetuous torrents and grand water-falls, constantly presenting such scenes as would have inspired the pencil of Salvator Rosa. The mountain system here does not form a continuous range, but consists of a succession of table-lands, like the Dovrefjeld, and of detached mountains rising from elevated bases. The length of this series of elevations — mountains and plateaus — is that of the entire peninsula from the North Cape to Christiania, some twelve hundred miles, which gives to the mountains of Norway and Sweden an area larger than the Alps, the Apennines, and Pyrenees combined; while the lakes, waterfalls, and cascades far surpass those of the rest of Europe. It has been said, somewhat extravagantly, by those familiar with the geography of Scandinavia, that could it be flattened out into plains, it would make as large a division of the earth as is now represented by either of the four principal continents.

The ratio of arable land to the entire area of Norway is not more than one to ten, and were it not that the support of the people came mainly from the sea, the country would not sustain one-quarter of its present population. Undismayed, however, by the prevalence of rocks, cliffs, and chasms, the people utilize every available rod of land to the utmost. The surroundings of many habitations seem severe and desolate, even when viewed beneath the summer sun; what, then, must be their appearance during the long and trying winters of their frosty regions?

It is not uncommon to see on the Norwegian coast, farm-houses surrounded by a few low buildings, perched among rocks away up on some green terrace, so high, indeed, as to make them seem scarcely larger than an eagle's nest. To anybody but a mountaineer these spots are inaccessible, and every article of subsistence, except what is raised upon the few acres of available earth surrounding the dwelling, must be carried up there upon men's backs. A few goats and sheep must constitute the animal stock, added to which are generally some domestic fowls. These dwellings are constructed of logs, cut in the lofty gulches, and drawn by hand to the spot, one by one. It would seem that such energetic industry applied in some inviting neighborhood would insure a more desirable result.

CHAPTER XVI.

BERGEN is situated some two hundred miles northwest of Christiania, and may be reached from thence by a carriole (a peculiar native vehicle) journey across the country, over excellent roads, or by steamboat doubling the Naze. The latter route, though three times as far, is most frequently adopted by travellers as being less expensive and troublesome. Another, and perhaps the most common, route taken by tourists is by the way of Lake Mjösen, called the Valders route. It involves railroad, steamer, and carriole modes of conveyance, and in all covers a distance of at least three hundred and fifty miles.

Bergen was the capital of Norway when it was under Danish rule, and was even up to a late period the commercial rival of the present capital, Christiania. The town rises from the bay nearly in the form of a crescent, nestling at the foot of surrounding hills on the west coast, between those two broad and famous arms of the sea, — the Sognefjord and the Hardangerfjord. The first-named indents the coast to a distance of over one hundred miles, the latter seventy miles, — the first being north, and the last south of Bergen. The excellent situation of the harbor and its direct steam communication with European ports gives this ancient city an extensive commerce in proportion to the number of inhabitants, who do not aggregate over forty thousand. A large portion of the town is built upon a promontory, between which and the mainland on its north side is the harbor, which is rarely frozen over, owing to the influence of the Gulf Stream, while the harbor of St. Petersburg (Russia), in about the same latitude, is closed annually by ice for at least three months.

We see here more of the traditional Norwegian customs than are to be met with either at Gottenburg or Christiania. Some of the old men who come from inland are particularly noticeable, forming vivid pictures and artistic groups, with their long, snowy hair flowing freely about face and neck in patriarchal fashion. They wear red worsted caps, open shirt-collars, and knee-breeches, together with jackets and vests decked by a profusion of silver buttons. The women wear black jackets, bright red bodices, and scarlet petticoats, with white linen aprons. On the street called the Strandgade many Norse costumes mingle like various colors in a kaleidoscope.

The staple commodity of Bergen is dried fish, mostly cod, supplemented by large quantities of cod-liver oil, lumber, and wood cut for fuel. A considerable portion of what is called cod-liver oil is produced from sharks' livers, which, in fact, are believed to possess the same medicinal qualities as those of the cod. At all events, with this object, sharks are sought for along the upper coast of Norway, especially in the region of the Lofoden Islands, and their livers are used as described. An average-sized shark will yield thirty gallons of merchantable oil, but this article would not obtain a market except under the more popular name of cod-liver oil. Catching sharks is not an employment entirely devoid of danger, as they are large and powerful, often measuring twenty feet and more in length. The shark, like the whale, when it is first struck with the harpoon, must be given plenty of line, or it will drag down the fishermen's boat in its rapid descent to deep water. Sometimes the struggle to capture the fish is a long and serious one, as it must thoroughly exhaust itself before it will yield. When it is finally drawn to the side of the boat, a heavy, well-directed blow upon the nose completely stuns the creature, and the capture is then complete.

There are here some neat public squares, a public park, wherein a military band plays occasionally, and half a dozen churches. There is also a theatre, royal palace, musical institute, public library, and museum; but there is hardly a trace of architectural beauty in Norway, with the exception of the cathedral at Tröndhjem, which is formed of a mixture of orders, the Norman predominating. The Church of St. Mary at Bergen is only interesting for its antiquity, dating as it does from the twelfth century. Its curious and grotesque front bears the date A.D. 1118.

The shops are filled with odd antique articles, mostly for domestic use, such as old plate, drinking-cups, spoons, and silver goblets bearing the marks of age, and the date of centuries past. A little experience is apt to create doubt, in the genuineness of these articles, which, like those found in the curiosity shops of Japan, are very generally manufactured in this present year of our Lord, however they may be dated.

A drive of a few miles inland upon the charming roads in any direction will fill the stranger with delight, and afford characteristic pictures of great beauty. The farmers hang their cut grass upon frames of wood to dry, as we do clothes upon a rope on washing-days. These frames are placed in the mowing-fields, in rows of a hundred feet in length and a hundred feet apart, and are about five feet in height. Agricultural tools used upon the farms are of the most primitive character; the ploughs in many parts of the country are single-handed, and as awkward as the rude implement used for the purpose to-day in Egypt. The country houses are low and mostly thatched, the roof being often covered with soil, and are not infrequently rendered attractive with blooming heather and little blue and pink blossoms planted by Nature's hand, — the hieroglyphics in which she writes her impromptu poetry. In the meadows between the hills are sprinkled harebells, as blue as the azure veins on a delicate face; while here and there patches of large red clover-heads are seen nodding heavily with their wealth of golden sweets. Further away, in solitary glens, white anemones delight the eye, in company with ferns of tropical variety in form and color. The blossoms of the multebaer, almost identical with that of the strawberry, are abundant. The humidity of the atmosphere favors floral development. All through Scandinavia one meets these bright mosaics of the soil with a sense of surprise, they are so delicate, so frail, creations of such short life, yet lovely beyond compare, born upon the verge of constant frost.

While rambling afield one meets occasionally a peasant who bows low, removing his hat as the stranger passes. Without evincing the servility of the common people of Japan, they yet exhibit all their native courtesy. Now and again the road passes through pine forests, still and aromatic, the soil carpeted with leaves, where, if one pauses to listen, there comes a low, undefined murmur of vegetable and insect life, like the sound that greets the ear when applied to an empty sea-shell. Some wood-paths are found sprinkled with dog-violets, saxifrage, and with purple heart's-ease. Song-birds are rarely to be seen and one cannot but wish for their delicious notes amid such suggestive surroundings.

The country lying between Bergen and Christiania, and indeed nearly every part of Norway, presents great attractions to the angler, who must, however, go prepared to rough it: but if he be a true lover of the sport, this will enhance rather than detract from the pleasure. The country is thinly inhabited, and affords only rude accommodations for the wandering pedestrian who does not confine himself to the regular post-route. The lakes, rivers, and streams, swarm with trout, grayling, and salmon.

Strangers visit with more than passing interest the admirable free school for girls, which is established at Bergen. Here girls from eight to sixteen years of age are taught the domestic industries practically, under circumstances void of every onerous regulation, and they are to be seen in cheerful groups at work upon all sorts of garments, supervised by competent teachers of their own sex. Possessed of these prudential and educational appreciations, it is not surprising that Bergen has sent forth some eminent representatives in science, art, and literature. Among these we recall the names of Ole Bull, the famous musician; Ludwig Holberg, the accomplished traveller; Johann Wtlhaven, the Norse poet; and J. C. C. Dahl, the celebrated painter.

Tröndhjem is situated on a fjord of the same name occupying a peninsula formed by the river Nid, and is surrounded by picturesque scenery. A delightful view of the town and its environs may be had from the old fort of Kristiansten. Here resided the kings of Norway in the olden time. It is now a thriving but small city, having a population of about twenty-five thousand, and is the seat of a bishopric. There is here an academy of sciences, a museum, and a public library. The Cathedral of St. Olaf is famous, being the finest Gothic edifice in Scandinavia, and the only local object of special interest. In the eleventh and twelfth centuries the kings of Norway were buried here.

Tröndhjem was founded about a thousand years ago by King Olaf Trygvason, upon the site of a much older city named Nidaros, but there is certainly nothing visible to indicate its great antiquity. The adventurous life of King Olaf, which occurs to us in this connection, may be outlined in a few words, and is more romantic than that of any other ruler of Norway which is generally known. Born a prince, he barely escaped assassination in childhood at the hands of the usurper of his rights, by fleeing from the country in charge of his mother. They were captured at sea by pirates, separated, and sold into slavery. Then followed a period of deprivation and hardship; but at a comparatively early age Olaf was discovered and ransomed by a relative who had never ceased to search for the missing youth. He soon after became a distinguished sea-king, of that class whom we call pirates. His career in this field of adventure is represented to have been one of daring and reckless hardihood, characterized by merciless aggression and great success. Finally Olaf married an Irish princess, embraced Christianity, and fought his way to the throne of Norway, assuming the crown in the year of our Lord 991. From this time he became a zealous missionary, propagating his faith by the sword, and like many other religious zealots he was guilty of outrageous cruelty. Seven years subsequent to the last-named date he destroyed the Pagan temples of Thor and Odin at Tröndhjem.

Upon the site of this temple he built a Christian church, making the city his seat of government, and so it remained the capital down to the union with Denmark. Olaf was slain in battle while fighting for his throne, and was declared a saint by the Church, his tomb at Tröndhjem being a Mecca for pious pilgrims from all parts of Europe for centuries. In such veneration were the memory and services of this reformed pirate held by a certain class of religionists, that churches were erected in his name at Constantinople and elsewhere. His ashes lie entombed beneath the present cathedral of Tröndhjem.

A short walk from the town brings one to Hlade, where stands the castle of the infamous Jarl Hakon, whence, in the olden time, he ruled over the surrounding country with an iron hand. He was a savage heathen, believing in and practising human sacrifices, evidences of which are still extant. About a mile from the town, in the fjord, is the island of Munkholm, once the site of a Benedictine monastery, as its name indicates, and which was erected in 1028. The mouldering and moss-grown base of one of its towers is all that now remains. Victor Hugo gives a graphic description of this spot in his book entitled "Han d'Islande." Here the famous minister of Christian V., Griffenfeldt by name, was confined for a period of many weary years. He was guilty of no crime, his incarceration being the result of political intrigue. When he was finally brought to the scaffold for execution, a messenger interrupted the headsman at the last moment and announced a pardon from the king. "The pardon," said the worn-out sufferer, "is severer than the penalty."

The usual route of those who seek to gain a view of the "midnight sun"—that is, of witnessing the phenomenon of the sun passing round the horizon without sinking beneath it — is to depart from Tröndhjem by sea, for the North Cape, skirting the ironbound coast for a distance of about seven hundred miles.

As we sail northward, the rapid lengthening of the days becomes more and more apparent. At Lund, in the extreme south of Sweden, the longest day experienced is seventeen hours and a half; at Stockholm, two hundred miles further north, the longest day of the year is eighteen hours and a half; at Bergen, in Norway, three hundred miles north of Lund, the longest day is twenty-one hours. Above this point of latitude to the North Cape, there is virtually no night at all during the brief summer season, as the sun is visible, or nearly so, for the whole twenty-four hours. From early in May until about the first of August, north of Tröndhjem, the stars take a vacation, or at least they are not visible, while the moon is so pale as to give no light. Even the Great Bear puts by his seven lustres, and the diamond belt of Orion is unseen. But the heavenly lamps revive by the first of September, and after a short period are supplemented by the marvellous and beautiful radiations of the Aurora Borealis, or Northern Lights. Winter now sets in, the sun disappears entirely from sight, and night reigns supreme, the heavens shining only with a subdued light. Were it not for the brilliancy of the Auroral light the fishermen could hardly pursue their winter business, that being the harvest time with them, and midnight is considered to be the best period of the twenty-four hours for successful fishing in these regions. In and about Lofoden Islands alone, five thousand boats are thus regularly employed, giving occupation to twenty thousand men in the boats and a couple of thousand on the shore.

The coast of Norway is bordered by innumerable rocky islands, and also by deep fjords, winding inland from ten to fifty miles each, among masses of rock forming perpendicular walls often towering a thousand feet or more in height. The turbulent waves of the North Atlantic and Arctic Oceans, hurled against the coast for thousands of years, have steadily worn into the land and thus formed these remarkable fjords; or perhaps after they were begun by volcanic or glacial action, the wearing of the waters has gradually brought about their present condition. The coast of Sweden, on the other hand, is formed by the Baltic Sea and the Gulf of Bothnia, both of which are inland waters, and though there are many islands on the Swedish coast, there are no fjords worthy of mention. Notwithstanding that the extreme length of Norway, from north to south, is hardly twelve hundred miles, yet so numerous and extensive are these peculiar arms of the sea, that its coast-line is estimated to measure over three thousand miles, which gives to these deep indentures altogether a length of eighteen hundred miles.

The peninsula known as Scandinavia is composed of Norway, Sweden, and a small portion of the Russian possessions in the northeast. This division of country supports a population of little less than seven millions, and contains in round numbers three hundred thousand square miles. The mountains of this section of the globe are mostly of primitive rock, presenting as near as possible the same form as when they were first solidified, standing forth as tangible evidence of the great antiquity of this region.

In her course northward the steamer, upon which we embarked at Tröndhjem, winds in and out among the many islands and fjords, touching occasionally at small settlements on the mainland to discharge light freight and to land or to take an occasional passenger. The few persons who come from the little cluster of houses, which are not sufficient in number to be called a village, are found to be of more than ordinary intelligence, and many of them speak English fluently. Even in these sparsely inhabited regions education is provided for by what is termed the "ambulatory system"; that is, one able teacher instructs the youth of three or four neighboring districts, meeting the convenience of all by suitable variations regarding time and place in holding school sessions.

There is but one day in the year when the phenomenon of the midnight sun can be seen at the imaginary line which we designate as the Arctic Circle, a point in the watery waste or on the land, twenty-three degrees and twenty-eight minutes from the North Pole; but by sailing some three hundred miles further northward, to the North Cape, the projecting point of the extreme north of Norway, it may be observed under favorable circumstances — that is, when not obscured by clouds — for over two months, dating from the middle of May. Soon after entering the Arctic Circle, fourteen hundred and eight geographical miles from the North Pole, a singularly formed island is observed, called by the natives Hestmandö, or Horseman's Island, — a rocky and mountainous formation of some two thousand feet in height, more or less. On approaching the island from the west, by aid of the imagination one can discern the colossal figure of a horseman wrapped in his cloak and mounted upon a charger. The island forms a well-known landmark for seamen navigating the coast. It is believed that the summit has never been reached by human feet.

We touch on our way at the little fishing-village of Bodöe. Louis Philippe lived here for a brief period when travelling as an exile under the name of Müller, and visitors are shown the room which he occupied. It is the chief town of Nordland, and has fifteen hundred inhabitants. After leaving Bodöe the course of the steamer is directly across the Vestfjord to the group of the Lofoden Islands. Owing to the remarkable clearness of the atmosphere as seen from Bodöe, they appear to be about fifteen or twenty miles away on the edge of the horizon, though the real distance is about fifty. The play of light and shade is here so different from that of lower latitudes that distances are very deceptive.

A little to the westward of the steamer's course in coming from the mainland lies the famous whirlpool known as the Maelström, the subject of many a romantic and wild conjecture which lives in the memory of us all. At certain stages of the wind and tide a fierce eddy is formed here which is somewhat dangerous for small boats to cross, but the presumed risk to vessels of the size of the coasting-craft usually employed here, is an error. At some stages of the tide it is difficult to even detect the exact spot which is at other times so disturbed. Thus we find that another legend of the credulous past has but a very thin substratum of fact for its foundation. The tragedies recorded in connection with the Venetian Bridge of Sighs are proven to be without reliable foundation; the episode of Tell and the apple is not historical, but a poetical fabrication; and now we know that neither ships nor whales were ever drawn into the Norwegian Maelström to their destruction. There are several other similar rapids in and about these pinnacled islands, identical in their nature, though the one here referred to is the most restless and formidable.

On close examination the Lofodens are found to consist of a maze of irregular mountain-peaks and precipices, often between two and three thousand feet in height, the passage between them being very tortuous, winding amid straits interspersed with hundreds of rocky islets which are the home of large flocks of sea-birds. Dwarf-trees, small patches of green grass, and velvety moss grow near the water's edge, and carpet here and there a few acres of soil, but the high ridges are bleak and bare rock, covered in spots with never-melting snow. These islands are composed mainly of granite, and for wonderful peaks and oddly pointed shapes, deep and far-reaching gulches, are unequalled elsewhere. It seems marvellous that a steamer can be safely navigated through such narrow passages and among such myriads of sunken rocks. These elevations from beneath the sea vary from mere turtle-backs, as sailors call them, just visible above the water, to mountains with sky-kissing peaks. For a vessel to run upon one of these low hummocks would simply be destruction, as the water alongside of them is rarely less than two or three hundred fathoms in depth.

The total length of these remarkable islands is about a hundred and thirty miles, and the area is computed at fifteen hundred and sixty square miles. The population will not vary much from twenty thousand, and the entire occupation of the people is fishing, curing the fish, and shipping them southward.

The hardy fishermen work nearly all winter at their rough occupation, braving the tempestuous Northern Ocean in frail, undecked boats, which to an inexperienced eye seem to be utterly unfit for such exposed service. The harvest time to the cod-fishers here is from January to the middle of April. Casualties, of course, are more or less frequent, but do not exceed those encountered by our fishermen on the banks of Newfoundland. In the year 1848, a terrible hurricane visited the Lofodens, and in a few hours swept over five hundred fishermen into eternity. The men engaged in this service come from all parts of Norway, returning to their homes in summer and engaging in other occupations.

As we leave the group and steer towards the mainland, it is remembered that the coast of Norway extends three hundred miles north of the Arctic Circle, projecting itself boldly into the Polar Sea. Two hundred miles and more of this distance is north of the Lofoden Islands. Now and then portions of country are passed on the mainland, affording striking and beautiful landscape effects, where valleys open towards the sea, presenting views sometimes capped by glaciers high up towards the overhanging sky, where they form immense level fields of ice embracing hundreds of square miles.

The varied and ever present attractions of Norway to the artist are many, and in a great measure they are unique, especially in the immediate vicinity of the west coast. No two of the many abrupt elevations resemble each other. All are peculiar; some like Alpine cathedrals rear their fretted spires far heavenward, where they echo the hoarse anthems played by the winter's storms. One would think that Nature in a wayward mood had tried her hand sportively at architecture, sculpture, and castle-building, constructing now a high monumental column or a mounted warrior, and now a Gothic fane amid regions strange, lonely, and savage. There are grand mountains and glaciers in Switzerland and other countries, but they do not rise directly out of the water as they often do in Scandinavia; and as to the scenery afforded by the innumerable fjords winding inland amid forests, cliffs, and impetuous waterfalls, nowhere else can we find such remarkable scenes.

Like rivers, and yet so unlike them in width, depth, and placidity, with their broad mouths guarded by clustering islands, one can find nothing in nature more grand, solemn, and impressive than a Norwegian fjord. Now and again the shores are lined for short distances by the greenest of green pastures, dotted with little red houses and groups of domestic animals, forming charming bits of verdant foreground backed by dark and shadowy gorges. Down precipitous cliffs leap cascades which are fed by ice-fields hidden in the lofty mountains. These are not merely pretty spouts, like many a little Swiss device, but grand, plunging, restless torrents, conveying heavy volumes of foaming water.

CHAPTER XVII.

AS we advance northward, our experiences become more and more peculiar. It seems as if humanity, like nature, is possessed by a certain sleeplessness in these regions during the constant reign of daylight. People are wide awake and busy at their various occupations during all hours, while the drowsy god appears to have departed on a vacation to the southward. The apparent incongruity of starting upon a fresh enterprise at midnight is only realized on consulting one's watch.

All along the coast the birds are nearly as numerous as the fishes, and many islands are solely occupied by them as breeding-places. Their numbers are beyond calculation, consisting of petrels, swans, geese, pelicans, auks, gulls, and divers. These last are more particularly of the duck family, of which there are over thirty distinct species in and about this immediate region. Curlews, ptarmigans, cormorants, and ospreys are also seen in greater or less numbers.

The steamer lands us for a few hours at Tromsöe, a small island in latitude 69° 38' north, a thriving place of six thousand inhabitants, a goodly number for a town within the Arctic Circle. It is the capital of Norwegian Lapland. Both to the north and south of the town snow-clad mountains shut off distant views. During the winter months there are only four hours of daylight here out of the twenty-four, — that is, from about ten o'clock A.M. until two o'clock p.m.,—but the long nights are made comparatively light by the glowing splendor of the Aurora Borealis. The birch-trees in and about Tromsöe are of a remarkably developed species, and form a marked feature of the place.

Just outside of the town a field is seen golden with buttercups, making it difficult to realize that we are in the Arctic regions. A pink-blooming heather also covers other fields, and we are surprised by a tiny cloud of butterflies, so abundant in the warm sunshine, and presenting such transparency of color as to suggest the idea that a rainbow has been shattered, and is floating in myriad particles in the air.

The short-lived summer perhaps makes flowers all the more carefully tended. In the rudest domestic quarters a few pet plants are seen whose arrangement and nurture show womanly care. Every window in the humble dwellings has its living screen of drooping, many-colored fuchsias, geraniums, forget-me-nots, and monthly roses. The ivy is especially prized here, and is picturesquely trained to hang about the window-frames. The fragrant sweet-pea, with its snow-white and peach-blossom hues, is often mingled prettily with the dark green of the ivy, the climbing propensities of each making them fitting mates. Surely there must be an innate sense of refinement among the people of these frost-imbued regions, whatever their seeming, when they are actuated by such delicate tastes.

One of the most interesting subjects of study to the traveller on the journey northward is to mark his progress by the products of the forest. The trees will prove, if intelligently observed, a means of fixing his position. From the region of the date and the palm we come to that of the fig and the olive; thence to the orange, the almond, and the myrtle. Succeeding these we find the walnut, the poplar, and the lime; and again there comes the region of the elm, the oak, and the sycamore. These will be succeeded by the larch, the fir, the pine, the birch, and their companions. After this point we look for no change of species, but a diminution in size of these last named. The variety of trees is the result of altitude as well as of latitude, since there are mountain regions of Southern Europe, as well as in America, where one may pass in a few hours from the region of the olive to that of the stunted fir.

From Tromsöe vessels are fitted for exploration towards the North Pole; some for the capture of seals and walruses among the ice-fields, and also on the coast of Spitzbergen. A small propeller is seen lying in the harbor fitted with a forecastle gun, whence to fire a lance at whales — a species of big fishing, so to speak, which is made profitable here. Little row-boats with high bows and sterns flit about the bay like sea-birds on the wing, and ride as lightly upon the water. These are often "manned" by a couple of sturdy women who row with great precision, their faces glowing with animation. These boats, of the same model as that ancient Viking ship at Christiania, sit very low in the water amidship, but are remarkable for buoyancy and the ease with which they are propelled.

The Lapps in their quaint and picturesque costumes of deer-skins surround the newly arrived steamer, in boats, offering furs, carved horn implements, moccasins, walrus-teeth, and the like for sale. These wares are of the rudest type, and of no possible use except as mementos of the traveller's visit to these far northern latitudes. This people are very shrewd in matters of trade, and are not without plenty of low cunning hidden behind their brown, withered, expressionless faces. They are small in stature, being generally under five feet in height, with prominent cheek bones, snub noses, oblique Mongolian eyes, big mouths, large, ill-formed heads, hair like meadow hay, and very scanty beards. Such is a pen portrait of a people who once ruled the whole of Scandinavia. A short trip inland brings us to the summer encampment of the Lapps, formed of a few rude huts, outside of which they live except in the winter months. A Lapp sleeps wherever fatigue overcomes him, preferring the ground, but often lying on the snow. They are a wandering race, their wealth consisting solely in their herds of reindeer, to procure sustenance for which necessitates frequent changes of locality. A Laplander is rich provided he owns enough of these animals to support himself and family. A herd that can afford thirty full-grown deer annually for slaughter, and say ten more to be sold or bartered, makes a family of a dozen persons comfortably well off. Some are destroyed every year by wolves and bears, notwithstanding all the precautions taken to prevent it, while in severe winters a large number are sure to die of starvation.

The herds live almost entirely on the so-called reindeer moss, but this failing them, they eat the young twigs of the trees. When the snow covers the ground to a depth of not more than three or four feet, these intelligent creatures dig holes in it so as to reach the moss, and guided by instinct they rarely fail to do so in just the right place. The Lapps themselves would be entirely at a loss for any indication as to where this food should be sought when covered by the deep snow. The reindeer will carry, lashed to its back, a hundred and thirty pounds, or drag upon the snow, when harnessed to a sledge, two hundred and fifty pounds, travelling ten miles an hour for several consecutive hours, without apparent fatigue. The country over which these people roam is included in Northern Norway and Sweden, with a portion of Northwestern Russia and Finland, extending over about seven thousand square miles, but the whole race will hardly number thirty thousand. Lapland, in general terms, may be said to be the region lying between the Polar Ocean and the Arctic Circle, the eastern and western boundaries being the Atlantic Ocean and the White Sea, two-thirds of which territory belongs to Russia, and one-third is about equally divided between Norway and Sweden.

In the winter season the Lapps retire far inland, where they build temporary huts of the branches of the trees, plastered with clay and banked up with snow, leaving a hole at the top as a chimney for the smoke, the fire being always built upon a broad, flat stone in the centre of the hut. In these rude, and, according to our estimate, comfortless cabins, they hibernate, rather than live the life of civilized human beings, for eight months of the year.

After leaving Tromsöe our course is north-northeast, crossing wild fjords and skirting the mainland. Along the shore at intervals little clusters of fishermen's huts are seen, with a small sprinkling of herbage and patches of bright verdure. As we glide along among the islands which line the shore, we are pretty sure to fall in with one of the little propellers, with a small swivel gun at the bow, in search of whales. The projectile which is used consists of a barbed harpoon, to which a short chain is affixed, and to that a strong line. This harpoon has barbs which expand as soon as they enter the body of the animal and he pulls upon the line, stopping at a certain angle, which renders the withdrawal of the weapon impossible. Besides this, an explosive shell is so attached that it quickly bursts within the monster, producing instant death. A cable is then fastened to the head, and the whale is towed into harbor to be cut up, and the blubber tried out on shore.

The objects which attract the eye are constantly changing. Large black geese, too heavy for lofty flying, rise awkwardly from the waves and skim across the fjords, just clearing the surface of the dark blue waters. Oyster-catchers, as they are familiarly called, decked with scarlet bills and legs, are abundant. Now and then that daring highwayman among birds, the skua, or robber-gull, is seen on the watch for a victim. He is quite dark in plumage, almost black, and gets a robber's living by attacking and causing other birds to drop what they have caught up from the sea, seizing which as it falls, he sails away to consume at leisure his stolen prize.

Long before we reach Hammerfest our watches seem to have become bewitched, for it must be remembered that here it is broad daylight throughout the twenty-four hours (in midsummer) which constitute day and night elsewhere. To sleep becomes a useless effort, and our eyes are unusually wide open.

The Gulf Stream, emerging from the tropics thousands of miles away, constantly laves the shores, and consequently ice is not seen. At first it seems a little strange that there are no icebergs here in latitude 70° north, when we have them on the coast of America in certain seasons at 41°. The entire west coast of Norway is warmer by at least twenty degrees than most other localities in the same latitude, owing to the presence of the Gulf Stream, — that heated, mysterious river in the midst of the ocean. It brings to these far-away regions quantities of floating material, such as the trunks of palm-trees, and other substances suitable for fuel, to which useful purpose they are put at the Lofoden Islands, and by the fishermen along the shore of the mainland. By the same agency West Indian seeds and woods are often found floating on the west coast of Scotland and Ireland.

Hammerfest, the capital of the province of Finmark, is situated in latitude 70° 40' north, upon the island of Kvaloe, or "Whale Island." It is overshadowed by Tyvfjeld, — that is, "Thief Mountain,"— thus fancifully named because it robs the place of the little sunshine it might enjoy, were this high elevation not at all times intervening. It is the most northerly town in Europe, and is about sixty-five miles southwest of the North Cape. It is a town of about three thousand inhabitants, who appear to be industrious and intelligent. Even here, in this region of frost and darkness, we are glad to say, there are plenty of good schools and able teachers.

From Hammerfest we continue our voyage northward along the coast. The land is now seen to be useless for agricultural purposes; habitations first become rare, then cease altogether, bleakness reigning supreme, while we seem to be creeping higher and higher on the earth. In ascending mountains of the Himalayan range, we realize that there are heights still above us; but in approaching the North Cape, a feeling is experienced that we are gradually getting to the very apex of the globe. Everything seems to be beneath our feet; the broad, deep, unbounded ocean alone marks the horizon. Day and night cease to be relative terms.

The North Cape, which is finally reached, is an island projecting itself far into the Polar Sea, separated from the mainland by a narrow strait. The highest point which has ever been reached by the daring Arctic explorer, is 83° 24' north latitude; this cape is in latitude 71° 10' north. The island is named Mageröe, which signifies a barren place, and it is certainly well named, for a wilder, bleaker, or more desolate spot cannot be found on the face of the earth. Only a few hares, ermine, and sea-birds manage to subsist upon its sterile soil. The western and northern sides are absolutely inaccessible owing to their precipitous character. The Arctic Sea thunders hoarsely against the Cape as we approach the rough, weather-worn cliff in a small landing-boat. It is near the midnight hour, yet the warmth of the sun's direct rays envelops us. For half an hour we struggle upwards at an angle of nearly forty-five degrees, amid loose rocks and over uneven ground, until the summit is finally reached, and we stand a thousand feet above the level of the sea, literally upon the threshold of the unknown.

No difference is observed between the broad light of this Polar night and the noon of a sunny summer's day in other latitudes. The sky is all aglow, and the rays of the sun are warm and penetrating, though a certain chill in the atmosphere at this exposed elevation renders thick clothing indispensable. This is the objective point, to reach which we have voyaged thousands of miles from another hemisphere. We look about us in silent wonder and awe. To the northward is that unknown region to solve whose mystery so many gallant lives have been sacrificed. Far to the eastward is Asia; in the distant west lies America; and southward are Europe and Africa. Such an experience may occur once in a lifetime, but rarely can it be repeated. The surface of the cliff is quite level where we stand, and beneath our feet is a soft gray reindeer moss which yields to the tread like a carpet of velvet. There is no other vegetation, not even a spear of grass. Close at hand, in all directions, are frightful fissures and sheer precipices, except on the side where we have ascended. Presently the boom of a distant gun floats faintly upwards, the cautionary signal from the ship now seen floating far below us, a mere speck upon that Polar Sea.

The hands of the watch indicate that it is near the hour of twelve, midnight. The great luminary has sunk slowly amid a glory of light to within three or four degrees of the horizon, where it seems to hover for a single moment like some monster bird about to alight, then changing its mind slowly begins its upward movement. This is exactly at midnight, always a solemn hour; but amid the glare of sunlight and the glowing immensity of sea and sky, how strange and weird it is! Notwithstanding they are so closely mingled, the difference between the gorgeous coloring of the setting and the fresh hues of the rising sun seem to be clearly though delicately defined. True, the sun had not really set at all on the occasion we describe. It was constantly visible, so that the human eye could not rest upon it for one moment. It was the mingling of the golden haze of evening with the radiant, roseate flush of the blushing morn.

After returning to Christiania we take the cars of the railroad which crosses the peninsula by way of Charlottenborg, the frontier town of Sweden. Here there is a custom-house examination of our baggage; for although Norway and Sweden are under one crown, yet they have separate tariffs, import and export fees being enforced between them. In crossing the peninsula by rail one does not enjoy the picturesque scenery which is seen on the Gotha Canal route. The railroad journey takes us through a region of lake and forest, however, by no means devoid of interest, and which is rich in mines of iron and other ores. As we approach Lake Maelaren on the east coast, a more highly cultivated country is traversed, until Stockholm is finally reached; a noble capital, and in many respects exceptionally so. It is situated on the Baltic, at the outlet of Lake Maelaren, and is built on several islands, all of which are connected by substantial bridges. The city has a population of over a hundred and eighty thousand, covering an area of five square miles, and, taken as a whole, certainly forms one of the most cleanly and interesting capitals in Europe. It is a city of canals, public gardens, broad squares, and gay cafés, with two excellent harbors, one on the Baltic and one on Lake Maelaren.

Wars, conflagrations, and the steady progress of civilization have entirely changed the city from what it was in the days of Gustavus Vasa; that is, about the year 1496. It was he who founded the dynasty which has survived for three hundred years. The streets in the older sections of the town are often crooked and narrow, but in the modern-built parts there are fine straight avenues, with large and imposing public and private edifices.

Stockholm is the centre of the social and literary activity of Scandinavia, hardly second in this respect to Copenhagen. It has its full share of scientific, artistic, and benevolent institutions such as befit a great European capital. The stranger should as soon as convenient after arriving, ascend an elevation of the town called the Mosebacke, where has been erected a lofty iron framework and lookout, which is ascended by means of a steam elevator. From this structure an admirable view of the city is obtained, and its topography fixed clearly upon the mind. At a single glance, as it were, one takes in the charming marine view of the Baltic with its busy traffic, and in the opposite direction the many islands that dot Lake Maclaren form a widespread picture of varied beauty. The bird's-eye view obtained of the environs is unique, since in the immediate vicinity lies the primeval forest, undisturbed and unimproved for agricultural purposes.

Though Sweden, unlike Norway, has no heroic age, so to speak, connecting her earliest exploits with the fate of other countries, still no secondary European power has acted so brilliant a part in modern history as have those famous Swedish monarchs, Gustavus Vasa, Gustavus Adolphus, and Charles XII. The last-named monarch fought all Europe, — Danes, Russians, Poles, and Germans, — and gave away a kingdom before he was twenty years of age.

The Royal Palace of Stockholm is a very plain edifice externally, though it is quite large. Its present master, King Oscar II., is an accomplished artist, poet, musician, and linguist, nobly fulfilling the requirements of his responsible position. He has been called the ideal sovereign of our period. His court, while it is one of the least pretentious in Europe, is yet one of the most refined. The State departments of the palace are very elegant, and are freely shown to strangers at all suitable times. In the grand State Hall is the throne of silver originally occupied by Queen Christiana, while the Hall of Mirrors appears as though it might have come from Aladdin's palace. Amid all the varied attractions of art and historic associations which are here exhibited, one simple chamber seems most impressive. It is the bedroom of Charles XIV. (Marshal Bernadotte), which has remained unchanged and unused since the time of his death, his old campaign cloak of Swedish blue still lying upon the bed. The clock upon the mantel-piece significantly points to the hour and minute of his death. The life and remarkable career of the dead king flashes across the memory as we stand for a moment beside these suggestive tokens of personal wear. We recall how he began life as a common soldier in the French army, rising rapidly from the ranks by reason of his military genius to be a marshal of France, and finally to sit upon the throne of Sweden. Bernadotte, Prince of Ponte Corvo, is the only one of Napoleon's generals whose descendants still occupy a throne.

The shops on the principal streets are elegantly arrayed; there are none better in Paris or New York. A ceaseless activity reigns along the thoroughfares, among the little steamboats upon the many water-ways, and on the myriads of passenger steamers which ply upon the lake. The Royal Opera House is a plain substantial structure, built by Gustavus III. in 1775. The late Jenny Lind made her first appearance in public in this house, and so did Christine Nilsson, both of these renowned vocalists being Scandinavians. It was in this theatre, at a gay masquerade ball, on the morning of March 15, 1792, that Gustavus III. was fatally wounded by a shot from an assassin, who was one of the conspirators among the nobility.

Norway and Sweden are undoubtedly poor in worldly riches, but they expend larger sums of money for educational purposes, in proportion to the number of inhabitants, than any other country, except America. The result is manifest in a marked degree of intelligence diffused among all classes. One is naturally reminded in this Swedish capital of Linnæus, and also of Swedenborg, both of whom were Swedes. The latter graduated at the famous University of Upsala; the former in the greater school of outdoor nature. Upsala is the oldest town in the country, as well as the historical and educational centre of the kingdom. It is situated fifty miles from Stockholm. It was the royal capital of the county for more than a thousand years, and was the locality of the great temple of Thor, now replaced by a Christian cathedral, almost a duplicate of Notre Dame in Paris, and which was designed by the same architect.

Upsala has often been the scene of fierce and bloody conflicts. Saint Eric was slain here in 1161. It has its university and its historic associations, but it has neither trade nor commerce of any sort beyond that of a small inland town — its streets never being disturbed by business activity, though there is a population of at least fifteen thousand. The university, founded in 1477, and richly endowed by Gustavus Adolphus, is the just pride of the country, having to-day some fifteen hundred students and forty-eight professors attendant upon its daily sessions. No one can enter the profession of the law, medicine, or divinity in Sweden, who has not graduated at this institution or that at Lund. Its library contains nearly two hundred thousand volumes, and over seven thousand most valuable and rare manuscripts. Linnæus, the great naturalist, was a professor of botany and zoölogy at this university for nearly forty years. This humble shoemaker, by force of his genius, rose to be a prince in the kingdom of science. Botany and zoölogy have never known a more eminent exponent than the lowly born Karl von Linné, whom the Swedes very properly denominate the King of Flowers. A certain degree of knowledge relative to plants and natural history, forms a part of all primary education in Sweden.

About three miles from the university is the village of Old Upsala, where there is an ancient church of small dimensions, built of rough stones, containing a monument erected to the memory of Anders Celsius, the Swedish astronomer. There are also exhibited to the visitor here some curious pagan idols in wood. What a venerable and miraculously preserved old pile it is!

We return to Stockholm, — bright, cheerful, sunny Stockholm, — where, during the brief summer months, everything wears a holiday aspect, where life is seen at its gayest in the many public gardens, cleanly streets, and open squares. Even the big white sea-gulls that swoop gracefully over the many water-ways of the town — rather queer visitors to a populous city — seem to be uttering cries of bird merriment.

CHAPTER XVIII.

IN pursuing our course towards St. Petersburg, Russia, from Stockholm, we cross the Baltic,—that Mediterranean of the North, but which is in reality a remote branch of the Atlantic Ocean, with which it is connected by two gulfs, the Kattegat and the Skagger Rack. It reaches from the southern extremity of the Danish Archipelago up to the latitude of Stockholm, where it extends a right and left arm,—each of great size,—the former being the Gulf of Finland, and the latter the Gulf of Bothnia, the whole forming the most remarkable basin of navigable inland water in the world. The Finnish Gulf is two hundred miles long by an average width of sixty miles, and that of Bothnia is four hundred miles long, averaging a hundred in width.

The peninsula of Denmark, known under the name of Jutland, stands like a barrier between the two extremes of the western formation of the continent of Europe. We have called the Baltic the Mediterranean of the North, but it has no such depth as that classic inland sea, which finds its bed in a cleft of marvellous depression between Europe and Africa. One thousand fathoms of sounding-line off Gibraltar will not reach the bottom, and two thousand fathoms fail to find it a few miles east of Malta. The greatest depth of the Baltic, on the contrary, is only a hundred and fifty fathoms.

It is a curious, though not unfamiliar fact, that the

Baltic, or rather the bottom of the basin in which it lies, is rich in amber, which the agitated waters cast upon the shores in large quantities annually, — a process which has been going on for three or four centuries. We all know that amber is a hardened fossil resin produced by an extinct species of pine; so that it is evident that where these waters now ebb and flow there were once flourishing forests of amber-producing pines. These were doubtless gradually submerged by the encroachment of the sea, or suddenly engulfed by some grand volcanic action of nature. Pieces of the bark and of the cones of the pine-trees are often found adhering to the amber, and insects of a kind unknown to our day are also found embedded in it. The largest piece of amber extant is preserved in the British Museum in London, and is about the size of a year-old infant's head.

It is known that the peninsula of Scandinavia is gradually becoming elevated above the surrounding waters at the north, and depressed in an equal ratio in the extreme south, — a fact of great interest to geologists. The total change in the level has been carefully observed and recorded by scientific commissions, the aggregate certified to being a trifle over three feet, brought about in a period of a hundred and eighteen years.

We take passage on a coasting steamer which plies between Stockholm and St. Petersburg by way of Åbo and Helsingfors, a distance of about six hundred miles. By this route, after crossing the open sea we pass through an almost endless labyrinth of beautiful islands in the Gulf of Finland, including the archipelago, known as the Aland Islands, besides many isolated ones quite near the Finnish coast. This forms a delightful sail, the passage being almost always smooth, except during a few hours of exposure in the open Gulf. By and by we enter the fjord which leads up to Åbo, which is also dotted here and there by charming garden-like islands, upon which are built many pretty cottages, forming the summer homes of the citizens of Finmark's former capital.

The town of Åbo has a population of about twenty-five thousand, who are mostly of Swedish descent. It is thrifty, cleanly, and wears an aspect of quiet prosperity. The place is venerable in years, having a record reaching back for over seven centuries. Here the Russian flag — red, blue, and white — first begins to greet us from all appropriate points. The most prominent building to catch the stranger's eye on entering the harbor is the long barrack-like prison upon a hillside. In front of us looms up the famous old castle of Åbo, awkward and irregular in its shape, and snow-white in texture. Here, in the olden time, Gustavas Vasa, Eric XIV. and John III. held royal court. The streets are few but very broad, causing the town to cover an area quite out of proportion to the number of its inhabitants.

Helsingfors is situated still further up the Gulf, facing the ancient town of Revel on the Esthonian coast, and is reached from Åbo in about twelve hours' sail, also through a labyrinth of islands so numerous as to be quite confusing, but whose picturesque beauty will not easily be forgotten. This is the present capital of Finland, and it contains a little over fifty thousand inhabitants; it has been several times partially destroyed by plague, famine, and fire. It was founded by Gustavus Vasa of Sweden, in the sixteenth century. The university is represented to be of a high standard of excellence, and contains a library of about two hundred thousand volumes. The most striking feature of Helsingfors, as one approaches it from the sea, is the large Greek church, with its fifteen domes and minarets, each capped by a glittering cross and crescent, with pendant chains in gilt metal; and as it is built upon high ground, the whole is very effective. The Lutheran church is also picturesque and notable, with its five domes sparkling with gilded stars upon a dark green ground.

Though Finland is a dependency of Russia, still it is nearly as independent as is Norway of Sweden. It is ruled by a governor-general assisted by the Imperial Senate, over which a representative of the Emperor of Russia presides. The country pays no pecuniary tribute to Russia, but imposes its own taxes, and frames its own code of laws. When the country was joined to Russia, Alexander I. assured the people that the integrity of their constitution and religion should be protected, and this promise has thus far been honestly kept by the dominant power.

The port of Helsingfors is defended by the large and remarkable fortress of Sweaborg, which repelled the English and French fleets during the Crimean War. It was constructed by the Swedish General Ehrenswärd, who was a poet as well as an excellent military engineer. This fort is considered to be one of the strongest ever built, and is situated upon seven islands, each being connected with the main fortress by tunnels under the water of the harbor, constructed at great labor and cost.

After leaving Helsingfors we next come to Cronstadt, being a series of low islands, about five miles long by one broad, all fortified, and forming the key to St. Petersburg, as well as being the chief naval station of the Empire. The two fortifications of Sweaborg and Cronstadt insure to

Russia the possession of the Gulf of Finland, no matter what force is brought against them. The arsenals and docks are here very extensive and unsurpassed in completeness. The best machinists in the world find employment in them, and the latest inventions a sure and profitable market. In all facilities for marine armament Russia is fully abreast of, if it does not surpass, the rest of Europe.

The sail up the Neva, queen of northern rivers, affords the greatest pleasure. Passenger steamers are seen flitting about with well-filled decks, noisy tug-boats puff and whistle while towing heavily laden barges, naval cutters propelled by dozens of white-clad oarsmen and steered by officers in dazzling uniforms, small sailing-yachts containing merry parties of both sexes glance hither and thither, all giving animation to the scene. Here and there on the river's course long reaches of sandy shoals appear, covered by myriads of sea-gulls, scores of which occasionally rise, hover over our steamer, and settle in the water. As we approach nearer to St. Petersburg, hundreds of gilded domes and towers flashing in the warm sunlight come swiftly into view. Some of the spires are of such great height in proportion to their diameter as to appear needle-like. Among those reaching so far heavenward are the slender spire of the Cathedral of Peter and Paul, nearly four hundred feet in height, and the lofty pinnacle of the Admiralty Building. Notwithstanding its giddy towers and looming palaces rising above the level of the capital, the want of a little diversity in the grade of the low-lying city is keenly felt. Like Berlin and Havana, it is built upon a perfect level, which is the most trying of positions as to general aspect.

St. Petersburg is the grandest city of Northern Europe.

By ascending the tower of the Admiralty, a superb and comprehensive view of the capital is obtained. The streets are broad, the open squares vast in size, the avenues interminable, the river wide and rapid; while the lines of grand architecture are seemingly endless. The view from this elevation is indeed superb, studded with azure domes decked with stars of silver and gilded minarets. A grand city of palaces and spacious boulevards lies spread out before the eye. The quays of the Neva above and below the bridges are seen to present as animated a prospect as the busy thoroughfares. A portion of this Admiralty Building is devoted to schoolrooms for the education of naval cadets. The rest is occupied by the offices of the civil department of this service, and a marine museum.

There are over two hundred churches and chapels in the city, most of which are crowned with four or five fantastic cupolas each, and whose interiors are rich in gold, silver, and precious stones, together with a large array of priestly vestments elaborately embroidered with gold and ornamented with a profusion of gems. It is, indeed, a city of churches and palaces. Peter the Great and Catharine II., who has been called the female Peter the Great, made this brilliant capital what it is. Everything that meets the eye is colossal. The superb Alexander Column, erected about fifty years ago, is a solid shaft of red granite, and the loftiest single-stone column in the world. On its pedestal is inscribed this simple line : " To Alexander I. — Grateful Russia." It is surmounted by an angelic figure, the whole structure being one hundred and fifty-four feet high, and the column itself fourteen feet in diameter at the base; but so large is the square in which it stands that the shaft loses much of its colossal effect. Opposite the Alexander

THE CATHEDRAL OF ST. ISAACS AT ST. PETERSBURG.

To face p. 280.

Column, on the same wide area, are situated the Winter Palace, with the Hermitage on one side as a sort of annex, and on the other side in half-moon shape are the State buildings containing the bureaus of the several ministers, whose quarters are each a palace in itself. There is not one of the many spacious squares of the city which is not ornamented with bronze statues of more or less merit, embracing monuments to Peter the Great, Catharine, Nicholas, Alexander I., and others.

The Nevsky Prospect is the most fashionable thoroughfare, and the one devoted to the best shops. It is over a hundred feet in width, and extends for a distance of three miles in a nearly straight line to the Alexander Nevsky Monastery, forming a most magnificent avenue. On this street may be seen the churches of several sects of different faiths, such as Roman Catholics, Protestants, Armenians, and a Mahometan mosque. Here also are the Imperial Library, the Alexander Theatre, and the Foreign Office. The cosmopolitan character of the population of St. Petersburg is indicated by the fact that preaching occurs weekly in twelve different languages. The Nevsky Prospect is a street of alternating shops, palaces, and churches. Four canals cross but do not intercept this boulevard. These water-ways are lined their whole lengths by substantial granite quays, and are gay with the life imparted to them by pleasure and small freighting boats constantly furrowing their surface. Large barges are seen containing cut wood, piled fifteen feet high above their decks, delivering the winter's important supply of fuel all along the banks of the canals. Others, with their hulls quite hidden from sight, appear like great floating haystacks moving mysteriously to their destination with horse-fodder for the city stables. From one o'clock to five in the afternoon the Nevsky Prospect, with the tide of humanity pouring in either direction through its broad road-way, is like the Rue Rivoli, Paris, on a holiday.

The Imperial Library of St. Petersburg is justly entitled to more than a mere mention; for it is one of the richest collections of books in all Europe, both in quality and quantity. The bound volumes number a little over one million, while it is especially rich in most interesting and important manuscripts. In a room devoted to the purpose there is a collection of books printed previous to the year 1500, which is considered unique. The Alexander Theatre and the library both look down upon a broad square which contains a fine statue of Catharine II. in bronze. This composition seems to breathe the very spirit of the profligate and cruel original, whose ambitious plans were ever in conflict with her enslaving passions. History is compelled to admit her great ability, while it causes us to blush for her infamy.

St. Petersburg is the fifth city in point of population in Europe, but its very existence seems to be constantly threatened on account of its low situation between two vast bodies of water. A westerly gale and high tide in the Gulf of Finland occurring at the time of the annual breaking up of the ice in the Neva would surely submerge this beautiful capital, and cause an enormous loss of life. The Neva, which comes sweeping through the city with such resistless force, is fed by that large body of water, Lake Ladoga, which covers an area of over six thousand square miles at a level of about sixty feet above that of the sea. However, St. Petersburg has existed in security for nearly two centuries, and it may possibly exist as much longer, independent of possible floods. What the Gotha Canal is to Sweden, the Neva and its joining waters are to Russia. Through Lake Ladoga and its ramifications of connecting canals and rivers, it opens communication with an almost unlimited region of inland territory, while the mouth of this river receives through the gulf the commerce of the world.

As regards popular amusements, Sunday is the favorite day of the seven at the public gardens, on which occasion, day and evening, theatrical performances take place. The Greek churches, like the Roman Catholic, are always open through the entire week, so that the devoutly inclined can turn aside at any hour and bow before the altar, which to him typifies all that is holy. Sunday is therefore regarded here, as in Rome, Paris, or Seville, in the light of a holiday as well as a holy-day. After having attended early morning service, a member of either church unhesitatingly seeks his favorite amusement. The horse-races of Paris, the bull-fights of Madrid, and the grand military parades of St. Petersburg, all take place on Sunday. Few European communities find that repose and calmness in the day which best accords with American sentiment.

The one vehicle of Russian cities is the drosky, the most uncomfortable and inconvenient vehicle ever constructed for the use of man, but of which there are, nevertheless, over fifteen thousand in the streets of the imperial city. It has very low wheels, a heavy, awkward body, and is as noisy as a hard-running Concord coach. Some one describes it as being a cross between a cab and an instrument of torture. There is no rest for the occupant's back; and while the seat is more than large enough for one, it is not large enough for two persons. It is a sort of sledge on wheels. The noise made by these low-running conveyances as they are hurried over the uneven pavements is almost deafening.

The winter season, which sets in about the first of November, changes the aspect of everything in the Russian capital, and lasts until the end of April, when the ice generally breaks up. In the meantime the Neva freezes to a depth of six feet. But keen as is the winter cold, the Russians do not suffer much from it, being universally clad in furs. Even the peasant class necessarily wear warm sheep-skins with the fleece on, otherwise they would often freeze to death on a very brief exposure to the low temperature which prevails in winter. Doubtless there must be poverty and wretchedness existing here, but it certainly is not obvious to the stranger. There is no street-begging, and no half-clad, half-starved women or children obstruct the way as is so often the case in London or Naples.

The five islands of the city, separated by the Nevka and Neva, are called the "Garden Islands," and they form the pleasure-drive of the town, having quite a country aspect, forming a series of parks where fine roads wind through shady woods, cross green meadows, and skirt transparent lakes. Here every variety of villa is seen embowered in attractive verdure, and a highly rural effect is obtained within city limits.

St. Petersburg is the most spacious capital ever built by the hand of man, and one cannot but feel that many of its grand squares, presided over by some famous monument, are yet dismally empty. As we look upon it to-day, it probably bears little resemblance to the city left by the great Peter, its founder, except in its general plan, and yet it extends so little way into the past as to have comparatively no root in history. The magnificent granite quays, the gorgeous palaces, the costly churches and monuments do not date previous to the reign of Catharine II. The choice of the locality, and the building of the capital upon it, is naturally a wonder to those who have not thought carefully about it, since it seems to have been contrary to all reason, and to have been steadily pursued in the face of difficulties which would have discouraged and defeated most similar enterprises. Ten thousand lives and more were sacrificed among the laborers annually, while the work was going on, owing to its unhealthy nature, but still the autocratic designer held to his purpose, until finally a respectable but not unobjectionable foundation may be said to have been obtained upon this Finland marsh. Yet there are those who believe that all was foreseen by the energetic founder, that he had a grand and definite object in view of which he never lost sight, and moreover that the object which he aimed at has been fully consummated.

The Winter Palace is grand in every respect. Its size may be divined when we realize that it accommodates six thousand persons connected with the royal household. With the exception of the Vatican at Rome, and Versailles near Paris, it is the largest habitable palace in existence, and is made up of suits of splendid apartments, reception saloons, drawing-rooms, throne rooms, banqueting-halls, etc. The gem of them all is the Salle Blanche, or White Hall, so called because the fittings and decorations are all in white and gold, by means of which an aerial lightness and fascination of effect is produced which is difficult to describe. It is in this apartment that the court festivals take place, and there are probably no royal entertainments in Europe which quite equal in splendor those given in the Winter Palace. One becomes almost dazed by the glare of gilt and bronze, the number of polished columns of marble and porphyry, the gorgeous hangings, the mosaics, mirrors, and candelabra. Many of the painted ceilings are wonderfully perfect in design and execution, while choice works of art are so abundant on all sides as to lose effect. The famous banqueting-hall measures two hundred feet in length by one hundred in breadth. As we come forth from the palace through the grand entrance upon the square, it is natural to turn and scan the magnificent front as a whole, and to remember that from the gate of this palace Catharine II. went forth on horseback with a drawn sword in her hand, to put herself at the head of her army.

The Hermitage, of which the world has read so much, is a spacious building adjoining the Winter Palace, with which it is connected by a covered gallery, and is five hundred feet long where it fronts upon the square containing the Alexander Column. It is not, as its name might indicate, a solitude, but a grand and elaborate palace in itself, built by Catharine II. for a picture gallery, a museum, and a resort of pleasure. It contains to-day one of the largest as well as the most precious collections of paintings in the world, not forgetting those of Rome, Florence, Paris, and Madrid. The catalogue shows twenty original pictures by Murillo, six by Velasquez, sixty by Rubens, thirty-three by Vandyke, forty by Teniers, the same number by Rembrandt, six by Raphael, and many other invaluable examples by famous masters.

Here are also preserved the private libraries that once belonged to Zimmermann, Voltaire, and Diderot, besides those of several other remarkable men of letters. There is a royal theatre under the same roof, where plays used to be performed by amateurs from the court circles for the gratification of the empress, the text of the plays being sometimes written by herself. This royal lady indulged her fancy to the fullest extent. On the roof of the Hermitage was created a marvellous garden planted with choicest flowers, shrubs, and even trees of considerable size, all together forming a grand floral conservatory which was heated by subterranean fires in winter, and sheltered by a complete covering of glass.

CHAPTER XIX.

THE Palace of Peterhoff is situated about sixteen miles from St. Petersburg, on the shore of the Neva where the river expands to a width of eight or ten miles. This place has always been celebrated for the magnificent entertainments given here since the days when it was first built by Peter the Great. The main structure has no special merit in point of architecture, but the location and the surroundings are extremely beautiful. From the terrace of the great yellow palace built upon a natural elevation, one gets a fine though distant view of the coast of Finland, — a portion of the Tzar's dominion which alone exceeds in size Great Britain and Ireland, a wide-spread barren land of lakes and granite rocks, but peopled by over two millions of souls. The parks, gardens, fountains, hothouses, groves, and embowered paths of Peterhoff are kept in the most perfect order by a small army of household attendants. The artificial water-works are after the style of those at St. Cloud, and are nearly equal to those of Versailles.

Here the famous Peter used to retire and stroll about the gardens with his humble favorite, a Polish girl, forgetting the cares of state. This lowly companion, besides great personal beauty, possessed much force of character, and exercised great influence over her melancholic and morose master. Long before her final elevation to the throne, many instances are related of her interference in behalf of mercy, which showed a kind and loving nature. Peterhoff is the favorite summer resort of the royal family.

The Tzar's dominion embraces every phase of religion and of civilization. Portions of the empire are as barbaric as Central Africa, others are semi-civilized, while a large share of the people inhabiting the cities assume the highest outward appearance of refinement and culture. This diversity of character spreads over a country extending from the Great Wall of China on one side to the borders of Germany on the other; from the Crimea in the south to the Polar Ocean in the far north.

The distance from St. Petersburg to Moscow is about four hundred miles; the cars upon this route take us directly towards the heart of Russia. Thirty years ago there were but about eight hundred miles of railroad in the country; to-day there are twenty thousand and more. On this trip one passes through scenery of the most monotonous and melancholy character, flat and featureless, made up of forests of fir-trees, interspersed with the white birch, and long reaches of wide, deserted plains.

The forest forms a very prominent feature of Russia north of the line of travel between the two great cities, covering in that region fully a third part of the country; the largest forest in Europe is that of Volskoniki, which commences near the source of the Volga. But to the south of Moscow the vast plains, or steppes, are quite free from wood, consisting merely of sandy deserts, unfit for habitation. No country is more thinly inhabited or more wearisomely tame. Now and again a few sheep are seen cropping the thin brown moss and straggling verdure, tended by a boy clad in a fur cap and skin jacket, forming a strong contrast to his bare legs and feet.

Though sparsely inhabited by fierce and active races for centuries, the appearance is that of primitiveness; the log-cabins seem to be only temporary expedients, — wooden tents, as it were. The men and women who are seen at the railroad stations are of the Tartar type, the ugliest of all humanity, with high cheekbones, flattened noses, dull gray eyes, copper-colored hair, and bronzed complexions. Their food is not of a character to develop much physical comeliness. The one vegetable which the Russian peasant cultivates is cabbage; this, mixed with dried mushrooms, and rarely anything else, makes a soup upon which he lives. Add to this soup a porridge made of meal, and we have about the entire substance of his regular food. If they produce some pork and corn, butter and cheese, they are seldom indulged in for their own subsistence, but are sold at the nearest market, as a certain amount of ready money must be had when the tax-gatherer makes his annual visit. We are speaking of the masses, but of course there are exceptions. Some thrifty peasants manage much better than this. No other country is richer in horses, mines of gold, silver, copper, and precious stones; or in the useful articles of iron, lead, and zinc. Though the Russians are famous for having large families, still the inhabitants average but fifteen to the square mile, while in Germany there are eighty, and in England over four hundred to the square mile.

Forests of such density as to be impenetrable to man frequently line the railroad for many miles together, but the loneliness of the way is relieved by occasional glimpses of wild-flowers scattered along the roadside in great variety, diffusing indescribable freshness. Among them now and again a tall scarlet poppy rears its gaudy head, nodding lazily in the currents of air and leading us to wonder how it came here in such company. A peculiar little blue flower is frequently observed with yellow petals, seeming to look up from the surrounding nakedness and desolation with the appealing expression of human eyes. Snow-white daisies and delicate little harebells come into view at intervals, struggling for a brief and lonely existence. The railroad stations are beautified by floral displays of no mean character. It seems that professional gardeners travel on the line, remaining long enough at each place to organize the skilful culture of garden-plants by the keeper's family during the few weeks of summer; but one shudders to think what must be the aspect of this region during the long frost-locked Russian winter.

On reaching the city of Tver, we cross, by a high iron bridge, the river Volga, — one of the greatest in the world, — the Mississippi of Russia. From this point the river is navigable for over two thousand miles to Astrakhan. In a country so extensive and which possesses so small a portion of seaboard, rivers have a great importance, and until the introduction of railroads they formed nearly the only available means of transportation. The canals, rivers, and lakes are no longer navigated by barges drawn by horse-power. Steam-tugs and small passenger steamers now tow great numbers of flat-boats of large capacity; and transportation by this mode of conveyance is very cheap. The Volga is the largest river in Europe. Measured through its entire windings it has a length of twenty-four hundred miles from its rise in the Valdai Hills, five hundred and fifty feet above sea-level, to its outlet into the Caspian Sea. Many cities and thriving towns are situated upon its banks. At Nijni-Novgorod it is joined by the Oka

River. In addition to these water-ways there are also the Obi, the Yenisee, the Lena, the Don, and the Dnieper, all rivers of the first class, whose entire course from source to mouth is within the Russian territory, saying nothing of the several rivers tributary to these. Nor should we forget those frontier rivers, the Danube, the Amoor, and the Oxus, all of which are auxiliary to the great system of canals that connects the important rivers of the empire. The Volga by this system communicates with the White Sea, the Baltic, and the Euxine.

While we are narrating these interesting facts relating to the material greatness of Russia, we are also approaching its ancient capital. It stands upon a vast plain through which winds the Moskva River, from which the city derives its name. The villages naturally become more populous as we advance, and gilded domes and cupolas occasionally loom up above the tree-tops on either side of the road, indicating a Greek church here and there. As in approaching Cairo in Egypt, one sees first and while far away the pyramids of Ghizeh, and afterwards the graceful minarets and towers of the Oriental city gleaming through the golden haze; so as we gradually emerge from the thinly inhabited Russian plains and draw near the capital, first there comes into view the massive towers of the Kremlin and the Church of Our Saviour with its golden dome, followed by the hundreds of glittering steeples, belfries, towers, and star-gilded domes of this extremely interesting and ancient city.

Though some of these religious temples have simply a cupola in the shape of an inverted bowl, terminating in a gilded point capped by a cross and crescent, few of them have less than five or six, and some have sixteen superstructures of the most whimsical device, with gilded chains depending from each apex and affixed at the base. A bird's-eye view of Moscow is far more picturesque than that of St. Petersburg, the older city being located upon very uneven ground, is in some places quite hilly. St. Petersburg is European, while Moscow is Tartar. The latter has been three times nearly destroyed: first by the Tartars in the thirteenth century; next, by the Poles, in the seventeenth century; and again at the time of the French invasion under Napoleon, in 1812. Still it has sprung from its ashes each time as if by magic, and has never lost its original character, being now a more splendid and prosperous capital than ever before, rapidly increasing in population. The romantic character of its history, so mingled with protracted wars, civil conflicts, sieges, and conflagrations, makes it seem half fabulous. The population is not much, if any less than that of St. Petersburg,—eight hundred thousand,—while the territory which it covers measures over twenty miles in circumference.

Moscow is to the Russian what Mecca is to the pious Moslem, and he calls it by the endearing name of "mother." Like Kief and the Trortzkoi (sacred monastery), it is the object of pious pilgrimage to thousands annually, who come from long distances on foot.

The Kremlin, which crowns a hill, is the central point of the city, and is enclosed by high walls, battlement rising upon battlement, flanked by massive towers. The name is Tartar and signifies a fortress. As such it is unequalled for its vastness, its historical associations, and the wealth of its sanctuaries. It was founded five or six hundred years ago, and is an enclosure studded with cathedrals, and embracing broad streets and spacious squares,—a citadel and city within itself, being to Moscow what the Acropolis was to Athens. The various buildings are a strange conglomerate of architecture, including Tartar, Hindu, Chinese, and Gothic exhibited in noble cathedrals, chapels, towers, convents, and palaces. There are about twenty churches within the walls of the Kremlin. The Cathedral of the Assumption is perhaps the most noteworthy, teeming as it does with historic interest, and being filled with tombs and pictures from its dark agate floor to the base of the vast cupola. Here, from the time of Ivan the Great to that of the present Emperor, the Tzars have all been crowned, and here Peter placed the royal insignia upon the head of his second wife, the peasant-girl of Livonia.

The venerable walls of the Kremlin, which measure about two miles in circumference, are pierced by five gates of an imposing character, to each of which is attributed a religious or historical importance. Often have invading hosts battered at these gates, and sometimes gained an entrance; but, strange to say, they have always in the end been worsted by the faithful Muscovites. Over the Redeemer's Gate, so called, is affixed a wonder-working picture of the Saviour, which is an object of great veneration. No one, not even the Emperor, passes beneath it without removing his hat and bowing the head. A miracle is supposed to have been wrought in connection with this picture of the Redeemer at the time when the retreating French made a vain attempt to blow up the Kremlin, and hence the special reverence given to it.

The most strikingly fantastic structure in Moscow is the Cathedral of St. Basil, which is top-heavy with spires, domes, and minarets, ornamented in the most irregular and unprecedented manner. Yet, as a whole, the structure is not inharmonious with its unique surroundings, — the semi-Oriental, semi-barbaric atmosphere in which it stands. It is not within the walls of the Kremlin, but is just outside, near the Redeemer's Gate, from which point the best view of it may be enjoyed. No two of its towering projections are alike, either in height, shape, or ornamentation. The coloring throughout is as various as the shape, being in yellow, green, blue, red, gilt, and silver. Each spire and dome has its glittering cross; and when the sun shines upon the group, it is in effect like the bursting of a rocket at night, against a dark blue background.

In front of this many-domed cathedral is a circular stone whence the Tzars of old were accustomed to proclaim their edicts; and it is also known as "The Place of the Scull," because of the many executions which have taken place upon it. Ivan the Terrible rendered the spot infamous by the series of executions which he ordered to take place here, the victims being mostly innocent of any crimes. Here Prince Scheviref was impaled by order of this same tyrant, and here several other members of the royal family were ruthlessly put to death after being barbarously tortured.

The treasury of the Kremlin, erected so late as 1851, is a historical museum of crowns, thrones, state costumes, and regalia generally; including in the latter department the royal robes of Peter the Great as well as his crown, in which there are about nine hundred diamonds; and that of his widow Catharine I., which contains three thousand of these precious stones. One comes away from the labyrinth of palaces, churches, arsenals, museums, and the treasury, after viewing their accumulation of riches, quite dazed and surfeited. To examine the latter properly requires more than a single day. It is a marvel of accumulated riches, including the crowns of many now defunct kingdoms, such as those of Kazan, Georgia, Astrakhan, and Poland, — all heavy with precious stones. The crown jewels of England and Germany combined would not equal in value these treasures. The most venerable of the crowns is that of Monomachus, brought from Byzantium more than eight hundred years ago. This emblem is covered with jewels of the choicest character, among which are steel-white diamonds and rubies of pigeon's-blood hue, such as are rarely obtainable in our day.

While viewing the many attractions of Moscow one is apt to recall a page from history and remember the heroic, self-sacrificing means which the people of this Asiatic city adopted to repel the invading and victorious enemy. It was an act of sublime desperation to place the torch within the sanctuary of Russia and destroy all, sacred and profane, so that the enemy should also be destroyed. It was the grandest sacrifice ever made to national honor by any people. "Who would have thought that a nation would burn its own capital?" said Napoleon.

Strangers are hardly prepared to find Moscow so great a manufacturing centre, more than fifty thousand of the population being regularly employed in manufacturing establishments. There are over a hundred cotton mills within the limits of the city, between fifty and sixty woollen mills, over thirty silk mills, and other kindred establishments, though enterprise in this direction is mostly confined to textile fabrics. The city is fast becoming the centre of a great railroad system, affording the means of rapid and easy distribution for the several products of these mills.

The favorite seat of learning is the Moscow University, founded by Peter the Great in 1755, its four principal faculties being those of history, physics, jurisprudence, and medicine. It is a State institution, and has at this time some two thousand students. The terms of admission as regards cost to the pupils are merely nominal, the advantages being open to all youth above seventeen who can pass a satisfactory examination. Here, also, is another large and valuable library open at all times to the public, containing over two hundred thousand well-chosen volumes. This liberal multiplication of educational advantages in the very heart of Oriental Russia is an indisputable evidence of progressive civilization.

One is struck by the multitude of pigeons seen in and about the city. They are held in great reverence by the common people, and no Russian will harm them. Indeed, they are as sacred here as monkeys in Benares, or doves in Venice, being considered emblems of the Holy Ghost and under protection of the Church. They wheel about in large blue flocks through the air, so dense as to cast shadows, like swift-moving clouds, alighting fearlessly where they choose, to share the beggar's crumbs or the rich man's bounty. It is a notable fact that this bird was also considered sacred by the old Scandinavians, who believed that for a certain period after death the soul of the deceased assumed this form to visit and watch the behavior of the mourners.

Beggary is sadly prevalent in the streets of Moscow, the number of maimed and wretched-looking human beings recalling the same scenes in Spain and Italy, especially in the former country, where beggary seems to be the occupation of one-third of the people.

CHAPTER XX.

WE must travel by railway three hundred miles further towards the centre of the empire and in a northerly direction, to reach Nijni Novgorod, that is, Lower Novgorod, being so called to distinguish it from the famous place of the same name located on the Volkhov, and known as Novgorod the Great. This journey is made in the night, and the cars, which are supposed to afford sleeping accommodations, are furnished with reclining chairs only. However, we get along very well, and fatigue is pretty sure to make one sleep soundly, notwithstanding the want of inviting conveniences. Having arrived at Nijni-Novgorod early in the morning, we find it to be a peculiar city. The residence of the governor of the district, the courts of law, and the citadel are within the Kremlin, where there is also a fine monument to the memory of Mininn and Pojarski, the two patriots who liberated the country from the Poles in 1612.

The Kremlin, like that at Moscow, is situated on an elevation overlooking the town and the broad valley of the Volga. As we view the scene, a vast alluvial plain is spread out before the eye, covered with fertile fields and thrifty woods, through which from northwest to southeast flows the river, like a silver thread upon a verdant ground, extending from horizon to horizon. On this river, the main artery of Central Russia, are seen scores of swift-moving steamers, while a forest of shipping is gathered about the wharves of the lower town, and also upon the Oka River, which here joins the Volga. From this outlook we count over two hundred steamers in sight at the same time, all side-wheelers and clipper-built, drawn hither by the exigencies of the local trade growing out of the great annual fair. The first of these steamboats was built in the United States and transported to Russian waters, since which it has served as a model to builders, who have furnished many hundreds for river service.

The flat-boats or barges, which have been towed hither by the steamers from various distances, having been unloaded, are anchored in a shallow bend of the river, where they cover an area of a mile square. On most of these barges entire families live, it being their only home; and wherever freight is to be transported, thither they go; whether it is towards the Ural Mountains or the Caspian Sea, it is all the same to them: the Arabs of the desert are not more roving than they.

The Volga has a course of twenty-four hundred, and the Oka of eight hundred and fifty miles. As the Missouri and the Mississippi rivers have together made St. Louis in this country, so these two rivers have made Nijni-Novgorod. This great mart lies at the very centre of the water communication which joins the Caspian and the Black seas to the Baltic and the White seas; besides which, it has direct railroad connection with Moscow, and thence with all Eastern Europe. The Volga and its tributaries pour into its lap the wealth of the Ural Mountains and that of the vast region of Siberia and Central Asia. It thus becomes very apparent why and how this ancient city is the point of business contact between European industry and Asiatic wealth.

The attraction which draws most travellers so far into the centre of Russia, lies in the novelty of the great annual fair held here for a period of about eight weeks, and which gathers together for the time being some two hundred thousand people, traders and spectators, merchants and rogues, who come from the most distant provinces and countries of Asia, as well as from immediate regions round about. The variety of merchandise brought hither is something to astonish one. Jewelry of such beauty and fashion as would grace the best stores of Paris is here offered for sale, beside the cheapest ornaments manufactured by the bushel-basketful at Birmingham, England. Choice old silverware is exposed along with iron sauce-pans, tin dippers, and cheap crockery — variety and incongruity, gold and tinsel, everywhere side by side. There is an abundance of iron and copper from the Urals, dried fish in tall piles from the Caspian, tea from China, cotton from India, silk and rugs from Persia, heavy furs and sables from Siberia, wool in the raw state from Cashmere, together with the varied products of the trans-Causcasian provinces, even including droves of wild horses. Fancy goods are here displayed from England as well as from Paris and Vienna, toys from Nuremberg, ornaments of jade and lapis-lazuli from Kashgar, precious stones from Ceylon, and gems from pearl-producing Penang. Variety, indeed! Then what a conglomerate of odors permeates everything, — boiled cabbage, coffee, tea, and tanned leather, — dominated by the all-pervading musk; but all this is quite in consonance with the queer surroundings which meet the eye, where everything presents itself through an Oriental haze.

If any business purpose actuates the visitor, let him

keep his wits about him, and, above all, remain cool, for it requires an effort not to be confused by the ceaseless buzzing of such a crowded hive of human beings. Sharpers are not unrepresented here, but may be seen in full force seeking to take advantage of every opportunity for imposition, so that many who come hither thrive solely by dishonesty. It is a sort of thieves' paradise — and Asiatic thieves are marvellously expert. Most of these are itinerants, having no booths, tables, or fixtures, except a satchel or box hung about their necks, from which they offer trifling articles at low prices, a specious disguise under which to prosecute their real design.

The period of great differences in prices at localities wide apart has, generally speaking, passed away, and nearly everywhere the true value of things is known. Circumstances may favor sellers and buyers by turns, but intrinsic values are fixed all over the world. Nothing is found especially cheap at this great Russian-Asiatic fair except such articles as no one wants, though occasionally a dealer who is particularly anxious to get cash will offer his goods at a low price to effect the desired sale. The Tartar merchant from the central provinces of Asia knows the true worth of his goods, though in exchange he pays liberal prices for Parisian and English luxuries. Gems which are offered so abundantly here can only be bought at somewhat near to their just value in the markets of the world. All the tricks of trade are known and resorted to at these gatherings. The merchant begins by demanding a price ridiculously above the amount for which he is willing to sell. No dealer has a fixed price at Nijni-Novgorod. The Asiatic enjoys dickering — it is to him the very life of his occupation, and adds zest, if not profit, to his business transactions.

It is curious to watch the various features, the physical development, the dress, manners, customs, and languages of the throng. It would be impossible to convey an idea of the ceaseless Babel of noise which prevails;—the cries designating certain goods, the bartering going on in shrill voices, the laughter mingled with sportive exclamations, and the frequent disputes which fill the air. But there is no actual quarrelling; the Russian police are too vigilant, too much feared, too summary for that. Open violence is instantly suppressed, and woe betide the culprit!

Such is this unique fair, which presents one of the rude and ancient Eastern forms of trade —a form which was once also prevalent throughout Europe, but now rapidly disappearing by the introduction of railroads, even in the East. The glory of Nijni-Novgorod is already beginning to wane; but it would seem that the fair still represents all the gayest features of the olden time, having been held here annually since 1366, tradition pointing even to an earlier date.

The large and populous city formed here, though so temporary, is divided into long and broad streets lined with booths, shops, restaurants, tents, and even minor theatres, while the wharves of the rivers are crowded with bales of rags, grain, hides, skins, casks of wine, madder, and cotton. The total value of the goods disposed of at these annual fairs is estimated as high as eighty million dollars. It is the only notable gathering of the sort now to be seen in Russia. With the close of the day business is mostly laid aside, dancing-girls appear in the cafés, and rude musical instruments are brought forth, each nationality amusing itself after its own fashion. Strange and not inharmonious airs fall upon the ear, supplemented by songs, the words of which are utterly unintelligible, except to the circle of participants. The whole scene forms a strange picture, as parti-colored as Harlequin's costume, while the whole is watched by the ever-present Russian police.

A couple of days at the fair serves to acquaint us sufficiently with all of its peculiarities, and we return to the ancient capital of the empire by night train.

It is a long and rather dreary journey from Moscow to Warsaw, in Russian Poland, the distance being some seven hundred miles by rail, and the route very monotonous. The country through which we pass is heavily wooded, and affords some attractive sport to foreigners, who resort here especially for wolf-shooting. In the summer season these creatures are seldom dangerous to men, except when they go mad, which, in fact, they are rather liable to do. When in this condition, they rush through field and forest, heedless of hunters, dogs, or aught else, biting every creature they meet, and such victims are pretty sure to die of hydrophobia. The wolves are at all seasons more or less destructive to small domestic stock, and sometimes in the severity of a hard winter they will gather in large numbers and attack human beings, though as a rule they are timid and keep out of the way of men. There are also some desirable game-birds in these forests. The wild bison still exists here, though it is forbidden to shoot them, as they are considered to belong to the Crown. If they were not fed by man during the long winters, they would surely starve.

In the last portion of this journey the country puts on a more agreeable aspect. The beautiful lavender color of the flax-fields interspersed with the peach-bloom of broad, level acres of buckwheat, produces a pleasant and thrifty aspect.

These fields are alternated by miles of intensely green oats, rye, and other cereals. No finer display of growing grain is to be found, except in Western America. The hay-makers, in picturesque groups, are busy along the line of the railroad as we pass, nine-tenths of them being women. The borders of Poland exhibit a scene of great fertility and successful agricultural enterprise. As we cross the frontier, a difference in the dress of the common people becomes noticeable. Men no longer wear red shirts outside of their pantaloons, and scarlet disappears from the dress of the women, giving place to more subdued hues. The stolid, square faces of the Russian peasantry are replaced by a more intelligent cast of features, while many representatives of the Jewish race begin to appear, especially about the railway stations, where they offer trifling articles for sale. The dwelling-houses which now come into view are of a superior class to those left behind in Russia proper. Log cabins disappear entirely, and thatched roofs are rarely seen; good, substantial frame houses appropriately painted become numerous. Small, trim flower-plats are seen fenced in, adjoining the dwellings. Lines of beehives find place near these cheerful homes, where the surroundings generally are suggestive of thrift and industry.

In passing through Poland the country presents almost one unbroken plain admirably adapted to agriculture, so much so that it has been called the granary of Europe. The Polish peasants are extremely ignorant, if possible even more so than the Russians proper of the same class; but they are a fine-looking race, strongly built, tall, active, and well formed. There are schools in the various districts, but the Polish language is forbidden to be taught in them: only the Russian tongue is permitted. The peasantry have pride enough to resist this arbitrary measure in the only way which is open to them; that is, by keeping their children out of the schools. Education not being compulsory here as it is in Norway and Sweden, little benefit is consequently derived from the schools. With a view to utterly obliterate the Polish language it is even made a penal offence by Russian law to use it in commercial transactions.

The Polish peasantry as a whole are by no means a prepossessing race. Naturally dull, they are furthermore demoralized and degraded by a love of spirituous liquors, these being unfortunately both cheap and potent. As regards the nationality of Poland, her fate is certainly decided for many years to come, if, indeed, it be not settled for all time. Dismembered as she is, every new generation must amalgamate her more and more completely with the three powers who have appropriated her territory and divided the control of her people among them. We continue to speak of Poland as a distinct country, though the name is all that remains of its ancient independence. The map of Europe has long since been reconstructed in this region, — Austria, Germany, and Russia coolly absorbing the six millions of Poles, Warsaw becoming thus the capital of Russian Poland.

We enter the city by the Praga suburb, crossing the lofty iron bridge which here stretches over the Vistula, nearly two thousand feet in length.

The city extends about six miles along the left bank of the Vistula, and upon very high ground. The river is navigable at most seasons of the year, extending the whole length of Poland from north to south, its source being the Carpathian Mountains, and its mouth at Dantzig. The city covers a great surface in proportion to the number of inhabitants, and is enclosed by ramparts pierced by ten gates, all being defended by a strong castle of modern construction. The fortifications are kept at all times up to a war standard, and are very complete in the department of modern artillery. The city has nearly half a million inhabitants, one-third of whom are Jews, who monopolize the main branches of trade.

From the top of the railway station in the Praga district one gets an admirable view. On the opposite side of the river is seen the citadel, the oldest portion of the town, with its narrow streets and lofty houses, the castle and its beautiful gardens, as well as the newer section of the city, including the public promenade and groves about the royal villa of Lazienki. Viewed from Praga, as it slopes upward, the effect of the city is very pleasing, and a closer examination of its churches, former palaces, and fine public buildings confirms the favorable impression. This view should be supplemented by one of a bird's-eye character to be obtained from the cupola of the Lutheran Church, which more clearly reveals the several large squares and main arteries, bordered by graceful lime-trees.

In spite of its misfortunes, Warsaw ranks to-day as the third city in importance as well as population in the Russian Empire. It was not made the capital of Poland until 1566, when it succeeded Cracow. It is now the residence of a viceroy representing the Emperor of Russia, and the place is strongly garrisoned by the soldiers of the Tzar. War and devastation have deprived it of many of its national and patriotic monuments, but its squares are still ornamented with numerous admirable statues, and with a grand array of fine public buildings. In the square of the royal castle there is a colossal bronze statue of Sigismund III.; in another quarter a bronze statue of Copernicus is found. It will be remembered that he was a Pole by birth and was educated at Cracow, his name being Latinized from Kopernik. There is a thirteenth century cathedral close by, whose pure Gothic contrasts strongly with the Tartar style which we have so lately left behind in Russia. This old church is very gray and crumbling, very dirty, and very offensive to the sense of smell, partly accounted for by obvious causes, since about the doors, inside and out, swarm a vile-smelling horde of ragged men, women, and children, sad and pitiful to behold.

Here we find the finest public buildings and most elegant residences strangely mingled with wooden hovels; magnificence and squalor side by side, inexorably jumbled together. No other city in all Europe has so many private palaces and elegant mansions as may be seen in an hour's stroll about Warsaw; but the architecture is often gaudy and in bad taste. Here for centuries there were but two classes or grades of society; namely, the noble, and the peasant. A Polish noble was by law a person who possessed a freehold estate, and who could prove his descent from ancestors formerly possessing a freehold, who followed no trade or commerce, and who was at liberty to choose his own habitation. This description, therefore, included all persons who were above the rank of tradesmen or peasants.

The "Avenues" is the popular drive and promenade of the citizens of Warsaw. It is bordered by long lines of trees, and surrounded by elegant private residences. Here also are inviting public gardens where popular entertainments are presented, and where cafés dispense ices, favorite drinks, and other refreshments. The Botanical Gardens are close at hand, forming a pleasant resort for the lovers of floral beauty. Just beyond these gardens is the Lazienki Park, containing the suburban palace built by King Stanislaus Poniatovski in the middle of the last century, and which is now the temporary residence of the Emperor of Russia when he visits Warsaw. These grounds are very spacious, affording complete seclusion and shady drives. Though it so closely adjoins the city, it has the effect of a wild forest of ancient trees. The royal villa stands in the midst of a stately grove, surrounded by graceful fountains, tiny lakes, and delightful flower-gardens. There are some fine groups of marble statuary picturesquely disposed among the tropical plants.

One is hardly prepared to see so much commercial prosperity and rapidity of growth as is evinced in Warsaw. In matters of current business and industrial affairs it appears to be in advance of St. Petersburg. The large number of distilleries and breweries are unpleasantly suggestive of the intemperate habits of the people. The political division of Poland, to which we have referred, was undoubtedly a great outrage on the part of the three powers who confiscated her territory, but it has certainly resulted in decided benefit as regards the interests of the common people. There are those who see in the fate of Poland that retributive justice which Heaven metes out to nations as well as to individuals. In past ages she was a country ever aggressive upon her neighbors, and it was not until she was sadly torn and weakened by internal dissensions that Catharine II. first invaded her territory. Nine-tenths of the populace were no better than slaves, in much the same condition as the Russian serfs before the late emancipation took place. They were acknowledged retainers, owing their service to, and holding their farms at the option of the upper class; namely, the so-called nobility of the country. This overmastering class prided itself on the fact of neither promoting nor being engaged in any kind of business; indeed, this uselessness was one condition attached to its patent of nobility. These autocratic rulers knew no other interest or occupation than that of the sword. War and devastation constituted their profession, while the common people for ages reaped the fruit of famine and slaughter. Even in what were called times of peace, the court and nobles were constantly engaged in intrigues and quarrels. However hard these reflections may seem, they are substantiated by historical facts, and are frankly admitted by the intelligent citizens of Warsaw to-day.

That there is shameful despotism exercised by the present ruling powers all must allow; but that peace, individual liberty, and great commercial prosperity now reign in Poland is equally obvious. In the days which are popularly denominated those of Polish independence the nobility were always divided into bitter factions. Revolutions were as frequent as they are to-day in South America or Mexico, and the strongest party disposed of the crown, ruling amid tumult and bloodshed.

CHAPTER XXI.

FROM Warsaw we turn towards Munich, the capital of Bavaria, reaching the quaint old city by way of Vienna, a description of which we have given in a previous chapter. Munich has a population of about two hundred thousand, and it possesses many noble institutions devoted to charitable, literary, and art purposes. The accumulation of art treasures is of the choicest character, not exceeded in number or importance by any other city of Germany, if we except Dresden. Many of its churches, centuries in age, are of great interest. Nearly all of our modern bronze statues have been cast in the famous founderies of Munich. The university, in the University Platz, takes first rank among the educational institutions of the old world. The English Garden, so-called, is a beautiful and extensive park which was established just one century ago; it is about four miles long by half a mile in width. Here is seen an admirable statue of Count Rumford, the founder of the garden. In clear weather the distant Alps are visible from here.

The public library of Munich is remarkably comprehensive, and contains about nine hundred thousand volumes, besides twenty-four thousand valuable manuscripts. Few collections in the world are so important. The Bavarian national museum embraces a magnificent array of objects illustrating the progress of civilization and art. Munich is strongly marked in its general aspect, manners, and customs. A considerable share of the most menial as well as of the most trying physical labor devolves upon the women. It is very repulsive to an American to see them, as one does here, ascending high ladders with buckets of mortar or bricks for building purposes. The stranger is unpleasantly impressed with the fact that more beer is drunk in Munich than in any other community composed of the same number of people. The obvious trouble with those who consume so much malt liquor is that they keep half tipsy all of the time, and their muddled brains are never in possession of their full mental capacity. There is not much absolute drunkenness to be seen in the streets of this capital, but the bloated faces and bleared eyes of the masses show only too plainly their vulgar and unwholesome indulgence.

From Munich we proceed to Frankfort-on-the-Main, an ancient and important city of Germany, containing a population of one hundred and twenty thousand. The difference in large communities is remarkable. While some cities with three hundred thousand inhabitants seem drowsy and "slow," another, like this of Frankfort, with not half that population, presents the aspect of much more life, activity, and volume of business. Here we have fine, cleanly streets, and stores almost Parisian in elegance and richness of display. The older portions of the town have the usual narrow lanes and dark alleys of past centuries, with quaint, overhanging fronts to the houses. The city is surrounded on three sides by very beautiful public gardens. The venerable town hall is an object of universal interest. One visits also the house from which Luther addressed the multitude in the Dom Platz, or square: nor should another famous residence be forgotten; namely, that in which Goethe was born, in memory of whom a colossal bronze statue stands in the Goethe Platz. There is also a group here of three statues in honor of Gutenberg, Faust, and Schöffer, inventors of printing. In the Schiller Platz is a bronze statue of Schiller. The public library has a hundred and thirty thousand volumes, and there is a museum of natural history, an art gallery of choice paintings, and all the usual philanthropic organizations appropriate to a populous Christian capital. Frankfort is a great money centre, and is the residence of many very rich bankers. In the grounds attached to the residence of one of these wealthy men is exhibited, in a suitable building, the famous marble statue of Ariadne, by Dannecker. There is also here a fine botanical garden with a collection of choice plants open to the public. Thus it will be seen that Frankfort, upon the whole, though comparatively small, is yet an extremely pleasing city, thriving, cleanly, and attractive.

Our next place to visit is Cologne, a city situated on the left bank of the Rhine. It was a famous and prosperous Roman colony fifteen hundred years ago, containing amphitheatres, temples, and aqueducts. The passage-ways in the ancient portions of the city are remarkably small, but there are some fine modern streets, arcades, and open squares, which present a busy aspect, with an active population of one hundred and sixty thousand. The Rhine is here crossed by a substantial iron bridge, as also by a bridge of boats. The one most prominent attraction of Cologne is its grand, and in some respects unequalled, cathedral, which was over six hundred years in process of building. It was not completed until so late as 1880, representing an enormous amount of elaborate masonry.

The towers are over five hundred feet high. The effect of the interior, with its vast height, noble pillars, niches, chapels, and stained glass windows is most impressive, and by many travellers is thought to be unequalled elsewhere. The exterior, with its immense flying buttresses and myriads of pinnacles, is truly awe-inspiring. There are other old and interesting churches here. That of St. Gereon is said to contain the bones of the hundreds of martyrs of the Theban Legion who were slain by order of the Emperor Diocletian in the year 286. The Church of St. Peter's, where Rubens was baptized, contains his famous picture entitled the "Crucifixion of St. Peter," painted a short time before the artist's death. The stranger is shown the house at No. 10 Sternengasse, where Maria d' Medici died in 1642. Rubens lived in this same house when a boy of ten years. There is a choice and comprehensive gallery of paintings at Cologne.

From this city we turn our steps towards Paris, by the way of Antwerp, Belgium, which is remarkable for its many churches, convents, and noble public buildings, beautiful parks, and open squares. It has a population of fully three hundred thousand, owing its attraction mostly to the fact that here are gathered so many masterpieces of painting. The great influence of Rubens can hardly be fully appreciated without a visit to this Flemish capital, where he lived so long, where he died, and where his ashes rest in the Church of St. Jacques. Here is the burial place of many noble families, and among them that of Rubens, his tomb being situated just back of the high altar. Above it is a painting by his own hand, intended to represent the Holy Family, but its object is also well understood as being to perpetuate a series of likenesses of the Rubens family; namely, of himself, his two wives, and his daughter, besides his father and grandfather. Vandyke and Teniers were also natives of Antwerp, where their best works still remain, and where the state has erected fitting monuments to their memory. Jordaens, the younger Teniers, and Denis Calvart, the art master of Guido, the great Italian painter, were also natives of this city.

The Cathedral of Antwerp, more remarkable for its exterior than interior, is of the pointed style. Did it not contain Rubens' world-renowned pictures, the Descent from the Cross, the Elevation of the Cross, and the Assumption, few people would care to visit it. In all the older portions of the town the houses have a queer way of standing with their gable ends to the street, as we see them in Amsterdam and Hamburg, showing it to be a Dutch fashion. Dogs are universally used here in place of donkeys for drawing small carts. Beggars there are none to be seen, to the credit of the city be it said.

From Antwerp we make our way to Paris, whence to take a brief trip into Switzerland, which, after a journey by rail of three hundred and twenty-five miles, we enter on the northwestern corner, at Bâle, a considerable city of nearly seventy thousand inhabitants, situated on the left bank of the Rhine. Its earliest history was that of a Roman colony; consequently there are many portions of the place especially "quaint and olden." Being situated at the junction of the frontiers of France, Germany, and Switzerland, it has a considerable trade and evinces much commercial life. It has many admirable institutions, a public library which contains about a hundred thousand volumes, and a justly famed university which also has a library of two hundred thousand volumes. The town hall is a curious old structure three centuries old and of the Gothic style. Most cities have some specialty in manufacturing, and Bâle is not without its peculiarity in this respect. It consists of the production of silk ribbons of exquisite finish and in great variety, which find their way to distant and profitable markets.

There is an admirably arranged picture gallery and art museum here, principally remarkable for the number of paintings by the younger Holbein, but containing, also, many other fine works of the modern painters. The cathedral dates back nearly nine hundred years, or, to be exact, to 1010. It was originally of the Byzantine order, but has been repaired and added to until it has assumed a Gothic shape. The material is red sandstone. It has two lofty towers, and the portal is ornamented with mounted statues of St. George and St. Martin. About six miles from Bâle, on the river near its confluence with the Ergolz, is Augst, upon the site of the great Roman city of Augusta Rauracorum, founded in the reign of Augustus. From these ruins have been taken many valuable relics which are deposited in the museum of Bâle.

From Bâle we take the railway southward to Lausanne, situated on the borders of Lake Geneva, where we find a population numbering some thirty-three thousand. This city occupies a beautiful and commanding situation overlooking the lake and valley. Its streets are hilly and irregular, but are well kept and cleanly. The view from the high points of the town is very fine, the Jura Mountains enclosing a portion of the landscape, which is vine-clad and varied in its systematic cultivation. If we stop at the Hotel Gibbon, which is a good house, we shall see in its garden overlooking the lake, the spot where the historian Gibbon completed his "Decline and Fall of the Roman Empire." Lausanne is a delightful summer resort, cool and healthful.

Geneva, with a population of about fifty thousand, is located on the same lake a short journey southward, being one of the largest and wealthiest towns in Switzerland. It is situated at the point where the river Rhone emerges from the lake, forming a favorite watering-place with large and admirable hotels, but many of the streets are steep, narrow, and crooked. The Rhone separates the town into two parts, and is here crossed by eight bridges. We get from Geneva a superb view of the Mont Blanc group, and the relative height of the several peaks is better realized than from a nearer point. Mont Blanc is upwards of fifteen thousand feet in height.

Geneva has few attractions except its position and scenery, being in the vicinity of the most famous mountains in Switzerland. The history of the place is, however, very interesting. Calvin resided here nearly thirty years. Rousseau was born here in 1712, and it has been the birthplace of other famous scholars, botanists, naturalists, and philosophers. Necker, financial minister to Louis XVI., and his daughter, Madame de Staël, were natives of Geneva. In the environs, say four miles from Geneva, Voltaire built a famous chateau, making it his home for a number of years. From here one goes to Chamouni, if disposed for mountain-climbing, — the immediate region of Mont Blanc.

The Lake of Geneva, or Lake Leman, the name by which it is best known, is forty-five miles long, varying from two to eight miles in width. We will cross the lake by steamer to the charming little town of Vevay, situated on the northern side, and containing some nine thousand inhabitants. A few miles from this point, where the Rhone enters the lake, stands the famous Castle of Chillon, connected with the shore by a drawbridge, — palace, castle, and prison, all in one. Some of its dark damp cells are hewn out of the solid rock beneath the surface of the lake. This fortress of the Middle Ages has been rendered familiar to us by Byron's poetic pen. It was built by Amedeus IV., Count of Savoy, in 1238. Here languished Bonnivard in his underground cell for six years, during which time he wore a prisoner's chains for his heroic defence of Genevan liberty.

A short journey northward by railway brings us to Berne, the capital of Switzerland, and which contains less than forty thousand inhabitants. It is situated upon a lofty promontory above the winding Aar, which nearly surrounds it, and is crossed here by two stone bridges. The view of the snow-capped Bernese Alps from Berne is remarkably fine and comprehensive. The town has all the usual charitable and educational organizations, with a public library containing fifty thousand volumes. Many of the business streets are lined by arcades for foot passengers. Fountains abound, each one being surmounted by some grotesque figure. The cathedral is a fine Gothic structure, dating from 1457. The bear, of whose name the word Berne is the German equivalent, forms the principal figure in the crest or arms of the city. Near the Aarburg gate is a small menagerie of these animals, kept up at all times, and at the public expense. The figure of a bear appears to one in all sorts of connections about the city. There is here a curious and famous clock-tower. Just as the hour is about to strike, a wooden figure of chanticleer appears and crows. He is followed by another puppet which strikes the hour upon a bell, and then come forth a number of bears from the interior of the clock, each one making an obeisance to an enthroned figure, which in turn inclines its sceptre and opens its mouth. The town is noted for the manufacture of choice musical boxes, which are sold all over Europe and America.

We go by railway from Berne to Lucerne, which is situated on the lake of the same name, and contains a population of twenty thousand. The ancient walls which served the town in olden times are still in good preservation. Lucerne is located between the Rigi and Pilatus (lofty mountains), while it faces the snow-clad Alps of Uri and Engelberg. Here the river Reuss issues from the lake with great force. The Schweizerhof Quay, beautifully ornamented with trees, borders the lake, and is a famous promenade for visitors. The chief object of interest, after the very remarkable scenery, is the lion-sculptured rock, in a garden adjoining the town, designed to commemorate the Swiss guard, who sacrificed themselves in fidelity to their royal master, the king of France, at the beginning of the French Revolution. It was modelled by Thorwaldsen. The lake of Lucerne is unsurpassed in Europe for its scenic beauty. It is twenty miles in length, and of irregular width; the greatest depth reaches five hundred feet.

A short trip northward brings us to Zurich, which has a population of eighty thousand, and is situated on the borders of the lake whose name it bears. It is recognized as the Athens of Switzerland, the intellectual capital of the country, as well as being one of the busiest of manufacturing centres, silk and cotton goods forming the staple. The educational facilities afforded at Zurich are recognized all over Europe. The scenery of the suburbs is very fine and peculiarly Swiss, the immediate neighborhood being highly cultivated, and the distance formed by snowy Alps. Lavater, the great physiognomist, Gesner, the celebrated naturalist, and Pestalozzi, the educational reformer, were born at Zurich. The shores of this beautiful lake are covered with vineyards, grain-fields, and pleasant gardens interspersed with the most picturesque cottages and capacious villas. Zurich is divided into two parts by the rapid river Limmat, somewhat as the Rhone divides Geneva. The Platz-promenade is an avenue of shady trees on the banks of the clear, swift river, which is much frequented by the populace. It terminates just where the small river Sihl joins the Limmat. The former is an insignificant stream except in the spring, when it assumes considerable importance through the body of water which it conducts into the bosom of the larger river.

Switzerland is but a small division of Europe. Its greatest length from east to west is about two hundred miles, and its width north and south is about one hundred and forty Two-thirds of its surface consists of lofty Alps, as we have shown, the scenery being thus marked by towering mountains, vast glaciers, beautiful lakes, fertile valleys, and glittering cascades. Owing to the great elevation of most of the country, the climate is uniformly rather cold. The population does not exceed three millions. The different languages spoken in Switzerland show that the people have no common origin, but come from different races. In the west, French is the language which is in common use, and these people are believed to have descended from the Burgundians; in the north, where German is spoken, a common origin is indicated with the Germans of Swabia; while in the south, both the language and the physical appearance of the people is that of the Italians.

On our way towards England from Zurich, we pass through Schaffhausen, about forty miles from the former city, on the right bank of the Rhine, having a population of about ten thousand. It is a place of considerable business activity, very quaint and antique in general aspect, the style of architecture reminding one of that seen in Chester, England. The chief object of attraction to strangers in this neighborhood is the famous falls of the Rhine, which form three tremendous cascades, where the river is three hundred feet in width, and the falls are eighty feet in height. Schaffhausen is the capital of the canton of the same name, and retains many of the ancient features of a Swabian town of the period of the Empire. The cathedral, an early Romanesque structure, bears the date of 1052. It contains a remarkable bell, which shows by its date that it was placed here about four hundred years ago.

TOWER OF THE HOUSE OF PARLIAMENT.

CHAPTER XXII.

WE shall speak only incidentally of London; to describe such a mammoth city even superficially would require an entire volume. It is situated on the river Thames, fifty miles from its mouth, containing a population of about five millions. It is consequently the largest metropolis in the world. Many of the older streets are confused, narrow, and intricate, but the modern portion of the city consists of broad, straight thoroughfares and fine substantial buildings. No capital is better supplied with public parks, the most notable being Hyde Park, covering about four hundred acres in the heart of London, and forming the most popular promenade and drive during the favorite hours of the day, when there is always a brilliant display of wealth and fashion.

It was in existence at the time of Cæsar's invasion and has flourished ever since. Of the many churches, new and old, that known as Westminster Abbey is the most interesting, being the shrine of England's illustrious dead. It has been a sacred temple and a royal sepulchre for many centuries; but the towers were completed by the famous English architect, Sir Christopher Wren, who also designed St. Paul's Cathedral, the grandest structure of its kind in the country. Old St. Paul's was destroyed by fire in 1665-6. A Christian church has occupied the same site from a very early period. The present edifice is five hundred feet long and more than one-fourth as wide. The height of the dome to the top of the cross is over three hundred and sixty feet, while the grand and harmonious proportions of the whole are beyond description. The Houses of Parliament form a very imposing architectural pile. The Victoria Tower is seventy-five feet square and nearly three hundred and fifty feet high. The clock-tower is forty feet square and three hundred and eighteen feet high. The face of the clock, placed at this great elevation, must be very large to be discernible upon the street, and is twenty-three feet in diameter.

The British Museum is a noble institution, both in its object and its general appearance. Its front measures three hundred and seventy feet in length, the central portion being decorated with a grand line of lofty columns in the Ionic style. These columns are five feet in diameter and forty-five feet in height. The collection of Greek and Roman antiquities, curiosities from all parts of the world, and valuable relics, undoubtedly exceed in interest and comprehensiveness any other similar museum. The library contains over a million volumes and thousands of precious manuscripts. The National Gallery of Paintings on Trafalgar Square has been formed at an enormous expense, and is worthy of the great metropolis, though it is exceeded in the number of examples and in the individual merit of many of the paintings by some of the continental galleries of Europe. The Zoölogical Garden, adjoining Regent's Park, is one of the great attractions to strangers, and of never-failing interest to the people, being probably the most complete and extensive collection of wild and domestic animals, quadrupeds, birds, and reptiles in the world. Regent's Park is even larger

THE TOWER OF LONDON.

than Hyde Park. Besides these noble, health-dispensing parks,— these breathing-places for a dense population,— the metropolis is dotted here and there with large squares, varying in extent from four to six acres each. The most notable of these are Belgrave Square, Trafalgar Square, Grosvenor Square, Portman Square, Eaton Square, and Russell Square.

Twelve bridges other than railroad bridges cross the river Thames within the city boundary. The largest manufacturing interest in London is that of the breweries, wherein eleven million bushels of malt are annually consumed.

Buckingham Palace, the town residence of Queen Victoria, occupies a location facing St. James's Park, and is a spacious building, but of no architectural pretention. The famous tower of London, according to tradition, was originally built by Julius Cæsar, and is situated on the east side of the city, on the left bank of the Thames. It is no longer used as a prison, but is a national armory and museum of warlike implements of antiquity. London has an underground railway running beneath the streets and houses by means of tunnels, and also through cuttings between high walls, forming a complete belt round the inner sections of the city, while branch lines diverge to the suburbs. Statistics show that the railway company which controls the line conveys about eighty millions of passengers annually, at an average rate of twopence each, or four cents of our American currency, per trip. There are over fifty regularly licensed theatrical establishments in the city. The charitable organizations of London are on a scale commensurate with its great wealth and population, while its educational facilities are on an equally extensive scale.

Travellers who land in England at Holyhead, on their way to London, go to the great metropolis by way of Chester, which is one of the most interesting cities in Great Britain. It has a population of a little over thirty thousand, and retains more of its ancient character than any other city of England. The old defences have been carefully preserved, and charming views of the surrounding country may be enjoyed from the promenade which follows the course of the wall. Many of the houses are so constructed that the second floors form a series of continuous galleries or covered ways for foot passengers, known as the "Rows." There is an ancient cathedral here of considerable interest, rendered familiar by the numerous pictures of its several parts which have been so often published. One of the most popular race-courses in England is situated just outside of the city walls of Chester. There is a fine modern Gothic residence in the environs, belonging to the Marquis of Westminster, known as Eaton Hall, and which people travel long distances to see, as it is considered one of the finest structures of its kind in the kingdom.

A railway journey of a hundred miles from London takes us into a beautiful portion of rural England, to that pleasant watering-place, the town of Leamington, where some natural springs exist which are believed to possess certain medical properties. There is a resident population of twenty thousand, which is largely increased during the attractive season of the year. This neighborhood is not only remarkable in a historical point of view, but also for the rural beauty and quiet charms of its scenery. There is here a public garden of twelve or fifteen acres in the middle of the town, under a high condition of cultivation.

It is but a short trip by rail from Leamington to Kenilworth Castle, or rather to its ruins. We need not narrate the historical associations of this place. Scott, in his admirable novel, "Kenilworth," has rendered the reading world familiar with it. The bare and crumbling walls are an eloquent monument of the days of chivalry. The castle is said to have been sufficiently extensive to have accommodated on one occasion Queen Elizabeth and four hundred lords and ladies attached to her household. It was left to the charming pen of Sir Walter Scott to fix the history of the time and place upon the memory more effectually than could be done by the pages of the professed historian.

From Leamington we may also make an excursion to Warwick Castle, one of the grandest and best preserved of mediæval structures to be seen in Great Britain, and which is occupied by the present Earl of Warwick. This relic of the past, perhaps quite as ancient as Kenilworth, of which only the ruins remain, is in a condition of perfect preservation, and we believe it has never ceased to be occupied by representatives or descendants of the same family. The castle contains a museum of antiquity, including a great variety of armor, battle-axes, swords, flags, and war implements generally, which were used by the ancestors of the present earl. There are some choice paintings in the spacious halls, while from the windows views may be enjoyed, fully depicting the beauties of English rural scenery.

Stratford-on-Avon — the birthplace of Shakespeare — is within a short distance by rail: it contains some four thousand inhabitants. Few foreign travellers fail to visit Stratford. We come to the suggestive spot on a bright, sunny day, and hasten at once to the old church where rest the mortal remains of Shakespeare. Just back of this ancient Gothic structure flows the quiet Avon in the same bed where it has glided for centuries. A group of haymakers lying idly upon the grass on the opposite bank are gossiping away the noon hour; a fisherman with pole and line is daintily sounding the shady nooks of the peaceful river; a few white swans glide gracefully in the shadow of the overhanging willows, while in the middle distance a flock of sheep nibble the rich green herbage. We find the interior of the church but little superior in architecture and ornamentation to most country churches. The tomb of the poet is in the chancel. Just over the grave, in a niche of the wall, is a bust of Shakespeare, which was placed there shortly after his death, and which is believed to be a good and true likeness of the original. He died at the comparatively early age of fifty-three. We take refreshment at the Red Horse Inn, rendered famous by Washington Irving, stroll thoughtfully through the quaint old village, and visit, with thrilling interest, the house in which Shakespeare was born.

From this remarkable vicinity we take passage over the Great Northern Railroad, by way of Preston and Carlisle, finally reaching Edinburgh, the thriving and pleasant capital of Scotland.

It is a peculiarly formed city, being built on three parallel ridges of considerable elevation, and is remarkable for the general excellence and elegance of its architecture. The older portion of the city is situated upon the loftiest of the ridges, and on which the houses rise to the height of nine and ten stories along the edges and on the steep slopes. The streets in the old town are narrow and irregular. The newer section occupies a lower ridge, being separated from the old by a valley which is improved as a public garden

EDINBURGH CASTLE.

and for business purposes. The public and private buildings are mostly constructed of a white stone resembling marble, which is quarried in the neighborhood. The population numbers about three hundred thousand, occupying a territory which measures just about two square miles. The longest street commences at the Palace of Holyrood and ends at Castle Hill, upon the summit of which is Edinburgh Castle, standing four hundred and fifty feet above the level of the sea.

This might appropriately be called the city of monuments. Among the most prominent are statues to Sir Walter Scott, Nelson, Playfair, Professor Wilson, Allan Ramsay, the Duke of Wellington, and Robert Burns. Scott's monument stands quite by itself on Princes Street, and rises to two hundred feet in height. Few monuments in the world equal this Gothic structure in architectural beauty. The citizens of Edinburgh may well be proud of their numerous educational institutions and charitable establishments, in which departments of noble liberality no city in Great Britain can surpass the Scotch metropolis. Near by Holyrood Palace are the ruins of the ancient abbey of the same name, founded by David I. nearly eight hundred years ago. In its chapel Queen Mary was married to Lord Darnley. In visiting the castle on the hill we are shown the small room wherein Queen Mary became the mother of James VI., who was afterwards king of England. The royal infant was lowered from the window of the little chamber in a basket, when friends received it and thus saved it from its scheming enemies.

In the High Street we visit the house where John Knox, the great Scottish reformer, lived. Close by, in White Horse Close, is the inn where Dr. Johnson lodged in

1773, while in the churchyard hard by are the graves of Adam Smith and Dugald Stewart. It is not possible to feel indifferent to such associations. No grander figure can be found in the history of the Reformation than that of John Knox. His biography reads like a romance. Whether serving a two years' sentence in the French galleys, enduring a siege in the castle of St. Andrews, being tried for treason by order of Queen Mary, haranguing from the pulpit against what he considered false religionists, or having his steps dogged by assassins, Knox never swerved from what he believed to be the path of duty.

In the immediate environs of the city, to the south of Holyrood, are Salisbury Crags and Arthur's Seat, always visited by strangers, besides being a favorite resort of the citizens of Edinburgh. There is a fine road-way which surrounds Arthur's Seat, known as "The Queen's Drive." Scott made this vicinity of more than passing interest by his "Heart of Mid-Lothian," and the local guides point out the spot where Jeanie Deans is represented to have met Robertson. The "Queen's Drive" affords from several points charmingly comprehensive views.

A drive of twenty miles through the hills and plains lying to the southeast of the city will take us to Melrose, a place only noted for its famous ruins of the Abbey. It was founded by David I., in 1136, for monks of the Cistercian order, and rebuilt in an elaborate and elegant style between the reign of Robert Bruce and James IV. It was the finest church, as it is the noblest ruin, in Scotland. Scott has rendered us familiar with it. From here we drive to Abbotsford, the home of Sir Walter, and which is still kept exactly in the condition in which the poet left it on the day of his death. We wander through the house, lingering in the library, sit in the chair before the table where he sat and wrote in prose and poetry; we examine the curious collection of armor and the various historical mementos which he gathered about him, among which are weapons once owned by Rob Roy and the Douglas, and those of other real characters about whom his genius has woven such romantic interest. Abbotsford House is large, imposing, and beautifully situated, the spacious grounds which are attached to it sloping gracefully down to the banks of the river Tweed, beyond which rise the beautiful Selkirk Hills.

In travelling about the rural districts of Scotland in the vicinity of Edinburgh, one is impressed by the thrifty appearance of the country, which seems to be cultivated with great care. We see many flocks of sheep. There is not much attempt at what is called gardening, but a few staples in grain are depended upon, and much attention is given to the raising of sheep, horses, and cattle. The men and women are of a strong, vigorous type, hospitable and kindly. The national characteristics of the Scotch exhibit themselves in the simplest transactions. They are a remarkably intelligent and well-educated people; steady-going, plodding, economical, very set in their ways and opinions, being rather slow according to American ideas, but uncommonly sure and reliable.

Glasgow differs from Edinburgh in many respects. Its situation is low, and the view is obstructed by a multiplicity of tall, smoky chimneys, with other tokens of manufacturing industry. It is the most populous city of Scotland, having over half a million of inhabitants, and is located on the banks of the river Clyde. Except in the manufacturing parts of the town, the architecture and streets are fine and attractive. Dressed freestone is the material most commonly used in the construction of the best dwelling-houses and the public buildings. The river is crossed by five noble bridges, — two of granite, one of iron, — and two are suspension bridges. The city reminds one forcibly of Pittsburgh in America. The chemical works, foundries, and workshops of all kinds, using such quantities of bituminous or soft coal, create an atmosphere of a dense, smoky character.

Glasgow contains four large and beautifully kept parks. The city is over a thousand years old, but we have no record of its earliest three or four centuries. Situated in the midst of a district abounding in coal and iron, and upon a river which insures it world-wide commerce, maritime enterprise has been a natural result. Here James Watt made his memorable improvements in the steam-engine, and here Henry Bell first demonstrated in the Old World the practicability of steam navigation. This was in 1812, four years after Fulton's successful experiments upon the Hudson River in this country, but of which Bell seems to have had no knowledge. Glasgow has many handsome and substantial blocks of dwelling-houses. Buchanan Street and Queen Street are both remarkably elegant thoroughfares; the former especially is notable for its large and attractive stores. Argyle Street is very broad and two miles long, one of the finest avenues in Great Britain. Here, as in Edinburgh, there are numerous public monuments, among which we observe the equestrian statues of William III., the Duke of Wellington, in front of the Royal Exchange; and that of Queen Victoria, in George's Square. There is also an obelisk one hundred and forty feet high, erected to the honor of Nelson, besides others of Sir Walter Scott, Sir John Moore, James Watt, Sir Robert Peel, etc.

There are two chimneys in the city designed to carry off the poisonous gases from the chemical works, which are respectively four hundred and sixty, and four hundred and fifty feet in height, the latter carrying off the vapor from St. Rollox, the largest chemical manufactory in the world. These buildings cover fifteen acres of ground, and the works give employment to over a thousand men. Cotton factories are also numerous here, and calico-printing establishments. Beer-brewing is one of the largest branches of manufacture, as it is also in London. In the building of iron steamships the port of Glasgow leads the world. For a long time there was an average of one steamer a day launched on the banks of the Clyde, in the vicinity, though this number is not quite kept up at the present time. Clyde steamers have a high reputation, and are given the preference for durability and general excellence of workmanship.

Greenock, with a population of about fifty thousand, is one of the finest seaports in Scotland, having also a large business in iron ship-building. This was the native place of James Watt, already spoken of, and here we observe an admirable statue reared to his memory. The city is situated a little over twenty miles from Glasgow, on the Firth of Clyde. From here we take passage in a steamer across the Irish Sea to Belfast, the principal city of Northern Ireland.

Belfast has a population of about two hundred thousand, and next to Dublin is the most important city of the country. It is comparatively modern, its tall chimneys, large factories, and spinning-mills speaking intelligibly of material prosperity. Queen's College is a large structure in the Tudor style, with a frontage of six hundred feet in length. There is an admirable museum on College Square containing a large collection of Irish antiquities. We also find an excellent botanical garden here, and there are no better school facilities in the United Kingdom than are to be enjoyed in this metropolis of Northern Ireland. From Cave Hill, in the suburbs, an elevation over a thousand feet in height, a most admirable view of the city and its surroundings may be enjoyed, the coast of Scotland being visible on the far horizon. The streets of Belfast are regular, broad, and cleanly, and many of the public buildings are superb in architectural effect. The city hall, the custom house, the Ulster Bank, and Linen Hall are all noble structures. This is the great headquarters of the Irish linen trade.

A short journey of about a hundred miles due south by railway will bring us to Dublin, the capital of Ireland. It has a population of about four hundred thousand, and is situated on the shore of Dublin Bay, with the river Liffey flowing through its centre. It is an attractive city with very beautiful surroundings. There are many grand public buildings, several large parks, a number of interesting old churches, and a cathedral, — St. Patrick's, — connected with which are the associations of six centuries. The remains of Dean Swift are buried here. Near by is the house where Thomas Moore, the poet, was born, and not far away is the birthplace of the Duke of Wellington. Dublin has its public library, its museum, its Royal College of Surgeons, and its famous Trinity College, where Goldsmith, Swift, Burke, and many others graduated. It has also many noble charitable organizations and societies for the diffusion of science. The zoölogical garden is one of the most extensive in Great Britain. Dublin Castle is near the centre of the city, on slightly elevated ground, containing an armory, a chapel, and various government offices. This city claims great antiquity, having existed as a capital since the days of Ptolemy. It was for centuries held by the Danes; in 1169 it was taken by the English under Strongbow, whose remains lie in Christ Church Cathedral.

From Dublin we take passage on board of a steamer for Liverpool, the commercial metropolis of England, which contains about seven hundred thousand inhabitants. It is situated on the river Mersey, four miles from the sea. To the traveller it presents few attractions save those of a great shipping depot, which is unsurpassed in the department of maritime enterprise.

The moral and physical character of the population, taken in mass, is rather low, though the city has many institutions and associations designed to promote intelligence and to fulfil all charitable demands. The exhibitions of intemperance to be met with upon the streets at all hours forms a disgraceful picture of humanity, in which respect Liverpool seems to be more sadly afflicted than are the lowest sections of London.

From here we sail for Nassau, New Providence, a British possession in the Bahama Islands, lying northeast from Cuba, the largest of the West Indian Islands.

CHAPTER XXIII.

UPON landing at Nassau we find everything quite different from our late experiences in the large European cities, and are brought face to face with nature, — with a tropical race and with tropical vegetation. Instead of palatial edifices we have low native huts, while the people we meet have the bronzed hue of Africans. This island, which was settled by Europeans as early as 1629, contains nearly a hundred square miles. The town has a small free library, several churches, a hospital, and a bank.

It seems singular that an island like New Providence, which is almost without soil, should be so productive in vegetation. It is surrounded by low-lying coral reefs, and is itself of the same formation. In a pulverized condition this limestone forms the earth out of which spring palm, banana, ceba, orange, lemon, tamarind, mahogany, and cocoanut trees, with various others, besides an almost endless variety of flowers. Science teaches us that all soils are but broken and decomposed rock pulverized by various agencies acting through long periods of time. So the molten lava which once poured from the fiery mouth of Vesuvius has become the soil of thriving vineyards which produce the choice grapes whence is made the priceless Lachryma Cristi wine of Naples. This transformation of lava into soil is not accomplished in the period of a single life.

The luscious pineapple, zapota, mango, pomegranate,

citron, custard-apple, and other fruits captivate the palate of the stranger, while the profuseness and variety of beautiful ferns and orchids delight the eye of the northerner. The negroes are mostly engaged in cultivating pineapples, yams, sweet potatoes, and other vegetables, and a large number of the males employ themselves in fishing and gathering sponges. From this locality comes the largest supply of coarse sponge which is used in England and America. There is also a considerable trade carried on in fine turtle-shell, which is polished in an exquisite manner by the patient natives. The Bahama sponges are not equal to those obtained in the Mediterranean. But they are marketable for certain uses, and Nassau exports half a million dollars' worth annually. It is said that sponges can be propagated by cuttings taken from living specimens, which, when properly attached to a piece of board and sunk in the sea, will increase and multiply. Thus the fine Mediterranean sponge can be successfully transported to the coral reefs of the Bahamas.

A short drive or walk inland over smooth roads, formed of smooth, levelled coral rocks, brings us to the extensive pineapple fields, where this handsome fruit may be seen in the several stages of growth, varying according to the season of the year and the purposes of its use. If intended for exportation, the fruit is gathered when well-grown but still in a green state; if designed for canning,—that is, preserving,—the riper it is, the better it is adapted to the purpose. Great quantities are put in tin cans carefully sealed for use in this and other countries. The visitor is sure to be impressed by the beauty and grace of the cocoanut-trees, their plume of leaves, often sixty feet from the ground, notwithstanding that the bare stem or trunk is rarely over two feet in thickness.

There are said to be six hundred of the Bahama Islands, large and small, of which Nassau is the capital, and here the English governor-general resides. Many are mere rocky islets, and not more than twenty have fixed inhabitants. The sea-gardens, as they are called, situated just off the shore of the main island, are extremely interesting. We go out a short distance in a row-boat, and by means of a simple contrivance of wood and glass we can look many fathoms below the surface of the sea. These water-glasses are easily made, being formed of a small wooden box three or four inches square, open at the top and having a water-tight glass bottom. With the glass portion slightly submerged one is able to see distinctly the beautiful coral reefs with their marvellous surroundings. There are displayed tiny caves and grottoes of white coral, star-fishes, sea-urchins, growing sponges, sea-fans, and bright-colored fishes, including the humming-bird fish, and others like butterflies with mottled fins and scales, together with that little oddity, the rainbow-fish. The prevailing color of this attractive creature is dark green, but the tinted margins of its scales so reflect the light as to show all the colors of the rainbow, and hence its name. When bottled in alcohol for preservation, these fish lose their native colors. This unique display is enhanced in beauty by the clearness of these waters, and the reflected lights from the snow-white sandy bottom, which is dotted here and there by delicate shells of various shapes and colors. One longs to descend among these coral bowers, — these mermaid gardens, — and pluck a bouquet of the submarine flora in its purple, yellow, and scarlet freshness.

The surface life of these clear waters is also extremely

interesting. Here the floating jelly-fish, called from its phosphorescence the glow-worm of the sea, is observed in great variety, sheltering little colonies of young fishes, which rush forth for a moment to capture some passing mite, and as quickly return again to their cover. If we take up a handful of the floating gulf-weed, we find within the pale yellow leaves and berries, tiny pipe-fish, sea-horses, and specimens of the little nest-building fishes. Thus this curious weed forms a home for parasites, crabs, and shell-fishes, being itself a sort of mistletoe of the ocean. The young of the mackerel and the herring glide rapidly about in shoals, just below the surface, near the shore, like myriad pieces of silver. Verily there would seem to be more of animal life below than above the surface of the waters, which is not an unreasonable conclusion when it is remembered that the whole surface of the globe is supposed to have an area of about two hundred million square miles, and that of these only about fifty millions are composed of dry land.

Much of the drinking-water, and certainly the best in use at Nassau, as well as on some of the neighboring islands, is procured in a remarkable manner from the sea. Not far from shore, on the coral reefs, there are never-failing fresh-water springs, bubbling up from the bottom through the salt water with such force as to clearly indicate their locality. Over these ocean springs the people place sunken barrels filled with sand, one above another, the bottoms and tops being first removed. The fresh water is thus conducted to the surface through the column of sand, which acts as a filter, the water being sweet and palatable, as well as remarkable for its crystal clearness. So on the arid shores of the Persian Gulf, where rain seldom falls, and where there are no rills to refresh the parched soil, fresh water is obtained from springs beneath the sea. There it is brought to the surface by employing divers, who descend with leather bags. The mouth of a bag is placed over the bubbling spring, quickly filled and closed again, being then drawn to the surface by persons awaiting the signal from the diver, who then hastens to rise for needed air. There is no mystery as to the source of these springs. The rain falls on the distant mountains, and finding its way through the rocky ledges, pursues its course until it gushes forth in the bed of the gulf.

A fortnightly steamer from New York, bound for Cuba, touches at Nassau on the southward trip to leave the mail, and we will avail ourselves of this opportunity to visit the "Queen of the Antilles," as this island is called. At first we steam to the north for half a day, in order to find a safe channel out of the Bahamas, where there is more of shoal than of navigable waters, and as we do so, we leave many islands behind us inhabited only by turtles, flamingoes, and sea-birds. But we are soon steaming due south again towards our destination, namely, the island of Cuba, five hundred miles away. San Salvador is sighted on our starboard bow (right-hand side), the spot where Columbus first landed in the New World. It will be found laid down on most English maps as Cat Island, and is now the home of two or three thousand colored people, the descendants of imported Africans. The island is nearly as large as New Providence. It is said that the oranges grown here are the sweetest and best that are known. The voyager in these latitudes is constantly saluted by gentle breezes full of tropical fragrance, intensified in effect by the distant view of cocoanut, palmetto, and banana trees, clothing the islands in a mantle of green, down to the very water's edge. As we glide along, gazing shoreward, now and again little groups of swallows seem to be flitting a few feet above the waves, then suddenly disappearing beneath the water. These are flying-fish enjoying an air-bath, either in frolic or in fear; pursued possibly by some dreaded enemy in the sea, which they are trying to escape.

It is interesting to remain on deck at night and watch the heavens as we glide through the phosphorescent sea. Is it possible that the moon, whose light renders objects so plain that one can see to read small print, shines solely by borrowed light? We know it to be so, and also that Venus, Mars, and perhaps Jupiter and Saturn shine in a similar manner with light reflected from the sun. It is interesting to adjust the telescope, and bring the starry system nearer to the vision. If we direct our gaze upon a planet, we find its disk or face sharply defined; change the direction, and let the object-glass rest upon a star, and we have only a point of light more or less brilliant. The glass reveals to us the fact that the "star-dust" which we call the Milky Way is an accumulation of innumerable single stars. Sweeping the blue expanse with the telescope, we find some stars are golden, some green, others purple, many silvery white, and some are twins. Our use of the words "first and second magnitude" relates mainly to distance. It is most likely only a question of distance which regulates our vision or capacity for seeing, and which makes these "lamps of the sky" look larger or smaller to us.

When the lonely lighthouse which marks Cape Maysi,

at the eastern point of Cuba, comes into view on the starboard bow, the dim form of the mountains of Hayti are visible on the opposite horizon. A subterranean connection is believed to exist between the mountain ranges of the two islands. We are now running through the Windward Passage, as it is called; by which one branch of the Gulf Stream finds its way northward. The Gulf Stream! Who can explain satisfactorily its ceaseless current? What keeps its tepid waters, in a course of thousands of miles, from mingling with the rest of the sea? And finally whence does it come? Maury, the great nautical authority, says the Gulf of Mexico is its fountain, and its mouth is the Arctic Sea. The maps make the eastern shore of Cuba terminate as sharp as a needle's point, but it proves to be very blunt in reality, where it forms one side of the gateway to the Caribbean Sea, and where the irregular coast line runs due north and south for the distance of many leagues.

The nights are mostly clear, soft, and lovely in this region. As we double Çape Maysi, and the ship is headed westward, the Southern Cross and the North Star blaze in the opposite horizons at the same time, the constellation on our port side (left-hand), and the North Star on the starboard side. Each day at noon the captain and his officers determine the exact position of the ship by "taking the sun," as it is termed. When the sun reaches the meridian, that is, the point directly overhead, the exact moment is indicated by the nautical instrument known as a quadrant, adjusted to the eye of the observer. The figures marked on the quadrant give the latitude of the ship at the moment of meridian. The ship's time is then made to correspond, — that is to say, it must indicate twelve o'clock noon,—after which it is compared with an exact timepiece called a chronometer, which keeps Greenwich (English) time, and the difference enables the observer to determine the longitude. As fifteen miles are allowed to the minute, there will be nine hundred miles to the hour. Thus, by means of the chronometer and the quadrant, the sailing-master is enabled to designate his exact situation upon the ocean chart.

Soon after passing the remarkably sheltered port of Guantanamo, which was for nearly a century the most notorious piratical rendezvous in the West Indies, the famous castle of Santiago is seen. It is called Moro Castle, but it is older than the better-known Moro of Havana, by nearly a hundred years. This antique, yellow, Moorish-looking stronghold, which modern gunnery would destroy in ten minutes or less, is picturesque to the last degree, with its crumbling, honey-combed battlements, and queer little flanking towers. It is built upon the face of a lofty, dun-colored rock, upon whose precipitous side the fortification is terraced. Its position is just at the entrance of the narrow river leading to the city, six or eight miles away, so that in passing up the channel one can speak from the ship's deck to any one who might be standing on the outer battlement of the Moro.

The winding channel which leads from the sea to the harbor passes through low hills and broad meadows covered with rank verdure, cocoanut groves, and fishing hamlets. Thrifty palms and intensely green bananas line the way, with here and there upon the pleasant banks a charming country-house in the midst of a garden fragrant with flowers. So close is the shore all the while that one seems to be navigating upon the land, gliding among trees and over greensward rather than upon blue water. Steaming slowly up the Santiago River, we presently pass a sharp angle of the hills, leading into a broad sheltered bay, upon whose banks stands the rambling old city of Santiago de Cuba, built on a hillside like Tangier, in Africa, and it is almost as Oriental as the capital of Morocco. The first and most conspicuous objects to meet the eye are the twin towers of the ancient cathedral, which have withstood so many earthquakes.

This city, once the capital of the island of Cuba, was founded by Velasquez, and is now gray with age and decay. The many-colored, one-story houses are ranged in narrow streets, which cross each other at right angles with considerable regularity, though the roadways are in an almost impassable condition. They were once paved with cobblestones, but are now dirty and neglected, a stream of offensive water flowing through their centres, in which little naked children, blacks and whites, are at play. No wonder that such numbers die here annually of yellow fever. The surprise is that it does not prevail all the year round.

Santiago dates back to the year 1514, making it the oldest city in the New World, next to San Domingo. From here Cortez sailed in 1518 to invade Mexico. Here has been the seat of modern rebellion against the arbitrary and bitterly oppressive rule of the home government of Spain. The city contains over forty thousand inhabitants, and is situated six hundred miles southeast of Havana; after Matanzas, it comes next in commercial importance, its exports reaching the annual aggregate of eight millions of dollars. After climbing and descending these narrow, dirty streets of Santiago, and watching the local characteristics for a few hours, one is glad to go on board ship again, and leave it all behind.

To reach Cienfuegos, our next destination, we take water conveyance, the common roads in this district being, if possible, a degree worse than elsewhere on the island. It is necessary to double Cape Cruz and make a coasting voyage along the southern shore of the island, for a distance of four hundred miles. This is really delightful sailing in any but the hurricane months; that is, between the middle of August and the middle of October.

Cienfuegos has some twenty-five thousand inhabitants, a large percentage of whom speak English, nine-tenths of its commerce being with this country. It was in this immediate neighborhood, as Columbus tells us, on the occasion of his second voyage from Spain, that he saw with astonishment the mysterious king who spoke to his people only by signs, and that group of men who wore long white tunics like the monks of mercy, while the rest of the people were entirely naked. The town is low and level, occupying a broad plain. The streets are wide and clean, while the harbor is an excellent and spacious one. It is pitiful to behold such an array of beggars, and it is strange, too, in so small a city. Here the maimed, the halt, and the blind meet us at every turn. Saturday is the harvest day for beggars in Cuban cities, on which occasion they go about by scores from door to door, carrying a large canvas bag. Each well-to-do family and shop is supplied on this day with a quantity of small rolls of bread, one of which is almost invariably given to any beggar who calls, and thus the mendicant's bag presently becomes full of rolls. These, mixed with a few vegetables, bits of fish, and sometimes meat and bones, are boiled into a soup which at least keeps soul and body together in the poor creatures until another Saturday comes round.

Cienfuegos is in the centre of a great sugar-producing district. Sugar-cane is cultivated much like Indian corn, which it also resembles in appearance. It is first planted in rows and weeded until it gets high enough to shade its roots, after which it is left pretty much to itself until it reaches maturity. This refers to the first laying out of a plantation, which will afterwards continue to throw up fresh stalks from the roots, with a little help from the hoe, for several years. When ripe the cane is of a light golden yellow, streaked here and there with red. The top is dark green, with long narrow leaves depending,—very much like those of corn,—from the centre of which shoots upward a silvery stem fifteen or eighteen inches in height, and from the tip grows a white-fringed plume. The effect of a large field at maturity lying under a torrid sun, and gently yielding to the breeze, is very fine.

Though the modern machinery for crushing, grinding, and extracting the sugar from the cane as lately adopted on the Cuban plantations is expensive, still the result obtained is so much superior to that of the old methods, that small planters are being driven from the market. The low price of sugar and the great competition in its production renders economy in the manufacture quite necessary, especially now that slave labor is abolished.

The delightful climate is exemplified by the abundance and variety of fruits and flowers. Let us visit a private garden in the environs of the city. Here the mango with its peach-like foliage is found, bending to the ground with the weight of its ripening fruit; the alligator-pear is wonderfully beautiful in its blossom, suggesting in form and color the passion-flower; the soft, delicate foliage of the tamarind is like our sensitive plant; the banana-trees are in full bearing, the deep green fruit (it is ripened and turns yellow off the tree), being in clusters of nearly a hundred, tipped at the same time by a single, pendent, glutinous bud nearly as large as a pineapple. Here we see also the star-apple-tree, remarkable for its uniform and graceful shape, full of green fruit, with here and there a ripening specimen. The zapota, in its rusty coat, hangs in tempting abundance. From low, broad-spreading trees hangs the grape fruit, as large as a baby's head and yellow as gold; while the orange and lemon trees, bearing blossoms, and green and ripening fruit all together, serve to charm the eye and to fill the garden with rich fragrance.

Let us examine one of these products in detail, selecting the banana as being the most familiar to us at the north. It seems that the female banana-tree (for we must remember that there are sexes in the vegetable as well as in the animal kingdom), bears more fruit than the male, but not so large. The average clusters of the former comprise about one hundred, but the latter rarely bears over sixty or seventy distinct specimens of this finger-shaped fruit. The stem grows to about ten feet in height; from the centre of its broad leaves, which gather palm-like at the top, there springs forth a large purple bud ten inches long, shaped like a huge acorn, though more pointed. This cone-like bud hangs suspended from a strong stem, upon which a leaf unfolds, displaying a cluster of young fruit. As soon as these are large enough to support the heat of the sun and the chill of the night dews, the sheltering leaf drops off, and another unfolds, exposing its little brood of fruit; and so the process goes on until six or eight rings of young bananas are started, which gradually develop to full size. The banana is a plant which dies down to the ground after fruiting, but it annually sprouts again from the same roots.

We will continue our journey towards Havana by way of Matanzas, crossing the island so as to penetrate at once into a section of luxuriant tropical nature, where we see the cactus in great variety, flowering trees, and ever-graceful palms, with occasional trees of the ceba family grown to vast size. Vegetation here, unlike human beings, seems never to grow old, never to falter in productiveness; crop succeeds crop, harvest follows harvest; it is an endless cycle of abundance. Miles upon miles of the bright, golden sugar-cane lie in all directions; among the plantations here and there is seen the little cluster of low buildings constituting the laborers' quarters, and near by is the tall, white chimney of the sugar-mill, emitting its thick volume of smoke, like the funnel of a steamship. A little on one side stands the planter's house, low and white, surrounded by shade-trees and flower-plats. Scores of dusky Africans give life to the scene, and the overseer, on his little Cuban pony, dashes hither and thither to keep all hands advantageously at work. One large gang is busy cutting the ripe cane with sword-like knives; some are loading the stalks upon ox-carts; some are driving loads to the mill; and some are feeding the cane between the great steel crushers, beneath which pours forth a continuous jelly-like stream which is conducted by iron pipes to the boilers. Men, women, and children are spreading the refuse to dry in the sun, after which it will be used as fuel beneath the boilers. Coopers are heading up hogsheads full of the manufactured article, and other laborers are rolling up empty ones to be filled. Formerly the overseers were never seen without the long-lashed whip, but slavery no longer exists as an institution. The negroes are free, though they work for very small wages.

Occasionally in the trip across the island we pass through a crude but picturesque hamlet, having the mouldering stamp of antiquity, with low straggling houses built of rude frames, covered at side and roof with palm-bark and leaves. Chimneys, there are none, — none even in the cities, — charcoal being alone used, and all cooking is done in the open air. About the doors of the long, irregular posada, or inn, a dozen saddle-horses are seen tied to a bar erected for the purpose, while their owners are smoking and drinking inside; but there are no wheeled vehicles to be seen. The roads are only passable for men on foot or horseback. The people, the cabins, and the horses all are stained with the red dust of the soil, recalling our Western Indians in their war paint. This pigment, or colored dirt, penetrates and adheres to everything, fills the railroad cars, and decorates the passengers with a dingy brick color. It is difficult to realize that these comparatively indifferent places through which we glide so swiftly are of any importance, and the permanent home of any one. When the cars stop at the small way-stations, they are instantly boarded by lottery-ticket sellers, boys with tempting fruit, green cocoanuts, ripe oranges, and bananas, all surprisingly cheap. Here, too, is the guava-seller, with neatly sealed tin cans of this favorite preserve. Indeed, it seems to rain guava jelly in Cuba. At a shanty beside the road where we stop at noon, a large mulatto woman retails coffee and island rum, while a score of native whites lounge about with slouched hats, hands in pockets, and puffing cigarettes,— pictures of idleness and indifference.

Stray dogs hang about the car-wheels and track to pick up the crumbs which passengers throw away from their lunch-baskets. Just over the wild pineapple hedge close at hand, half a dozen naked negro children hover round the door of a low cabin; the mother, fat and shining in her one garment, gazes with arms akimbo at the scene of which she forms a typical part. The engineer imbibes a penny drink of thin Cataline wine and hastens back to his post. The station bell rings, the steam whistle is sounded, and we are quickly on our way again, to repeat the picture six or eight leagues farther on.

As we approach Matanzas, the scene undergoes a radical change. Comfortable habitations are multiplied, good roads appear winding gracefully about the country, and groves and gardens come into view with small dairy farms. Superb specimens of the royal palm begin to multiply themselves, always suggestive of the Corinthian column. Scattered about the scene a few handsome cattle are observed cropping the rank verdure. There is no greensward in the tropics, grass is not cultivated, and hay is never made. Such fodder as is fed to domestic animals is cut green and brought into the city from day to day.

Notwithstanding the ceaseless novelty of the scene, one becomes a little fatigued by the long, hot ride; but as we draw nearer to Matanzas, the refreshing air from the Gulf suddenly comes to our relief, full of a bracing tonic which renders all things tolerable. The sight of the broad harbor, under such circumstances, lying with its flickering, shimmering surface under the afternoon sun, is very beautiful to behold.

CHAPTER XXIV.

THE island of Cuba was discovered by Columbus, in October of the year 1492; the continent of America was not discovered until six years later, — that is, in 1498. Columbus and his followers found the land inhabited by a peculiar race; hospitable, inoffensive, timid, fond of the dance, yet naturally indolent. They had some definite idea of God and heaven, and were governed by patriarchs whose age gave them precedence. They spoke the dialect of the Lucagos or Bahamas, from which islands it was thought they originated, but it would seem more reasonable to suppose that both the people of the Bahamas and of the West Indian islands originally came from the mainland; that is, either from north or south of the Isthmus of Panama.

The natives were at once subjected by the new-comers, who reduced them to a condition of slavery, and proving to be hard taskmasters, the poor overworked creatures died by hundreds, until they had nearly disappeared. They were of tawny complexion, and beardless, resembling in many respects our native Indians. As Columbus described them in his first letter sent to his royal patrons in Spain, they were "loving, tractable, and peaceable; though entirely naked, their manners were decorous and praiseworthy." The wonderful fertility of the soil, its range of noble mountains, its widespread and well-watered plains, with its extended coast-line and excellent harbors, all challenged the admiration of the discoverers, so that Columbus recorded in his journal these words: "It is the most beautiful island that the eyes of man ever beheld, full of excellent ports and deep rivers."

The Spaniards were surprised to see the natives using rude pipes, in which they smoked a certain dried leaf with apparent gratification. Tobacco was native to the soil, and in the use of this now well-nigh universal narcotic, these simple savages indulged in an original luxury, or habit, which the Spanish invaders were not slow in acquiring.

The flowers were strongly individualized. The frangipanni, tall, and almost leafless, with thick, flesh-like shoots, and decked with a small, white blossom, was fragrant and abundant. Here, also, was the wild passion-flower, in which the Spaniards thought they beheld the emblem of our Saviour's passion. The golden-hued peta was found beside the myriad-flowering oleander and the night-blooming cereus, while the luxuriant undergrowth was braided with the cactus and the aloe. They were also delighted by tropical fruits in confusing variety, of which they knew not even the names.

This was four hundred years ago, and to-day the same flowers and the same luscious fruits grow upon the soil in similar abundance. Nature in this land of endless summer puts forth strange eagerness, ever running to fruits, flowers, and fragrance, as if they were outlets for her exuberant fancy.

Diego Velasquez, the first governor of the island under Spanish rule, appears to have been an energetic magistrate, and to have ruled affairs with intelligence. He did not live, however, in a period when justice erred on the side of mercy, and his harsh and cruel treatment of the natives will always remain a blot upon his memory. Emigration was fostered by the home government, and cities were established in the several divisions of the island; but the new province was mainly considered in the light of a military station by the Spanish government in its operations against Mexico. Thus Cuba became the headquarters of the Spanish power in the west, forming the point of departure for those military expeditions which, though small in number, were yet so formidable in the energy of the leaders, and in the arms, discipline, courage, fanaticism, and avarice of their followers, that they were fully adequate to carry out the vast scheme of conquest for which they were designed.

The Spaniards who invaded Mexico encountered a people who had attained a far higher degree of civilization than their red brethren of the outlying Caribbean Islands, or those of the northeastern portion of the continent, now forming the United States. Vast pyramids, imposing sculptures, curious arms, fanciful garments, various kinds of manufactures, filled the invaders with surprise. There was much which was curious and strange in their religion, while the capital of the Mexican empire presented a fascinating spectacle to the eyes of Cortez and his followers. The rocky amphitheatre in the midst of which it was built still remains, but the great lake which was its grandest feature, traversed by causeways and covered with floating gardens, is gone. The Aztec dynasty was doomed. In vain did the inhabitants of the conquered city, roused to madness by the cruelty and extortion of the victors, expel them from their midst. Cortez refused to flee further than the shore; the light of his burning vessels rekindled the desperate valor of his followers, and Mexico fell, as a few years after did Peru beneath the sword of Pizarro, thus completing the scheme of conquest, and giving Spain a colonial empire more splendid than that of any power in Christendom.

In the meantime, under numerous and often-changed captains-general, the island of Cuba increased in population by free emigration from Spain, and by the constant cruel importation of slaves from Africa. It may be said to have been governed by a military despotism from the outset to the present time, and nothing short of such an arbitrary rule could have maintained the connection between the island and so exacting a mother country, situated more than three thousand miles across the ocean.

The form of the island is quite irregular, resembling the blade of a Turkish cimeter slightly curved back, or that of a long, narrow crescent. It stretches away in this shape from east to west, throwing its western end into a curve, and thus forming a partial barrier to the outlet of the Gulf of Mexico, as if at some ancient period it had been a part of the American continent, severed on its north side from the Florida Peninsula by the wearing of the Gulf Stream, and from Yucatan on its southwestern point by a current setting into the Gulf. Two channels are thus formed by which the Mexican Gulf is entered.

One neither departs from nor approaches the Cuban shore without crossing that remarkable ocean-river to which we have so often referred in these pages, — the Gulf Stream, — with banks and bottom of cold water, while its body and surface are warm. Its color in the region of the Gulf is indigo-blue, so distinct that the eye can follow its line of demarkation where it joins the common water of the sea. Its surface temperature on the coast of the United States is from 75° to 80°.

Its current, of a speed of four to five miles per hour, expends immense power in its course, and forms a body of water in the latitude of the Carolina coast fully two hundred miles wide. Its temperature diminishes very gradually, while it moves thousands of leagues, until one branch loses itself in Arctic regions, and the other breaks on the coast of Europe.

The sea-bottom, especially near the continents, resembles the neighboring land, and consists of hills, mountains, and valleys, like the earth upon which we live. A practical illustration of this fact is found in the soundings taken by the officers of our Coast Survey in the Caribbean Sea, where a valley was found giving a water-depth of three thousand fathoms, twenty-five miles south of Cuba. The Cayman Islands, in that neighborhood, are the summits of mountains bordering this deep valley at the bottom of the sea, which has been found, by a series of soundings, to extend over seven hundred miles from between Cuba and Jamaica nearly to the Bay of Honduras, with an average breadth of eighty miles. Thus the island of Grand Cayman, scarcely twenty feet above sea-level, is said to be a mountain-top twenty thousand five hundred and sixty feet above the bottom of the submarine valley beside which it rises, — an altitude exceeding that of any mountain on the North American continent. A little more than five miles, or say twenty-seven thousand feet, is the greatest depth yet sounded at sea.

Cuba is the most westerly of the West Indian Islands, and compared with the others has nearly twice as much superficial extent of territory, being about as large as England proper, without the principality of Wales. Its greatest length from east to west is very nearly eight hundred miles, its narrowest part is over twenty miles, and its average width fifty. The circumference is two thousand miles, and it contains over forty thousand square miles.

The nearest port of the island to this continent is Matanzas, lying due-south from Cape Sable, Florida, a distance of a hundred and thirty miles. Havana is situated some sixty miles west of Matanzas, and it is here that the island divides the entrance to the Gulf of Mexico, whose coast-line measures six thousand miles, finding the outlet for its commerce along the shore of Cuba, almost within range of the guns in Moro Castle. Lying thus at our very door, as it were, this island stands like a sentinel guarding the approaches to the Gulf of Mexico, whose waters wash the shores of five of the United States, and by virtue of the same position barring the entrance of the great river, the Mississippi, which drains half the continent of North America. So, also, Cuba keeps watch and ward over our communication with California by way of the Isthmus of Panama. It is not surprising, therefore, when we realize the commanding position of the island, that so much interest attaches to its ultimate destiny.

Matanzas is situated in one of the most fertile portions of the island, the city covering the picturesque hills by which the bay is surrounded. The fortifications are of a meagre character and could not withstand a well-directed attack for half an hour. The custom house is the most prominent building which strikes the eye on approaching the city by water. Though built of stone, it is only one story in height, and was erected at the commencement of the present century. The city is connected with Havana by railway, of which there are nearly a thousand miles in operation in the island.

Club life prevails at Matanzas, as usual at the expense of domestic or family ties; the same may be said of Havana, and both cities in this respect are like London. It is forbidden to discuss politics in these Cuban clubs, the hours being occupied mostly in playing cards, dominoes, chess, and checkers, for money. Gambling is as natural and national in Cuba as in China. Many Chinese are seen about the streets and stores of Matanzas, variously employed, and usually in a most forlorn and impoverished condition, — poor creatures who have survived their "apprenticeship" and are now free. They were brought here under the disguise of the Coolie system, as it is called, but which was only slavery in another form. These Chinese are peaceful, do not drink spirituous liquors, work hard, never meddle with politics, and live on one-half they can earn, so as to save enough to pay their passage home to their beloved land. Few succeed; eight-tenths of those imported into the island have been not only cheated out of the promised wages, but worked to death!

The famous afternoon drive and promenade of Matanzas was formerly the San Carlos Paseo. It has fine possibilities, and is lined and beautifully ornamented with thrifty Indian laurels. It overlooks the spacious harbor and outer bay, but is now entirely neglected and abandoned; even the roadway is green with vegetation, and gullied with deep hollows. It is the coolest place in the city at the evening hour, but the people have become so poor that there are hardly a dozen private vehicles in the city. Matanzas, like all the cities of Cuba, is under the shadow of depressed business, evidence of which meets one on every hand.

Havana is a thoroughly representative city, and is the centre of the talent, wealth, and population of the island. Moro Castle, with its Dahlgren guns peeping out through the yellow stones, and its tall lighthouse, stands guard over the narrow entrance of the harbor. The battery of La Punta, on the opposite shore, answers to the Moro. There are also the long range of cannon and barracks on the city side, and the massive fortress of the Cabanas crowning the hill behind the Moro. All these are decorated with the yellow flag of Spain, — the banner of gold and blood. These numerous and powerful fortifications show how important the home government regards this island, and yet modern gunnery renders these defences comparatively useless.

The city presents a large extent of public buildings, cathedrals, antique and venerable churches. It has been declared in its prosperity to be the richest city, for its number of square miles, in Christendom, but this cannot be truthfully said of it now. There is nothing grand in its appearance as we enter the harbor, though Baron Humboldt pronounced it the gayest and most picturesque sight in America. Its architecture is not remarkable, its enormous prison overshadowing all other public buildings. This structure is designed to contain five thousand prisoners at one time. The hills which make up the distant background are not sufficiently high to add much to the general effect. The few palm-trees which catch the eye here and there give an Oriental aspect to the scene, quite in harmony with the atmospheric tone of intense sunshine.

Havana contains numerous institutions of learning, but not of a high character. It has a medical and a law school, but education is at a low ebb. There is a Royal Seminary for girls, but it is scarcely more than a name. The means of obtaining a good education can hardly be said to exist, and most of the youth of both sexes belonging to the wealthier class are sent to this country for school purposes. The city was originally surrounded by a wall, though the population has long since extended its dwellings and business structures far into what was once the suburbs. A portion of the old wall is still extant, crumbling and decayed, but it has mostly disappeared. The narrow streets of the old town are paved or macadamized, and cross each other at right angles; but in their dimensions they recall those of Toledo in Spain, whose Moorish architecture is also followed here.

The Paseo is the favorite afternoon drive of the citizens, where the ladies in open carriages and the gentlemen on horseback pass and repass each other, gayly saluting, the ladies with a coquettish flourish of the fan, and the gentlemen with a peculiar wave of the hand. The Alameda, a promenade and garden combined, — every Spanish city has a spot so designated, — skirts the shore of the harbor on the city side, near the south end of Oficios Street, and is a favorite resort for promenaders, where a refreshing coolness is breathed from off the sea. This Alameda might be a continuation of the Neapolitan Chiaja (the afternoon resort of Naples). With characteristics quite different, still these shores remind us of the Mediterranean, Sorrento, Amalfi, and Capri, recalling the shadows which daily creep up the heights of San Elmo, and disappear with the setting sun behind the orange-groves.

The cathedral of Havana, on Empedrado Street, is a structure of much interest, its rude pillared front of defaced and moss-grown stone plainly telling of the wear of time. The two lofty towers are hung with many bells which daily call to morning and evening prayers, as they have done for a hundred years and more. The church is not elaborately ornamented, but strikes one as being unusually plain. It contains a few oil paintings of moderate merit; but most important of all is the tomb where the ashes of Columbus so long reposed. All that is visible of this tomb, which is on the right of the altar, is a marble tablet six feet square, upon which, in high relief, is a bust of the great discoverer.

As we view the scene, Military Mass begins. The congregation is very small, consisting almost exclusively of women, who seem to do penance for both sexes in Cuba. The military band, which leads the column of infantry, marches, playing an operatic air, while turning one side for the soldiery to pass on towards the altar. The time-keeping steps of the men upon the marble floor mingle with drum, fife, and organ. Over all, one catches now and then the subdued voice of the priest, reciting his prescribed part at the altar, where he kneels and reads alternately. The boys in white gowns busily swing incense vessels; the tall, flaring candles cast long shadows athwart the high altar; the files of soldiers kneel and rise at the tap of the drum; seen through an atmosphere clouded by the fumes of burning incense, all this combines to make up a picture which is sure to forcibly impress itself upon the memory.

It seems unreasonable that, when the generous, fruitful soil of Cuba is capable of producing two or three crops of vegetation annually, the agricultural interests of the island should be so poorly developed. Thousands of acres of virgin soil have never been broken. Cuba is capable of supporting a population of almost any density; certainly five or six millions of people might find goodly homes here, and yet the largest estimate of the present number of inhabitants gives only a million and a half. When we tread the fertile soil and behold the clustering fruits in such abundance, — the citron, the star-apple, the perfumed pineapple, the luscious banana, and others, — not forgetting the various noble woods which caused Columbus to exclaim with pleasure, we are forcibly struck with the thought of how much nature, and how little man, has done for this "Eden of the Gulf." We long to see it peopled by those who can appreciate the gifts of Providence, — men willing to do their part in grateful recognition of the possibilities so liberally bestowed by Heaven.

As we go on shipboard to sail for our American home, some reflections naturally occur to us. To visit Cuba is not merely to pass over a few degrees of latitude; it is to take a step from the nineteenth century back into the dark ages. In a climate of tropical luxuriance and endless summer, we are in a land of starless political darkness. Lying under the lee of a Republic, where every man is a sovereign, is a realm where the lives, liberties, and fortunes of all are held at the will of a single individual, who acknowledges no responsibility save to a nominal ruler more than three thousand miles away.

Healthful in climate, varied in productions, and most fortunately situated for commerce, there must yet be a grand future in store for Cuba. Washed by the Gulf Stream on half her border, she has the Mississippi pouring out its riches on one side, and the Amazon on the other. In such close proximity to the United States, and with so obvious a common interest, her place seems naturally to be within our own constellation of stars.

But as regards the final destiny of Cuba, that question will be settled by certain economic laws which are as sure in their operation as are those of gravitation. No matter what our individual wishes may be in this matter, such feelings are as nothing when arraigned against natural laws. The commerce of the island is a stronger factor in the problem than is mere politics; it is the active agent of civilization all over the world. It is not cannon, but ships; not gunpowder, but peaceful freights which set'le the great questions of mercantile communities. As the United States take over ninety per cent of her entire exports, towards this country Cuba naturally looks for fellowship and protection. The world's centre of commercial gravity is changing very fast by reason of the rapid development of the United States, and all lands surrounding the Union must conform, sooner or later, to the prevailing lines of motion.

www.ingramcontent.com/pod-product-compliance
Lightning Source LLC
Chambersburg PA
CBHW030555300426
44111CB00009B/982